HOUNDED!

My Lifelong Obsession with Sherlock Holmes

and *The Hound of the Baskervilles*

By

VINCE STADON

Paperback ISBN 978-1-78705-790-6
ePub ISBN 978-1-78705-791-3
PDF ISBN 978-1-78705-792-0

Published by Orange Pip Books
335 Princess Park Manor, Royal Drive,
London, N11 3GX
www.orangepipbooks.com

TO

My wife, Alex, who puts up with my nonsense.

AND

Jeff Niles, my Sherlock.

Shalom aleichem.

THANKS

Orange Pip Books and MX Publishing - Nicko Vaughn, Dessie, & Steve Emecz

The Fam – Terrence Keith Stadon & Linda May Stadon (RIP), John Stadon, Lee Stadon, Troy Stadon

The Kids – Tom Stadon, Catherine Stadon

Holmesian Help – 221 Be Here, The Arthur Conan Doyle Encyclopedia, Bert Coules, Howard Ostrom, Paul Thomas Miller, Sherlock Holmes Fans Facebook Group, Sherlock Holmes on Screens, The Sherlock Holmes Museum, Joshua Ziegler

Old Friends– Paul Symmons, Jeremy Wall, Neil Barrett, John Dacey, Vince Costigan, Chris Wildridge, Tony Carroll, Justin Wildridge, Ian Pool, Caroline Boogaard, Trevor Chisom, Kim Woo, Kev F Sutherland & Heather Tweed, Naomi Carter, John Lomas, Lewis Cook, Elie Hirschman, Valina Cutler, Wayne & Sparky Heyward, Joe J Thomas, Jonithan Patrick Russell

New Friends - Ralph Scott, Kendra Murray and the Petaluma Radio Players, Beth Barnard, Linda Hein, Baker Street West and the Baker Street Players, Stephanie Kempson & the Bristol Old Vic, Billy Quain, Peter Baker, Dan Adams, Little Epic Theatre, Morton L Duffy, The BFI, Monique Faith Boodram, Jose Angel Ortiz, Robin Bailes (Dark Corners), Jonathan Goodwin and Don't Go Into the Cellar Theatre, Paul Thomas Miller, Fazia Rizvi, Kyle Borcz, James Silk, Louise Wallace and the Rondo Theatre Company, The Sherlock Holmes Society of London

CONTENTS

INTRODUCTION
Baskerville 101

THIS IS A SILLY BOOK about my experiences with *The Hound of the Baskervilles*, but you aren't required to have any knowledge of me or the novel before reading it. In fact, those readers who've never read Arthur Conan Doyle's masterpiece might well enjoy this book more than those already familiar with it. As people say, ignorance is bliss, and I'm bound to have gotten things wrong. There's a fine, scholarly Sherlock Holmes fan community made up of experts on all things Sherlockian, and then there's me... I have a sketchy grasp of facts, I have no area of expertise other than Google, and I naturally shirk from any form of effort. All this means is that I do not lay claim to be authoritative and I fully expect more learned readers of this book, should there be any, to find blood-boiling blunders that immediately send them to their writing desks to fire off incensed emails beginning with "Dear Imbecile..." In fact, I welcome every correction, rant, and warning to keep away from the moor – not least because it might mean I can talk the publisher into releasing a second edition, and I've promised my wife a new fridge.

This is also a book about me, in part. I shall try not to bore the reader with the occasional autobiographical snippet pertinent to the subject of Sherlock Holmes and *The Hound of the Baskervilles*, but I can't guarantee everyone is going to fall for my charms. That said, this book welcomes everyone. There is the (very) occasional swear word and incredulous rant, but overall, this is a well-behaved, polite and positive book that you can take home to meet your mother.

With all that in mind, I feel it will be useful to begin with a breezy primer on Arthur Conan Doyle, Sherlock Holmes and *The Hound of the Baskervilles*, if only because it affords me the opportunity to make a few gags that I've been dying to get into print.

Let's start by meeting the creator...

ARISE, SIR ARTHUR!

Arthur Ignatius Conan Doyle was born in Edinburgh in 1859. He studied medicine and, after graduating and serving as a ship's surgeon, set up a medical practice in Plymouth with a scoundrel and crook, which failed miserably. He then moved to Southsea to open another practice – this time *without* going into partnership with a scoundrel and crook, and things went considerably better for him. Conan Doyle wrote as a side-gig – principally non-fiction – and was published in many journals and magazines. In 1886, he dreamed up Sherlock Holmes, Dr Watson and the first Holmes story – *A Study in Scarlet,* which was published the following year in *Beeton's Christmas Album.* After that, fiction became the bulk of his output. Sir Arthur moved to London to become an eye specialist. Meanwhile, in 1891, the *Strand* magazine published the first six Sherlock Holmes short stories. A second run of stories soon followed, and England succumbed to' Sherlockmania[1]'.

In 1893, *The Adventure of the Final Problem* sees Holmes fall to his death, along with Professor Moriarty, as the yin and yang of Victorian crime give up their brief-yet-celebrated clash of wits to instead punch each other to death other over the Reichenbach Falls in Switzerland – as all warring couples end up doing, of course. Doyle had tired of Holmes and wanted to concentrate on his historical novels, which is a bit like The

---

[1] A bit like 'Beatlemania', but with considerably less screaming.

Beatles abandoning hit pop songs like *Hey Jude* to concentrate exclusively on tracks like *Revolution 9*.

When his wife fell ill with tuberculosis, the Doyles moved to Surrey and, in 1900, Arthur signed up to become a volunteer army doctor in South Africa. On his return to England (with enteric fever), he wrote a propaganda piece in which he argued the case for England's involvement in the Boer War, for which he was knighted. He stood for parliament as a Liberal Unionist in Edinburgh Central, but lost by just over 500 votes to his own publisher, the Liberal candidate George Mackenzie Brown. Frankly, the man was robbed. If *I'd* been Doyle's campaign manager, I fancy I'd have secured him the win through some catchy sloganeering: "Doyle: The Elementary Choice!"; "ACD FTW!"; "When You've Eliminated the Impossible All that Remains is to Improbably Vote Conan Doyle!" And I'd have had actors dressed as Holmes and Watson knocking on doors and telling voters that the opposition candidate was an evil criminal mastermind who needed to be stopped at all costs. Vote Doyle!

Licking his wounds on a golfing holiday at an hotel in Cromer (as you do), Doyle and his young friend, Bertram Fletcher Robinson got to talking about local ghost stories and, particularly, those legends involving ghost dogs – or shucks, as local folklore terms them. Robinson, who became friends with Doyle because all men with three names strike up immediate friendships, lived in Devonshire and knew well the stories of spectral hounds. Doyle was inspired – he wanted to write a classic Victorian 'creeper' and was keen to collaborate with Robinson. But somehow (details are sketchy), Robinson never got to co-write the novel; Doyle wrote the book himself.

---

[2] This is a bit unfair because, unlike The Beatles, who set out with *Revolution 9* to make something provocative, *avant-garde* and unsettling, ACD only ever wrote popular, readable fiction designed for a mass readership. On the other hand, I rather like *Revolution 9*, but I can't sit through at least three of Conan Doyle's big historical epics.

The Hound of the Baskervilles was serialised monthly in the *Strand* magazine before its hardback release in 1902 which sold (and continues to sell) more copies than any book currently on my bookshelves other than *Clifford the Big Red Dog - Colouring Book*. You really can't beat the *Clifford the Big Red Dog - Colouring Book*, so that's fair enough.

And finally, for those who have sketchy memories of the big black dog on Dartmoor, here's my wife to explain the plot:

THE HOUND OF THE BASKERVILLES ACCORDING TO MY TIPSY WIFE (WHO HAS NEVER READ IT)

My wife loves reading. She's claimed *Nineteen Eighty-Four* by George Orwell and *The Hitchhiker's Guide to the Galaxy* by Douglas Adams for her favourite novels. She has not, however, read *The Hound of the Baskervilles*, nor any other Sherlock Holmes stories, nor any of ACD's other writings. By and large, my wife has avoided sitting through all the screen adaptations I binged for this book, save for the final version which she joined me in watching all the way through. She drank several glasses of wine as we watched the movie.

A few hours after it had finished, I asked my rather tipsy wife to relate the plot as best as she understood it to be. Feeling like Woodward and/or Bernstein hot on the Watergate scandal, I used a Nixonian recording device on my phone to capture my wife's explosive testimony on tape:

Me: What happens in *The Hound of the Baskervilles?*

My Wife: Um... There's, uh, Lord of the Baskervilles, who is found dead, um, and he was scared to death by a huge dog but, like, his friend keeps silent about it 'cause he thinks people won't believe him and the judges decide that he died of natural causes... But then his nephew comes over, and his friend (can't quite remember his name) gets worried and goes to Sherlock Holmes and says what's happened and that he's really scared for this, erm, Lord Henry, is it? The new one. And so Sherlock Holmes first of all says, 'Don't tell him,' but then he sends Watson down. *He* don't do nothing about it, Holmes, and says, 'I'm gonna stay here' and poor old *Watson* gets sent down with him – with these lot – to investigate it. And there's lots of wandering around the moors, there's an escaped prisoner who is hiding out in the big house, um, 'cause the butler and his wife, um, he's his wife's brother, so that all that adds a bit of intrigue to it. And the baddie is this doctor of archelogy bloke whose got a sister, but she's *not* his sister – she's his wife! Um, and first Watson gets a bit of the hots for her, and then this Lord Henry *definitely* gets the hots for her. And, um, yeah, they *see* the hound at some point and then, yeah, it goes after... Um, is it Sir Henry, or something? Anyway, it eventually gets shot by Watson and it w*as* a hound, but it wasn't a spectral hound. And it was the doctor who did it because he was actually a relation who was after the money, see, instead of this Lord Henry whatsiname...

Me: Baskerville.

My Wife: Yeah, him.

Me: Anything else you can remember?

My Wife: Yeah, I've just remembered there's another bottle in the kitchen.

There you have it – the bare bones of the plot laid out by a tipsy woman who couldn't care less about it. My wife didn't miss anything important, so I think her precis could be considered definitive.

Reader, you need know nothing else to enjoy this book. All will be explained.

Off we go!

CHAPTER ONE

Off the Leash

September 2020

GOOFS

A DENSE WHITE FOG closes in on me as I crouch in wait for the spectral hound. A terrifying howl rings out in the night and I share nervous glances with my companions. We double check that our guns are loaded. Dr Watson, to my left, hands me a violin. I stare long and hard at him, and he suddenly takes back the violin. Inspector Lestrade, to my right, starts coughing. I whisper to the Inspector to knock it off – we don't want our position revealed and for the villain to get away. Dr Watson hands me a large magnifying glass. I stare longer and harder at Dr Watson, who then once again takes back the object. Inspector Lestrade coughs again. I sigh. I wish I wasn't accompanied by idiots.

Another howl pierces the night, and I feel the hairs on the back of my neck stand on end. I gulp. There is silence. A moment later, an odd rustling sound and a sweet smell... I ponder what on earth it could be as Dr Watson hands me a meerschaum pipe. I am about to hit Dr Watson on the head with the meerschaum pipe when Inspector Lestrade pipes up.

"Want one?" He's proffering a half-eaten packet of Lockets Menthol Cough Sweets. I stare very very long and very very hard at Inspector Lestrade.

"I'll have one," says Dr Watson, reaching across to grab a cough sweet.

A third howl rings out, immediately followed by someone's phone blasting *I'm Too Sexy* by Right Said Fred.

"Sorry!" cries out Sir Henry Baskerville. "It's my mum, gotta take this!"

"For God's sake!" I cry.

I've had enough!

We are supposed to be enacting the dramatic, fog-drenched climax of *The Hound of the Baskervilles*, but nothing has gone right. For a start, where's the bloody fog? And why does the Hound sound more like Mutley from *Wacky Races* than a centuries-old demon roaming the wild moors? Sir Henry didn't even bother with a Canadian accent! It's a disaster! I am grateful that this is only a dry run through. Heaven knows what will happen when we do it for real on Dartmoor.

Dr Watson – my wife in a false moustache – gathers up the props. I'd asked her to play Dr Watson because she once volunteered for St John's Ambulance and has first aid training. That's near enough being a doctor in my book. I'd also asked her to take care of the props, because she's always telling me to put things away. I had not asked her to bring every single sodding prop with her to 'The Moor' (in reality, the small green opposite our home in Bristol), or to keep handing me different props at such a crucial moment.

"Remind me of the bit where Dr Watson hands Holmes a sodding violin when he's on Dartmoor, hunting the hound," I later ask.

"I can't," says my wife.

"Hah!"

"'Cause I've never read *The Hound of the Baskervilles*, and have absolutely no desire to ever do so," she continues before instructing me to wash the dishes and de-flea the cats. She says the Benedict Cumberbatch version is the only *Hound of the Baskervilles* she'll ever need and makes weak innuendo remarks about how she'd like to do some 'deducting' with him. I point out that that doesn't even make sense, but she's not listening.

But that was later.

Before we got to that conversation, I had gathered everybody together to give them some notes. I started with 'Sir Henry Baskerville', the Canadian heir to the Baskerville fortune, as played by my friend Naomi[3], also in a false moustache. Naomi has been to Canada several times and has watched a YouTube video about oversized dogs, so she is a close fit for the character. She is also in charge of the sound effects, howling and growling like a mad dog. But then, she often does.

"How many times," I smile at Naomi, "have I reminded you to put your phone on airplane mode? And what's with the Right Said Fred ring-tone?"

"Sorry," says Naomi who I can tell isn't remotely sorry. "Always forget that. I'll remember next time. And I'll do the accent, though I'm not sure if you can tell if dogs sound like they've got Canadian accents?"

"What?"

"Mind you, I had a neighbour who had a Yorkshire Terrier that you could really tell came from Yorkshire. Ay up wooof!"

I never know when Naomi is kidding. She does stand-up comedy.

"The Hound doesn't have a Canadian accent, Naomi, because it's a dog. On the other hand, Sir Henry has a Canadian accent, because he's

---

[3] Naomi Carter is an excellent actress, writer, and stand-up comic. She wrote and starred in the play *Barbara and Jeffrey* which is about a marriage under strain during the night their home is burgled by inept thieves.

from Canada," I tell her, just to be absolutely sure, "where they have Canadian accents."

Naomi nods and says she'll make a note on her phone. But then she has trouble switching her phone on, and we all waste five minutes discussing the best way to get it working again, and whether we need to find a charger, and if we'd need to go inside to plug in a charger if we found one, until the phone finally switches on and immediately rings. It's Naomi's mum. Naomi walks away to chat with her mum, and I take the opportunity to give notes to 'Inspector Lestrade' who is, in reality, my friend Lewis[4] who has a friend whose dad is a retired police officer from Glamorgan.

"You need to get that cough sorted before we get to the Moor," I tell him. He looks a bit ill, and I'm worried he won't make it to Dartmoor, and I'll have to find somebody else. I don't want to find anybody else because I've enough to deal with as it is. And we need his car.

"I'll be fine," rasps Lewis after a long and painful-sounding coughing fit. "It's the smoke; it's aggravating my throat."

I look at the small fire a few feet away, the barely perceptible smoke coming from it. "Yes," I say, "that's another thing - there's supposed to be a dense wall of white fog! Throw some more wood on the fire, let's get some smoke!"

Lewis nods and the nod turns into another coughing fit. He's still holding his gun as he coughs and accidentally fires, shooting me in the groin with a suction dart. It hurts. I stare very, very, *very* long and very, very, *very* hard at Lewis as Naomi returns and tells me that I seem to have a suction dart attached to my groin, and whether that's supposed to happen to Sherlock Holmes in *The Hound of the Baskervilles,* because she saw this film once where—

---

[4] Lewis Cook is an excellent actor, writer, and stand-up comic. He wrote the play *Good Little Boy*, about a cuckold who reaches his breaking point.

"Enough!" I shout. "Please, everybody, can you all be quiet just for a moment?"

There is quiet. Blissful silence. And then a cough. But it's a small cough, so I let it go.

I think about all the reasons why I've gathered this group to help me with this, and the long journey it's taken to get there. I think about how much further there is to go. I think about love. My love for *The Hound of the Baskervilles*, and for Sherlock Holmes. I think about the lyrics to *I'm Too Sexy*, and why Right Said Fred sing that they're too sexy for Milan, New York and Japan, and whether those were the only places on Earth that would consider Right Said Fred's sexiness to be too extreme, whereas everywhere else on the planet could only tolerate Right Said Fred's sexiness. There might be a global measurement of *too much sexiness*. I shrug off such nonsense and resolve to pull myself together and get this thing done. There's a spectral hound to kill.

"Right," I say, pulling the suction cup dart away with plop. "Let's do this thing! Where's the dog?"

My wife reaches into her box of props and pulls out a cuddly Goofy toy. I stare at it, then at her.

"This is supposed to be the Hound of the Baskervilles, is it? A terrifying, giant spectral beast that roams the moonlit foggy moor and rips open the throats of men, then gorges on their fresh blood?"

My wife shrugs. She's not into this. She wants to get this over with so we can go to the pub because on Tuesdays they do tapas and you get a free glass of wine with orders over £10.

"Goofy isn't even a dog, is he?" coughs Lewis. "Isn't he a bear?"

"Good point, Lewis," I say, and pat him on the back. Bad move. This leads to a coughing fit so raucous that it sets off a car alarm.

"Yeah, he's a dog," says Naomi, who has Googled. "And listen to this: his full name is G. G. Goofy Goof, but he sometimes goes by the name Goofus G Dawg, like a Grime artist."

"I don't care," I say. "I only care that he looks absolutely nothing like the Hound of the Baskervilles – not even remotely. Do you have something else? Anything else?"

"Yes, I have this," says my wife, reaching into the props box, and pulling out a cuddly K-9 from *Dr Who* just as the fire goes out.

We give up and go to the pub, but there's no tapas and free glass of wine because it's Wednesday and my wife has got the day wrong.

WHY?

"I'm going to watch every version of *The Hound of the Baskervilles*, all in one go. On Dartmoor. And I'm going to do some of the things that the characters in the book do."

This was me speaking to my friend Jeremy Wall[5] back in January 2020. We were having a pint or two in a cosy pub, and the conversation had turned to what my plans were for now that had I reached a milestone birthday: fifty years of age.

"Why?" my friend asked me, reasonably enough.

I thought about it. I'd been thinking about it for a while, but I'd never articulated it. Maybe it was a nostalgia thing - *The Hound of the Baskervilles* is a book that's been with me since I was a child. I must have read it dozens of times. I've watched many versions. I've written lots of things about it, albeit always in a light-hearted way. Sherlock Holmes has been a constant in my life. I've drawn him, dressed up as him, played him, written thousands of words about him. I've made money from him. Not much money, granted, but enough to buy my friend a drink, as long as it

---

[5] Stapleton Cricket Club Player of the Year 1988.

was a half.

It would be a joy to fully immerse myself in the fiction, to dress up and just be silly; to be unapologetically playful. It would be a lovely little task to marathon every single film and TV adaptation; to read pastiches; to listen to radio dramas; to play video games. I've heard that people who reach middle age often begin to reassess their lives and their place in the world. I know people who've spent their fiftieth year travelling the world, or volunteering at homeless shelters or learning new languages. The truth is we can do anything at any time, if circumstances permit. Reaching fifty should not be an excuse to suddenly decide to live life more freely or altruistically. Even so, I can't help but feel a little bit ashamed that my inclination is to put on a deerstalker and run around Dartmoor rather than to help save lives. It's selfish, it's hugely self-indulgent, it's completely barmy.

"Because I'm fifty," I said. "What else am I going to do?"

THIS BOOK

This, then, is a book detailing my experiences over the autumn and winter of 2020 and into the spring of 2021 when I undertook a marathon viewing session of every available filmed version of *The Hound of the Baskervilles*, as well as listening to audio play adaptations and narrated audiobooks, watching stage productions, playing a video game based on the book, completing a 1000 piece jigsaw puzzle depicting the Sidney Paget illustration of the Hound, reading pastiche novels, and making a pilgrimage to "the wild and empty" Dartmoor, following in the dogged footsteps of Mr Sherlock Holmes and Dr Watson. (I also wanted very much to travel to the Reichenbach Falls in Switzerland, where Holmes battled Professor Moriarty, but my wife insisted we need a new fridge freezer and pointed out that, since no part of *The Hound of the Baskervilles* takes place in Switzerland, I was pushing my luck and testing the limits of her patience.)

We must be careful with money. Why, just the other day I could barely conceal my astonishment and glee (I was at a funeral) when an alert popped up on my smartphone to let me know that the complete Jeremy Brett DVD series had been put up for sale by a buyer who was only asking £6 for it.

"Fucking hell, that's a bargain!" I cried out, rising from my seat. Of course, I immediately regretted my outburst and attempted to disguise my actions by turning it into a coughing fit. I think I got away with it. I certainly got the Jeremy Brett DVD boxset. I was the clear winner that day.

As I marathon versions of *The Hound of the Baskervilles,* I will be immersing myself in the fiction of the book. I will be applying Holmes's methods of deductive reasoning to make startling statements of inference that greatly impress and bewilder all manner of people, cutting up newspapers to create a threatening note to a visiting Canadian, and even taking aim at a ghostly dog (albeit one made of cardboard), etc. Since its serial publication in 1901 many excellent books have been written about *The Hound of the Baskervilles* (which will be mostly referred to as HOUN[6] henceforth to save me typing out the full title hundreds of times), discussing and analysing Sir Arthur Conan Doyle's work in splendid detail. But I can confidently state without fear of contradiction that there has never been a HOUN book quite like this.

WE'RE ALL GOING TO DIE!

This book was written during a pandemic, with all the resulting infections, deaths, restrictions, anxieties, dry pasta and toilet roll shortages

---

[6] The Sherlock Holmes fan community has adopted four letter abbreviations for all the stories. For instance, *The Problem of Thor Bridge* is the Marvel-like THOR, whilst *A Study in Scarlet* is the steamy Jackie Collins-like STUD.

from supermarkets that ensued. Everybody went a little bit crazy as every*thing* went a little bit crazy. If you think what I get up to in this book is mad (and you'd be right to think this), then please bear in mind where the world was at the time.

WOLFMAN

My first task was to source as many versions of HOUN as possible, across all media. This was not easy. This was not inexpensive. This was not harmonious to my marriage.

"What's this, £44.88 for a DVD?" My wife stabbed a shapely finger at our bank statement.

"Yeah, that included postage and packaging from the Ukraine, though."

"Forty-five quid for a DV-bloody-D?!" I could hear the exclamation mark. "What the hell is it?"

"It's, errr, Scooby Doo."

"Scooby Doo."

"Scoob and the gang investigate the Hound of the Baskervilles."

"Last week you said we couldn't go out to eat because we didn't have the money. Now I find you've spent it on a Scooby Doo DVD from Russia."

"The Ukraine."

"Wherever. What's next? A £70 DVD of Snoopy from Tasmania? Where will the madness end?"

I pointed out that there is no Snoopy version of *The Hound of the Baskervilles* and it would, therefore, not be possible for me to buy a DVD copy of it from Tasmania, or anywhere else really. But my wife had stopped listening halfway through my pedantry and missed my witty retort that even if there was a Snoopy version of HOUN on DVD, it would probably cost peanuts.

I slept on the couch that night, wondering how I was going to source the early silent film adaptations and some of the obscure foreign language versions. Astonishingly, I discovered that the 1937 German version, starring Bruno Güttner, is on YouTube. What an age of wonders we live in to find such a rare treat amongst make-up tutorials, angry rants by angry young men about girls being in *Star Wars*, and weird ASMR videos.

I bought my wife a bottle of wine, cooked her favourite meal, and pretended I was a perfectly normal man who wasn't going slightly barmy. I didn't fool her for a second.

"You're not having a midlife crisis, are you?" she asked, after forking down some prawn spaghetti.

"No, not at all. I'm a perfectly normal man who isn't going slightly barmy."

"Then why are you crying?"

"I'm just a bit sad that I'll never get to see Wolf Ackva."

"Who the hell is Wolf Ackva?"

"He played Holmes in a German television adaptation of *The Hound of the Baskervilles*, back in—"

"You *are* having a mid-life crisis. I thought last year was weird when you became obsessed with squirrels."

"I'm not *obsessed* with squirrels. I just find them a real comfort in this cold, dark, lonely world." I changed the subject and wondered if I might find any photos of Wolf Ackva to pin to my wall as a kind of memoriam.[7]

DANIEL CRAIG'S PANTS

It occurred to me that watching them in order might be out of the question – I couldn't source every version in time to begin the marathon and sitting through several silent German black and white movies, one after the other, might be so taxing that it could sap me of all enthusiasm and kill the project dead. I'm fond of Germany, and German cinema, even German silent cinema, but, like Reese Witherspoon's films, or Heinz beef and tomato cupasoups, you can only enjoy two in succession before you start to feel a bit overwhelmed.

Better, I reasoned, to mix things up. I wrote down the list and cut each entry into a strip of paper, which I then folded up and tipped into my deerstalker hat. I'd pick them out at random, in a lucky dip. That would be fun. If I picked out a version that I didn't have a copy of, I'd put it back in the hat and pick out another one. Otherwise, I'd stay firm and fair, and not discard versions I suspect (or know from previous viewings) to be dreadful in favour of ones I know are better.

It was a risky and dangerous stratagem, the lucky dip idea, but now that I had reached a half century, I needed some adrenaline-pumping activity in my life. With thinning hair, creaking bones, weak eyesight, and big belly, I was astonished to learn that I am younger than Daniel Craig (my wife is a bit obsessed with him, especially that bit where comes out of the sea in his blue swimming trunks in *Casino Royale*, 2005), and I can only surmise that Danny keeps himself in good shape by regular lucky dip sessions – perhaps of Bond films or British actors with two first names instead of a first name and a surname, or maybe he himself had embarked on a HOUN marathon of his own? (A quick Google search gave me the answer: no, he hasn't. Or at least, if he has – which is highly doubtful – he

---

[7] I did. Wolf looks a bit like Hugh Hefner.

hasn't made his findings public. But then again, he is a secret agent, which only muddies the waters.)

With many films and books sourced, travel arrangements booked, and a lucky dip system in place, I was ready to begin. The game was afoot!

My wife asked me to take the bins out first.

DOG'S BREAKFAST

I began, naturally and sensibly enough, with a re-reading of the book. I thought it might be nice to take my time and read the book over a period of several months, for I tend to hungrily devour the Sherlock Holmes stories in one bite.

Ominously locked down, England was draped in an autumnal shroud, and I was glad of the central heating kicking in as I reluctantly left the comfort of my bed, grumpily disturbing the fat lazy cats who sleep on top of me in the darker months. (I'm happy for them to slumber on top of me because they're very warm and snugly; that said, one of them snores very loudly and the other is reliably flatulent, so my sleep is often disturbed by loud noises and pungent odours. Happily, I can blame all nightly sound and sensory disruptions on them and escape a tetchy rebuke from my long-suffering wife).

I wolfed down some nutty muesli and decaf Tetley's tea as I started to read.

HOUN begins with Watson noting, with mild surprise, that Sherlock Holmes is already seated at the breakfast table. Watson is the early riser; Holmes rarely stirring to hear the clock chime nine o'clock. I wondered what Watson might have eaten for breakfast most mornings. A few minutes of Googling led me to discover *Dining with Sherlock Holmes: A Baker Street Cookbook* which contains such delicious-looking recipes that I immediately ordered a copy. If nothing else, at the end of this project I will have eaten well (adieu, diet, adieu!), assuming my culinary skills are up to the task of doing justice to these salivating dishes.

Dr Watson doesn't eat whatever's on the dining table because he is preoccupied with examining Dr Mortimer's walking stick. I really like how the novel begins: with our good friends amiably making a series of deductions (Watson has a decent stab at it; Holmes is spot-on in almost every regard) and how the innocent bite marks on the walking stick brilliantly prepares the ground for a gigantic hound's footprints. I also love how Holmes knows the dog is a spaniel, not because of his brilliant deductive reasoning, but because he's just caught sight of the animal through the window. Earlier, though his back was facing his friend, he had known Watson was examining Dr Mortimer's walking stick because he could see the reflection of his friend in a shiny coffee pot on the breakfast table. These little moments of warmth, which so splendidly give colour to their friendship, are some of my favourite things in all literature.

THE SMELL OF TOM BAKER

The Hound of the Baskervilles - Tom Baker (six-part BBC TV drama, 1982)

Here we go – my very first pick. Excited? Indeed! With keen anticipation, I grabbed my deerstalker and gave the folded slips of paper container therein a rigorous swirl. I said a silent prayer to the Gods of Marathoning as I nervously unfolded my first pick. Would it be a genuinely great film? Would the actor playing Sherlock Holmes be one of the more acclaimed versions? Would I start my adventure with a bona fide classic?

No. I got the dreary Tom Baker BBC TV serial from the 1980s. Arse.

Age has not been kind to the Tom Baker version. It was creaky and uninspiring at the time (I watched it as a kid on its first broadcast and fell asleep in front of the telly); it's positively corpse-like now. The entire cast seems to be performing *The Hound of the Baskervilles* as a Brecht play about people devoid of all life and emotion, though Terrance Rigby is playing Dr Watson as Nigel Bruce in a Brecht play about people devoid of all life and emotion. Nicholas Woodeson, as Sir Henry, is so short that even I, a short-arse, would tower over him, and I can't believe he'd survive the wilds of Canada or Dartmoor. Watching him share scenes with the six-foot two Tom Baker is like watching a child feed a giraffe. I don't know why a short Sir Henry annoys me. I may be admitting to a prejudice I never knew I had (and one I should take steps to abandon). If nothing else, this HOUN marathon is a learning experience.

It's not all bad, this version. It's great to see real Dartmoor as a filming location, even though it's filmed without much artistry. There's a very funny bit with Holmes and Watson in a cab, chasing Stapleton's cab through London, that's entirely filmed with a locked-off camera in the interior of the first cab and is over in about ten seconds; Tom Baker's Holmes explaining, with budget-saving aplomb, that they've lost their quarry. I wish the entire production had been made this way – with the camera close in on a seated Holmes and Watson and nobody and nothing else. Indeed, I think whole movies could be made this way. Imagine the savings!

I've met the great Tom Baker. Aside from sundry Sherlocks who have starred in my own silly plays, the fabulous Mr Baker is the only Sherlock Holmes actor I've met in the flesh. He was slightly tipsy, even in the middle of the afternoon, as he signed copies of his recently published autobiography *Who On Earth is Tom Baker?* and gulped down red wine.

This was 1997 – my son was still a baby and, because I had named him after Tom Baker, my wife and I brought Little Tom along with us to meet Big Tom. As we queued, Little Tom did a smelly in his nappy. The foul odour, more terrifying than the Hound itself, spread quickly throughout the bookstore. There was a mass shuffling of feet as people moved away. Happily, this resulted in us moving up the queue very quickly, indeed, and it occurred to me that this was a spectacularly successful way of speeding things along without waiting in queues. I wondered if it might be possible to make Little Tom do smellies in his nappy to order, perhaps by feeding him foodstuffs that would play havoc with his baby digestive system.

"Hi Tom, I named my son after you," I said to the Great Man. His hair was almost as big and white as his toothy smile.

"Well, naturally," he said, in that famous dark chocolate voice that had sold so many Zanussi appliances and scared away armies of Daleks. He was my favourite Dr Who, I told him, as we posed together for a photo ("Well, naturally!" he said once again, as if I was feeding him punchlines). I could smell the wine on Tom Baker's breath, and knew I'd always remember such a detail.

Tom Baker gulped more vino and moved on to the next person in the queue. We had to get out of the bookstore quickly because Little Tom's arse was now so toxic, I was beginning to think we would need to call out a Hazmat Team to safely dispose of it. But as we exited, I stole a glance back at Tom Baker just as he was raising his wine glass to his lips.

"Cheers, Tom," I said to myself.

Tom Baker is the first to admit that he had not been particularly good as Sherlock Holmes in this drab production of HOUN. In his autobiography, he cheerfully mentions that "the BBC apologised in *The Daily Telegraph* for my performance as Holmes." But I don't care. He's Tom Baker, and he smells of red wine and I love him.

STICKY SITUATION

Back to HOUN Chapter One. Though Sherlock Holmes smarmily deduces much about Dr Mortimer by examining the doctor's walking stick, it sounded easy to me. Piece of cake. Anyone could do it. A notch here, a hair there – one could learn a great deal just by observing. I decided to give it a go. I have a magnifying glass, a deerstalker, and a piece of cake.

Firstly, I needed to find a stranger's walking stick. I don't know anyone who uses one, but I had seen plenty of pensioners social distancing at the local post office; some of them were likely to use a stick. At any rate, I had legitimate business to deal with at the post office because I needed to send a parcel[8]. The people in my area are, by and large, a friendly bunch, always willing to chat and to help. Not so at the post office.

A queue of grumpy elderly men and women rebuffed all my advances. One particularly cantankerous old woman accused me of being a yob and threatened me with her stick, though luckily, I was out of reach two metres away. I immediately deduced that she was an awful person and wondered if she had a criminal record. Perhaps the authorities would be interested in an anonymous tip? I surreptitiously took a photo of the outlaw granny to send to Special Branch.

Back at home, I pondered a new plan of attack. Elderly people were too dangerous. Who else used walking sticks? Ramblers and farmers and other outdoorsy types. Also, Charlie Chaplin impersonators. And if we widened the field to include canes, then I could try pimps from the seventies and Willy Wonka. Unfortunately, none of them were any help to me.

I wondered if I might make do with some other kind of stick. A cheerleader's baton. A drum stick. A stick insect. A chicken drumstick. And then inspiration hit me! I knew exactly what stick, and where to find it. A 'selfie' stick – in my daughter's bedroom! Left behind by one of her friends.

---

[8] I had ordered a spectral Hound figurine from Amazon, and the fools had sent me a toy of a character named 'The Hound' from *Game of Thrones*. Idiots.

I had no idea which friend as I avoid them as much as possible (principally on my daughter's insistence, because I am 'weird' and 'embarrassing' and 'old'). I can find no convincing argument to counter those accusations, so I just stay away. My daughter is at university, so I dropped her a message.

"Hey, it's me,"

"Who?"

"Your dad."

"So?"

"You recall the 'selfie' stick that a friend left behind in your room? I'd like to examine it for clues and deduce what kind of person your friend is."

"Why?"

"It's for a thing."

"A thing with the squirrels?"

"No, a different thing. A *Hound of the Baskervilles* thing."

"K."

"Great. What is the password to get into your room?"

My daughter kindly sent me the access codes and I dived into the room, grabbed the 'selfie' stick, and got out of there, all within a minute (I took a stopwatch with me). Beat that, Tom Cruise, with your impossible Scientology missions!

I examined the 'selfie' stick. It was aluminium, with a telescopic motion that was pleasing to muck around with. There were scuff marks on the grip handle and the wrist strap was broken. There was a battery in the handle, but it had been drained of power. The 'selfie' stick smelled slightly of weed. I Googled and discovered it was Bluetooth (whatever that is!) and inexpensive. There were flakes of paint and short ginger hairs.

I munched on a chicken drumstick as I made a series of quite brilliant deductions. Then I messaged my daughter.

"Hi, it's me again."

"Who?"

"Your dad."

"So?"

"I've examined the 'selfie' stick and I can confidently state that your friend is a young woman of around five feet three. She has a ginger cat, a recreational drugs problem, and she sometimes wears pink nail polish. She is forgetful, careless, and most likely a student. Admit it, you're astonished!"

"Dad, no. It was given to me by Henry who works in IT for Avon and Somerset Constabulary, never taken drugs ever!"

"Oh. I take it he's a short-arse, like me?"

"No, the opposite."

"Ah. But he has a ginger cat and wears pink nail polish? Henry, I mean, not the ginger cat."

"No."

"Does he have a beard like a hipster?"

"Yes."

"Is it ginger?"

"A bit."

"Hah! I was right!"

"Bye, Dad."

CHAPTER TWO

Hair of the Dog

September 2020

INDIGESTION

A NEW MORNING, and I'm straight back to muesli, tea and HOUN.

Holmes smokes a cigarette before he examines Mortimer's walking stick; smokes a second as he listens to Dr Mortimer read aloud the Curse of the Baskervilles (and extinguishes this cigarette by tossing it into the fire); and, most alarmingly, he has smoked so many pipes of tobacco that when, at nine o'clock at night, Dr Watson returns to 221b Baker Street from an agreeable day spent at his gentleman's club[9], he initially believes the room to be ablaze – so thick and noxious is the smoke that fills the room. Holmes, who has been examining maps of the moor, admits that he has smoked "an incredible amount of tobacco," along with two large pots of coffee.

I could not even contemplate smoking that much tobacco or drinking that much coffee because it would kill me. I quit smoking a decade ago (like Dr Mortimer, I rolled my own) and I drink one or two

---

[9] I wondered if there were any Gentlemen's Clubs in Bristol that I could join. A Google search quickly dispelled this idea, and I made sure to wipe my browsing history.

cups of coffee a year. And, even then, I feel like I'm dancing with death.

I wondered how many he smokes a day, pipes and cigars included. Google sent me down another rabbit hole from which I emerged baffled by the Victorians and their decidedly queer notions of health products. Smoking was thought to relieve all manner of conditions, from asthma to bronchitis, though there were many in the medical profession who were concerned that smoking carried health risks. Dr Watson would likely have been aware of the arguments for and against smoking and had presumably sided with the former, because he enjoys the occasional cigar himself.

Dr Mortimer has brought a centuries old manuscript with him to Baker Street, detailing The Curse of the Baskervilles. Holmes had observed the manuscript in Mortimer's pocket, dating it to the early 18th Century, unless otherwise the work of a skilled forger. How is the detective able to accurately pinpoint the dating of a manuscript that has yet to be removed from a pocket? Why, because he has written a monograph on the subject.

I felt my pulse quicken at the mention of Holmes's 'little' monographs, though it may have been a result of indigestion from gulping down spoonfuls of nutty muesli... Here was another thing I could do, myself, to follow in the great detective's footsteps. I would write a monograph! But on what subject? And what exactly *was* a monograph?

I jotted down a few ideas for possible monographs ("Some Notes on the Flatulent Effects of Nutty Muesli"; "On Googling"; "A Study of Cartoon Vampire Ducks") and wondered if I risked a heart attack by brewing a cup of coffee. But then the post arrived – all bills, dismayingly – and I decided against it. Instead, I threw a log (and the crumpled-up bills) into the fireplace, got a hearty flame going, and dived back into HOUN.

DR MORTIMER COVETS YOUR SKULL

It should be remarked upon at this stage that Dr Mortimer, in addition to being rather forgetful, is rather weird. He has scarcely been in Holmes and Watson's shared room for two minutes, and uttered no more than three short sentences, when he states he is attracted to the detective's skull and wants to keep it. But first, Weirdo Mortimer wants to run his fingers over it - if Holmes has no objections. Holmes seems to take all this in his stride and offers Dr Mortimer a cigarette, but he doesn't give an answer. In fact, we never get an answer from him. It remains the biggest unsolved mystery in Conan Doyle's work: does Holmes have any objection to Dr Mortimer running his hands over Holmes's skull? I remain haunted by this mystery. And a little aroused by it. Not least because Sir Arthur describes Dr Mortimer as having "long, quivering fingers as agile and restless as the antennae of an insect." Phoarwh!

I tiptoed into the kitchen, where my wife was opening another bottle of wine. I moved as silently and stealthily as a cat burglar and was soon directly behind her. She had not seen or heard me. Excellent. I wanted to give her an erotic thrill by running my hands over her skull. I wanted to put some spice and spontaneity into our marriage. I wanted to show my wife that I could be sensual and mysterious. I reached out and very gently ran my hands over her skull. She screamed bloody murder and elbowed me in the face, making me cry out in agony.

"What the hell do you think you're doing?"

"I ding you'b broden by dose!" I spluttered. Blood was streaming out of my nostrils, and I was seeing stars. I'm queasy about the substance.

"What?"

"I ded I ding yo'b broden by dose!"

"Well, what do you expect, if you sneak up on me like that? What were you doing?"

"I wanded do run by hand ober your skull."

"What?"

I repeated my answer, many times, before resorting to writing it down on the shopping list pinned to the fridge with a dog bone-shaped magnet.

"For God's sake, why?"

"Do pud dome erodic spide bag indo our marriage," I said, "Like Dr Mordimer in Duh Houndb ob duh Baddervilled."

That sentence took forever to explain, even in written form, so eventually I showed my wife the relevant passage in my copy of *The Hound of the Baskervilles*. But, by then, she had lost all interest and was attacking the wine – an improvement, I had to admit, over her attacking my nose. My book now has a bloody thumb print on page 8[10].

I wiped away the blood, set aside my book, and got myself ready to watch some HOUN, for I was eager to continue my marathon. And also, it would keep me out of the way of my wife, who kept laughing when she saw me.

DON'T PANIC!

I think that in the weeks leading up to his death, Sir Charles was suffering from panic attacks on top of being hunted by a gigantic spectral hound. I could completely relate - even though, to the best of my knowledge, I am not being hunted by a giant ghost dog in the weeks leading up to my death.

About a decade ago, I started having severe panic attacks. The symptoms included thinking I was having a heart attack or a severe stroke, flashing vision, nausea, numbness throughout the body, heavy breathing and hyperventilation, dizziness, hot flushes, and a sudden, profound

---

[10] Pleasingly, precisely on the word 'forefinger'.

understanding of Franz Kafka.

At first, I didn't understand what I was experiencing. I didn't know I was having panic attacks – I thought I was dying. And I was a bit upset about that because I don't particularly want to die. It was a relief to discover that I wasn't dying. I simply had an anxiety disorder, hypertension, and arrhythmia. The panic attacks were sometimes brought on by high blood pressure, so it became important for my well-being that I found a way to calm down and not get too worked up about things.

When my anxiety disorder was at its worst, I would get severe panic attacks in public places. I went to the cinema with a friend to see *Interstellar* (2014) and about half-way through I suffered a horrible panic attack where I was sure I was having a stroke. I had to get out of the cinema, but felt very embarrassed and self-conscious, and... Well, it was horrible. Stumbling over people, increasingly desperate, I finally got the hell out of there and my friend drove me home. And he didn't even send me an invoice for the reimbursement of his cinema ticket. Or for petrol.

I still haven't watched *Interstellar*. I get a bit anxious thinking about it. And besides, Chris Nolan films give me a headache. But above all else, I couldn't face going to the cinema again. I couldn't be in there, in the dark, with all those people, the huge screen and the surround sound booming at me...

Perhaps the worst panic attack I could remember happened in a busy supermarket one Sunday afternoon. It was in Bedminster, so really it was my fault for going there[11]. But I couldn't face going to a supermarket again.

I had another panic attack in beautiful Wells Cathedral. I had a panic attack on a train. I had a panic attack in a bookshop. And in a library. I had a panic attack in the Japanese Garden of Peace and Remembrance,

---

[11] Rather unloved urban district of Bristol that desperately needs some care, attention, and money. The people are nice. The area isn't.

killing time before I attended a Coping with Anxiety therapy session. And yes, I'm completely aware of the irony, particularly since I was also on an Irony Awareness course[12].

My doctor recommended I join a therapy group and prescribed me daily medication for my blood pressure and for my anxiety.

At group therapy, I was taught to use Cognitive Behaviour Therapy (or CBT) techniques to change the way I think and behave when anxious. For example, after an attack, I would write down what I had felt, and what I had been feeling beforehand. Then, when I was feeling healthier, I could see that there was often a pattern to the build-up when I would be getting more and more stressed. I would then visualise this as a bucket, filled to the brim with water – some water needed to be let out before the bucket overfilled. When I next started to feel increasingly anxious, I would visualise the bucket, and start to control my breathing so that each deep breath I let out was calming me down. I could see the water level in the bucket falling and I would feel a bit better. It was all about identifying the thoughts that lead to feelings of anxiety, stepping back to see that these negative thoughts don't match the reality of a situation. By doing this I would feel as if I had regained a bit of my life. Sir Charles Baskerville couldn't do anything about the chronic anxiety he was living through in his final days, and I feel sorry for him. I would have liked to have stayed with him at Baskerville Hall, been there by his side in his darkest moments, telling him all about stress buckets and Chris Nolan films.

Other useful CBT techniques include realising I was "catastrophising"; that is, always thinking the worst possible thing was going to happen all the time, though to be fair this was usually the case when I was called on to help shut down a nuclear reactor that had gone critical in the middle of a war zone being ripped apart by guerrilla freedom fighters

---

[12] This is a gag, obviously, but I really hope that someday someone starts such a course.

on one side and an occupying army on the other.

Through the Anxiety Management course, I learned how little things I could do had a big impact in stopping full-blown anxiety attacks. Running my wrists under cold water, for instance, concentrating on being fully aware of the sensation of water on my skin. Being totally in the moment prevents the feeling of being overwhelmed. Similarly, occupying myself with a task, such as doing the washing up, where I would deliberately register the physical sensations of the water or the bubbles, the cloth, the dishes. Using a broom or a mop to clean the floor is also great, getting lost in the action of sweeping, allowing myself to feel calmer. I found, too, that I was unable to panic if my mind was occupied with an immediate problem, such as a chess move, playing against my computer, or outwitting the cats.

These little CBT techniques are quite meditative in a way and are a little bit like the practice of Mindfulness. I have found that I am not good at daily meditation sessions where you're supposed to sit cross-legged and empty your mind, feeling very zen and at peace and into hummus and muesli and lentils and listening to Sting pretentiously play a lute. I'm rubbish at all of that. But I do find the little CBT things helpful; I really do think there's a little bit of mindfulness involved.

Sometimes I'm in a bit of a depressive slump, uncommunicative and lethargic. I don't contact people, and I don't exercise. Could be days, could be weeks. I always feel a bit ashamed afterwards, like I've let everybody down. On the other hand, these periods of low energy and low mood are great for binge watching all the Basil Rathbone and Nigel Bruce Sherlock Holmes films, so it's not all bad.

THE WIND OF THE STADONS

Dr Mortimer reads the legend of the Curse of the Baskervilles to

Holmes and Watson; both men seem unimpressed. Perhaps they would have been more taken with my own family legend (that I've just made up) for I have in my pocket a manuscript which any half-decent consulting detective, having observed the inch or two of the document presented for inspection all the time I have been writing, would date to early last week. This manuscript is a statement of a certain legend which runs in the Stadon family:

"Of the origins of the Wind of the Stadons there have been many statements, yet as I come in a direct line from Terrence Keith Stadon, and as I had the story from my father, I have set it down with all belief that it occurred even as is here set forth.

Terrence was, like the 70's Blaxploitation 'Private Dick' John Shaft, a complicated man. He loved watching sport on the telly and going for a pint of bass with a whiskey chaser in his local, *The Fellowship*, on Filton Avenue, a cesspit of horror and depravity, with a knackered pool table in the lounge that would never return the white ball when you went in off, and a disappointing selection of John Smith's mild bitter. Terrence would tell his four young sons to each pull his finger, and then he would break wind four times, each more wicked and foul and profane, and he would be greatly amused by his mischief, and he would settle in his chair with his *Daily Mirror* and chuckle to himself until he fell asleep to *Pro-Celebrity Golf* on BBC2.

But he had a dark side which landed him in trouble with the authorities, along with a callous disregard for BBC weathermen, whom he would jeer at and pelt the screen with rotten fruit when he saw them. And if he were to chance upon them in the flesh, he would physically accost the unsuspecting celebrity meteorologists by approaching them from behind and tapping them on the shoulder, pretending he was innocent of the act when the weatherman – John Kettley[13], say, or Ian McCaskill, would look to see who had so boldly demanded their attention.

And so it was in the autumn of 1987, when Madonna was *Causing a Commotion* and M|A|R|R|S told us to *Pump Up The Volume*, that, on a whim, Terrence decided to construct an unnecessary porch extension for the back door of his home – a semi-detached council house with a wonky gate. He set to work, swearing and sweating as he sawed through planks and hammered in nails, measuring things half-heartedly, having to cut new pieces when the old ones didn't fit. As Terrence worked and swore, he steadfastly ignored all reasoned advice from his wife and sons, and from the Met Office – pioneers in the science of meteorology since its foundation in 1854, uniting scientific leaders from across the globe through their exceptional scientific, technological and operational expertise as the most trusted weather forecasters in the world – that things were looking a bit nippy and blustery and it might've been best to postpone the construction of his unnecessary porch extension until the South West saw a spell of much more clement weather conditions.

That night, as Terrence sat in his armchair with his *Daily Mirror* and Glenfiddich Single Malt, happy and content with his day's work on the unnecessary porch extension, there occurred a violent extratropical cyclone with hurricane-force winds, which caused casualties in the United Kingdom, France, and the Channel Islands as a severe depression in the Bay of Biscay moved northeast. Among the most damaged areas were Greater London, the East Anglian coast, the Home Counties, the west of Brittany, and the Cotentin Peninsula of Normandy, all of which weathered gusts typically with a return period of 1 in 200 years. Forests, parks, roads and railways were strewn with fallen trees and schools were closed. The British National Grid suffered heavy damage, leaving

---

[13] Immortalised in the novelty song *John Kettley (is a Weatherman)* by Sunderland-based band A Tribe of Toffs which peaked at 21 in the UK Singles Chart in December 1988.

thousands without power. At least 22 people were killed in England and France. The highest recorded gust in the UK was 122 mph. The storm has been termed a 'weather bomb' due to its rapid development.

Needless to say, Terrence Keith Stadon's unnecessary porch extension did not survive that night. It was, in fact, ripped from its moorings and hurled at 122 mph into a neighbour's greenhouse, smashing it to pieces and ruining a promising crop of runner beans. When the terrible storm had at last abated and it was once again safe to step outside, free from the destructive power of the Wind of the Stadons, Terrence examined the damage as his sons looked on in awe.

"Never speak of this," Terence instructed his boys. "Never speak of this ever again."

But oh, if only the boys had heeded the words of their father! For it was Vince Stadon, third youngest and most intelligent of the clan, sexy and appealing to women, who was next to suffer the cursed maelstrom that blighted the Stadons. Vince, now a handsome, intelligent, and interesting father of two incredibly sarcastic children, had inherited both his father's disdain for BBC weather presenters and his shoddy carpentry skills; both would factor in the story of his undoing.

Thirty years had passed since the Wind of the Stadons had turned Terrence's unnecessary porch extension into matchwood. Taylor Swift was asking us to *Look What You Made Me Do*, and Demi Lovato was *Sorry Not Sorry*, but Vince had long since stopped listening to chart music and had had to look up those songs on Wikipedia. Just as his father had done, Vince decided on a whim to tackle a shoddy and unnecessary carpentry project, though his woodworking effort – a box for a herb garden – was, it must be said, considerably less ambitious than his father's. He toiled all day on his box, sawing planks and hammering in nails and measuring things half-heartedly, necessitating in having to cut new pieces that actually fit. His long-suffering wife looked on, giggling to herself as

Vince whacked his thumb with a hammer or threw a plank of wood across the garden in anger because he'd gotten the measuring bit wrong once again. Maths was never his strong point, nor was patience, nor were practical abilities.

That night, as Vince read *The Hound of the Baskervilles*, heavy rain fell over the land and soaked into his terrible herb garden box which he had neglected to varnish, having tired quickly and completely of the ill-fated project. Within weeks, the box fell to bits and was blown away by the Wind of the Stadons which this time manifested itself as Storm Brian, one of the more minor autumnal weather events of that year. It trended on Twitter for at least a day or so, after which it died down pretty quickly, on the whole.

Such is the tale, my sons, of the coming of the wind which is said to have plagued the family so sorely ever since. To that Providence, my sons, I hereby commend you, and I counsel you by way of caution to forbear from shoddy and unnecessary woodworking projects in those dark hours when the weather is looking a bit nippy and blustery, and the Met Office is warning of potential disruptive weather conditions for the South West of England.

Only Making Plans For Nigel (Bruce)

The Hound of the Baskervilles starring Basil Rathbone (B&W film, USA, 1939)

With my second pick from the Deerstalker of Doom, I hit gold: the best version of all, the Basil Rathbone-starring version from 1939, a fog-drenched *bona fide* classic that stands comparison with the best that cinema has to offer. I scoffed down Doritos and chugged Tom Baker-smelling red wine as I lounged on the sofa and thoroughly enjoyed reacquainting myself with this masterpiece.

There's so much to love about this film, but I'll settle for picking just a few things: Lionel Atwill as Dr Mortimer[14], whose spaniel is already dead when he visits Baker Street. The iconic shot of Rathbone as Holmes in his dressing gown, picking up his violin, playing a few notes – much to Watson's dismay – before a thought occurs to him and he puts down his bow and swaps it for a newspaper clipping, announcing Sir Henry Baskerville arriving in England. Selden on the moor, throwing a huge, heavy boulder at Watson and Henry. The fantastic Moor studio set, drenched in fog; Amanda J Field writes in her book *England's Secret Weapon* that "a crew of 98 artisans spent seven months constructing a 300 by 200 feet moor on the studio's 'cyclorama' stage." This is a big budget Twentieth Century Fox production and all the money is up there on the screen. Rathbone disguised as a wizened, bedraggled asthmatic hobbling about the moor, selling musical instruments ("I'm jus' peddlin' me wares, sir!"), irritating Watson who gets to note that the old man limps away on his *other* leg[15]. Watson and the old man's second meeting, with Watson boasting that he is the famous detective Sherlock Holmes and Holmes, himself, playing a few notes on a zephyr that sounds uncannily like the opening guitar part from Led Zeppelin's *Stairway to Heaven*[16]. And huffy Watson, later in the same scene, tucking into a plate of sardines. This film is such a joy.

I'm always amused by the scene where Stapleton attempts to kill

---

[14] Atwill, a staple of Universal's splendid horror film series, pops up in the fourth Rathbone/Bruce outing, *Sherlock Holmes and the Secret Weapon* (1942) as a quite wonderful Professor Moriarty.
[15] Rathbone Holmes in disguise is one of my favourite things, and luckily for me there are many examples throughout the Rathbone/Bruce films. My favourites include Holmes disguised as a Vaudeville entertainer, singing *I Do Like to be Beside the Seaside* in *The Adventures of Sherlock Holmes* (1939), and Holmes as a cheeky cockney mailman winding up a grieving Dr Watson in *Spider Woman* (1943). From the same film, Holmes in black face as a disgraced Indian soldier is only to be regretted.
[16] *Stairway to Heaven*, of course, is the last song on Side One of *Led Zeppelin IV* (1971) ...which has, as its' kinetic opening track, the phenomenal *Black Dog*.

Sir Henry in London, presumably so he won't have to bother with any of the big scary dog nonsense – just shoot the Canadian heir in the face and be done with it! Even more amusing is the scene where a rock wrapped in the 'Beware the moor' note is lobbed through the window of Sir Henry's moving cab, nearly braining the man. Imagine if the stone had struck with lethal impact! That would have been an awkward conversation between the Stapletons back at their hotel:

"My god, Beryl, have you seen the headlines? Sir Henry Baskerville is dead!"

"What? No, Jack, it can't be! Did you kill him?"

"No, my love, I did not! I tried to, I wanted to, but someone beat me to it! I can't believe my luck."

"Then who? How?"

"There's a quote here from a policeman - one Inspector G Lestrade of Scotland Yard, who says, 'We are in the preliminary stages of our investigation into the murder of the Canadian tourist Henry Baskerville, and we have many lines of inquiry, chief amongst them the search for witnesses who may have seen the murderer throw a rock at the hansom cab, carrying Mr Baskerville as a passenger, as it raced eastwards along Great Portland Street.' My word! It seems, dear wife, that someone did for Henry with a rock! Hah! What do you say to that, Beryl? Beryl? Beryl, you've gone white!"

Also amusing is the sweet scene of Sir Henry arriving in England aboard a steamer, saying his farewells to passengers and crew, and being dogged by young English girl Betsy Rose and her formidable mother. They've taken a shine to the baronet and would very much like to develop the relationship.

"You'll keep in touch, won't you? We're staying at The Savoy..."

Bless them. Things would have gone very differently if Henry had reciprocated sweet Betsy Ann's affections. I wonder what happened to the young lady. Has anyone ever written about her, perhaps featured her as the lead in a short story or even a novel? I wonder if my publisher would be interested in *The Unrequited Loves and Murder Cases of Betsy Ann (and her Formidable Mother)*.

All the way through my viewing of this delightful film, I thought about poor Nigel Bruce. Poor, loveable old Nigel Bruce. Because Bruce's Dr Watson is loathed throughout sections of the Sherlockian fan community for being nothing like the capable, intelligent doctor from the books. Nigel Bruce is the first comedy Watson (or at least, he's positioned as such opposite Basil Rathbone's Holmes) and, as such, he is hated with a passion. But I love him as I love me a comedy Watson, so I set about writing a rubbish poem in his honour:

I propose we call an immediate truce

On the war surrounding Nigel Bruce

To hate on him is to be obtuse

Let's give some love to Nigel Bruce

For seventy years there's been division

And scorn, rejection, and derision

For this amiable sidekick to Basil Rathbone

The alpha Holmes of pure testosterone

But it's time for rancour to be cut loose

And we all learn to love Nigel Bruce

They called him 'bumbling', they called him 'duffer'

They wanted nothing more than to see him suffer

They wanted him gone without too much fuss

They nicknamed him 'Boobus Britannicus'

But they were wrong to dish out all that abuse

So, let's give some love to Nigel Bruce

From thirty-nine to forty-six

Despite the boos from sceptics

This one-time guest at Baskerville Hall

Battled Nazi spies all through the war

It is therefore elementary to deduce

That he was worth our love, was Nigel Bruce

This well-built man who stands six foot two

Towers over Lucy Liu

And in every film, he gave it his all

Though he's not as fit as Jude Law

There's a moose loose aboot this hoose

So, let's give some love to Nigel Bruce

WHEN I WAS TWELVE

My love for Nigel Bruce undoubtedly stems from him being my very first Dr Watson. Regardless of his merit, or lack of, in the part (and how it was written for him), he was the first one I set eyes on. And like favourite Dr Whos, James Bonds, or Secretary Generals of the TUC[17], it's only natural that you love the first one you ever saw.

I have a clear recollection of when and where I watched my first Sherlock Holmes film. I saw Nigel's impressive moustache from across a crowded living room one cold Friday early evening, in the first week of February 1982, when I was twelve. He was on Dartmoor, chasing the Hound in foggy BBC2 black and white. And brilliantly, he was back (with Sherlock Holmes, of course) the week after, and the week after that, and then every week through February, into March, then April. I can remember the crisp snow and hard ice of that very cold winter, watching Peter Davison's Dr Who[18] step out of his TARDIS for the very first time on telly. Early evenings lying on the carpet next to the three-bar electric heater in the living room, keeping company with these very British heroes: Basil's Holmes, Nigel's Watson, and Peter's Doctor.

In my memory, all three of them are chasing the Hound across Dartmoor as thick snow falls. Through the fog of memory and the rolling mists over the moor I see the flashing lamp on top of the Police Box as the TARDIS materialises, and the roar of time engines merges into the baying of the beast. The doors open to Sherlock Holmes and Dr Watson, both rushing out onto the moor, Watson muttering under his breath about the "confounded machine" before stumbling into the Grimpen Mire. "Good old Watson," says Basil's Holmes, pulling his friend out of the quicksand. And he *is* a good old Watson, that Nigel Bruce – a comforting,

---

[17] 1973 - 1983 Lionel Murray.
[18] I've always called the character Dr Who because, well, that's the character's name! My wonderful copy editor, however, corrected 'Dr Who' to 'The Doctor' and left the following charming note: "I will be correcting these as we don't want Whoovians (or, universe forbid, Superwholockians) to come for you with flaming pitchforks. Footnote: Nothing against Superwholockians, but they can be vicious creatures when tested. As a 2010s tumblr veteran, I should know." I've changed it back to Dr Who, not least because I'd love to be chased with flaming pitchforks (it's on my Bucket List!), but I've left the occasional corrected Doctor/The Doctor, just to be kind. And this footnote was suggested by friend Kim Woo, who delights in this kind of thing.

amusing, amiable companion.

I've kept him close to my heart ever since then and I entertain a mischievous appreciation for bumbling comedy Watsons who stumble through fog, muttering baffled protestations as they gamely try to keep up with the Best Brain in England.

PUZZLED

After the film, I spent the rest of the day writing and ignoring the cats. My wife was upstairs with a bottle of wine, 'zooming with the girls'. At supper time I decided to make inroads into the thousand-piece HOUN jigsaw puzzle. I cleared the dinner table, put on some soothing music, and set to work.

I started, as one is supposed to with jigsaw puzzles – by finding all the straight edged pieces. This process would have gone much smoother if one of the cats, Fergal, hadn't decided to go to sleep in the puzzle box. I lifted him out, putting him on the table. He was so annoyed by this that he engaged in a terror campaign against me, disrupting my puzzle making by pawing at the pieces, knocking them to the floor, hissing at me, yowling, and generally being horrid. Eventually I defrosted a chicken fillet, cut it up into small chunks, and fed it to him bit by bit as I worked on the outside of the puzzle. Fergal fell asleep on the table and, from that moment on, I made excellent progress; the entire outer edge was complete, aside from one corner piece. Yay!

As I rummaged in the box, looking for the corner piece, I congratulated myself on keeping calm. Puzzles have been known to bring out the worst in me.

Rummaging through the box of pieces proved fruitless. I needed a system. I decided to remove each piece one by one and put them in the lid of the box. Repeated this two times. No sign of the corner piece. Midnight was far-approaching and I was tired and frustrated. I was no longer calm. The piece must be on the floor. Fergal must have knocked it off and, unlike the other pieces which I retrieved, I must have missed this one. I crawled under the table and looked on the floor, but couldn't see anything. I got up, went into the study, retrieved my magnifying glass, and crawled back under the table. I imagined the floor under the table to be lined with a grid and moved around, spoking aloud which part of the 'grid' I had examined. I had just reached "F7" when my wife said:

"What the hell do you think you're doing?"

I banged my head on the underside of the table. I hadn't heard her come downstairs.

"Hello, dear, did you have a nice time?"

"Why are you crawling around on the floor? Why are you wearing a deerstalker hat?"

"I'm looking for a missing piece of the jigsaw. Fergal knocked it off the table. He's been a complete git."

Predictably, Fergal sauntered over to my wife and started rubbing his head against one of her legs, being ridiculously cute and adorable. My wife bent down to rub his ear.

"*This* piece?" she said. "It was on Fergal's tail, near his bum."

I emerged from under the table and got to my feet.

"Bloody cat," I said, taking the piece from her.

As my wife staggered up the stairs to the bathroom, I slotted in the final piece of the outside edges of the HOUN puzzle. There. It had only taken me three hours.

CHAPTER THREE

One Man and His Dog

October 2020

GRANGER THINGS

> *The Hound of the Baskervilles* starring Stewart Granger (TV movie, USA, 1972)

THE DEERSTALKER OF DOOM spews out the Stewart Granger *Hound of the Baskervilles,* a low-budget TV Movie adaptation intended as part of a short film series depicting famous detectives[19]. I'd never seen this version before, but I had read many scathing reviews. It couldn't be as bad as everybody said, could it? Yes. It could. In fact, reviews have been kind to it, for it's even worse than its terrible reputation. I came away from my viewing, having noted three things of interest:

1. Shatner! Yes, William Shatner is the villain in *The Hound of the Baskervilles (*1972)! Hooray! Shatner, a joyous screen presence,

---

[19] The others were *The Adventures of Nick Carter* (a 'dime novel' private detective created for comic strips by Ormond G Smith and John L Coryell), starring Robert Conrad in the title role, and *A Very Missing Person,* starring Eve Arden as Hildegarde Withers, a Bostonian schoolteacher who gets involved in whimsical mysteries, created by the novelist Stuart Palmer.

incapable of being boring[20], enlivens everything he's in. He's a complete hoot as Sir Hugo Baskerville in a big, scraggly black beard and long poodle hair, striding through Baskerville Hall in boots and breeches, roaring at his own wickedness. He's such good fun that he overshadows the rest of the movie. When he pops up on the moor as Stapleton, waving a butterfly net and trying not to wink at the camera, he can't help but be a bit disappointing. Overplaying Sir Hugo and underplaying Stapleton means that Shatner, in fact, steals the movie away from himself. You gotta admire that.

2. The Sets. This is clearly a low budget TV movie that can't afford filming in London. Instead, Baker Street is a backlot in California, under a blazing sun and populated with palm trees. It needs to be seen to be believed, frankly, and I found myself frequently replaying all the scenes set in London just to be sure I wasn't hallucinating. Then I felt bad about being so mean and wondered if there was any chance at all those palm trees might have lined the streets of Marylebone in 1889. I emailed my friend Alan, who is a botanist:

> Hi, I was wondering if it was possible for palm trees to grow in London during the late Victorian era? — Vince

> Vince, no, please stop bothering me. — Alan

I Googled instead, discovering that palm trees *can* grow in England. That is how I found myself ordering some seeds from an online gardening store to try and grow my very own palm trees in my garden, just for the

---

[20] My favourite story about the egocentric William Shatner is that during his *Star Trek* days he had it put into his contract that, on the credits, his name must always appear in a bigger typeface than his castmates. A production memo from 1966 says: "Please note that Leonard Nimoy's credit is to be no more than 75% of the type that we afford to William Shatner." I would love a t-shirt that has "25% Less Important than William Shatner!" printed on it.

hell of it[21].

More problematic than the unlikely foliage in Baker Street is the geography of this London - for in the background, atop a mighty hill, is St Paul's Cathedral (possibly with palm trees in its grounds). This means that, in a parallel Earth, London exists where a huge mound of earth towers over the west of the city, and Sir Christopher Wren decided that this gargantuan hill would be the perfect place to build a Cathedral. Mind you, this new layout of London – presumably, all traffic must go around the hill – might well be an improvement. The moor, meanwhile, is an obvious studio set with plastic rocks that Shatner no doubt patted with familiarity and fondness. Grimpen village is so clearly a standing set used for westerns that I kept expecting a drunken cowboy to be thrown out of the window of a saloon.

3. Sherlock Holmes is so boring anddeathly dull and tedious that I fell asleep during several of his scenes. He's played by Stewart Granger, aged 58 at the time of filming (a staggering 23 years older than the character from the novel!), tanned orange, with bright white hair and enormous white sideburns, making him look like a geriatric vampire made up of Roger Moore's tan and a cotton wool widow's peak. He wears a kind of Mississippi Gambler costume when he's not donning the Inverness cape and deerstalker and often looks drunk or bored (or both) as if he's turned up on set under heavy sedation. Seemingly devoid of any discernible personality or spark, this somnambulistic white fox may be the most boring Sherlock Holmes on screen.

More interesting than anything on screen is the tragedy which befell the director. A veteran director of US television serials (*Mission:*

---

[21] I bought a 'Grow Your Own Palm Tree' kit from an online seller which promises I can grow a Washingtonia Robusta in my garden. The kit comes in a biodegradable Ecocube Planter Ecocube pot, which naturally decomposes and turns into fertiliser. It cost me £19.95.

Impossible, Wonder Woman, The Incredible Hulk, etc.), Barry Crane was also a 13 time champion Bridge player – there's even a cup named after him. He was found dead by his housekeeper in July 1985. His body was wrapped in bedding on the floor of his garage, according to the Los Angeles police. The murder went unsolved for three decades until an arrest was made in 2019. The killer, Edwin Hiatt, admitted to killing Crane, but can offer no explanation for doing so as he allegedly cannot remember doing it. Weird.

Three HOUN adaptations down, with two that were resoundingly terrible. Sigh. A disappointing start. Any lesser man would have given up at this point, but I had made a promise to the cats that I was going to experience every version of HOUN ever produced, so I ploughed on.

But not before I watched *Enola Holmes*[22], which had just dropped on Netflix. It was excellent.

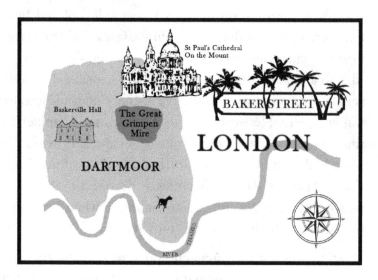

---

[22] Sherlock's younger daughter, played splendidly by Millie Bobby Brown. The film is adapted from Nancy Springer's series of Young Adult novels. Henry Cavill, Superman himself, plays Sherlock, though disappointingly without the 'S' logo on his chest, and his underpants on the outside of his trousers.

LIKE A DOG WITH A BONE

Wishbone / Season 1 Episode 8 / *The Slobbery Hound* (kids TV show, 1995)

The next pick, plucked from the Deerstalker of Doom, was *Wishbone*, a US Kids TV show with a literary/educational bent that ran for two seasons on Kids PBS. Each half hour-long show revolves around a classic book, with dramatizations bookended by sitcom shenanigans set in the present day.

I'd never heard of it before, but was pleased to discover a high-quality version on YouTube and even more pleased to discover that it's great fun. Wishbone, a wise-cracking Jack Russell, is an engaging character who manages to effectively and economically tell the story of HOUN in about fifteen short scenes. (How the production team get the dog to perform so professionally is a wonder - I've worked with actors who aren't half as cooperative or talented.)

Having a dog play Sherlock Holmes does throw up some deeply weird and disturbing images, however, such as having human-Dr Watson stroking dog-Holmes's head while said dog reclines in an armchair, smoking a pipe. Remember those freaky paintings of dogs playing pool? It's a bit like that.

I started thinking about dogs playing Holmes in other versions of HOUN, and before I knew it, I had created an illustration. I think my wife might be right. I am going slightly mad.

THE SIGHS OF MARTIN FREEMAN

Sherlock: The Hounds of Baskerville, starring Benedict Cumberbatch

(UK TV Serial, 2012)

Next up, I pick *Sherlock: The Hounds of Baskerville.* I wonder how I'm going to approach watching it, because the cultural impact of *Sherlock* is huge. It has a protective, creative and very charming fanbase. While the show may not be entirely my thing, I can't deny how important it is and how much it means to people. I reason that in order to do it justice.

I need help. From Twitter. I invite around ten of my meagre collection of followers to join in a 'tweetalong' (with cake), and I thankfully get a particularly good response (and only a couple of unfollows). These followers are from a diverse sampling as I'm interested in opinions that are far away from those of a white man in his fifties (though only just!) with an unhealthy obsession with squirrels and a broken nose that hurts like a bastard. I set a date and time, create a suitable hashtag (I later brag about this to my daughter), bake a Victoria Sponge with jam filling (which my wife confiscates), and off we go. You can read the full 'tweetalong' in Appendix Two.

It's worth me mentioning that I was in some small way responsible for Benedict Cumberbatch's casting as Sherlock. Well, in a sense. Alright, in no sense. But I *did* call for him to be cast in the part on a public message board[23] way back when a new BBC Sherlock Holmes television series was originally announced, several months before any casting news hit the media. So, go me!

Cumberbatch is terrific, though I'm not at all sold on this 'high functioning psychopath' Holmes, who sometimes comes across to me as a charmless and infantile boor. Martin Freeman is a fine Watson and the relationship between the two men feels authentic and charming. I believe them as friends and colleagues and flatmates. I like their onscreen

---

[23] Roobarb's DVD Forum, a charmingly grumpy message board devoted to UK TV, DVD and Blu-Ray collecting, etc.

chemistry, and I enjoy spending time with them when Holmes isn't being a complete dick.

The decision not to use Watson as a narrator, or to have him as a viewpoint figure throughout, is a mistake. We spend too much time in the company of Holmes, rather than his faithful chronicler (sorry, *blogger*). The Doyle stories aren't really about the plots – they're about Watson's opinions and thoughts about this most remarkable of men. Moffat and Gatiss[24] wisely decided to strip the Victoriana from the Sherlock Holmes stories, placing the relationship between Holmes and Watson centre stage, but they fudge it by making the characters subservient to complicated plots. There is, frankly, too much twisty-turny stuff going on in these episodes that ill-serves the characters who enter and exit scenes at the caprice of a plot point. Better, by far, to have the whole thing seen from Watson's viewpoint.

What *Sherlock* does best, for me, is make excellent use of London, depicting it as wild and exciting hunting ground. I was always intrigued to see how the series fares when it gets away from the capital to the wilds of Dartmoor, so I was pleased to discover that, on the whole, the photography of the moor is wonderful. Best of all, the inspired idea of having the fog itself be the 'monster' might be the best idea Mark Gatiss has ever had. Fog, on Dartmoor, at night – *Sherlock* knocks it out of the park.

Less good is the scene where Cumberbatch's Sherlock is seen to be enjoying watching Watson terrified out of his wits. It marks the detective out as cruel and uncaring, and undercuts the friendship that had been so deftly handled in previous episodes. Martin Freeman's Watson seems to spend the bulk of his time sighing, and it's no wonder. I don't

---

[24] Steven Moffat and Mark Gatiss, two of UK television's best-known writers (and in Gatiss's case – actor, broadcaster, and occasional director). Moffat oversaw the writing and production of *Dr Who* for a decade, with Gatiss regularly contributing scripts. The two men went on to create a new adaption of *Dracula*, broadcast in January 2020 on BBC1..

think any other version of Watson has been as badly treated as this one poor sod.

Sherlock has a 'mind palace', which is depicted on screen by having Cumberbatch stand still as the camera swoops around him and various bits of text and imagery is superimposed, then dismissed with swooshing sound effects as Cumberbatch swipes them away. At one point, a cut-out black and white portrait of the American composer John Philip Sousa is superimposed over Sherlock's face as we hear a snatch of his most famous piece of music, *The Liberty Bell* (better known to everyone and anyone who's ever eaten spam as the theme music to *Monty Python's Flying Circus*). This is very silly stuff, and *Sherlock*'s tone - flashy, self-reverential, bombastic - plays against the comedy, making it seem even sillier. That said, Watson gets some very witty lines in these sequences, not least his weary reply to Dr Stapleton's confusion as to why Sherlock would choose a palace of all things for his mind memory exercises:

> "Well, he would, wouldn't he?", deadpans Martin Freeman with a sigh.

I don't think I'll ever love *Sherlock*, but I do love how massively popular it was and how it turned so many people onto Sherlock Holmes. In its wake came a flourishing of Sherlock Holmes releases, including a second excellent big budget Sherlock Holmes movie, *Sherlock Holmes: A Game of Shadows* (2011) starring Robert Downey Jnr as a scruffy, physical Holmes, and Jude Law as a wonderful Watson. Then we have *Mr Holmes*, (2015), starring Ian McKellan as a retired Holmes, and *Elementary* (2012-2019), a US crime procedural starring Jonny Lee Miller and Lucy Liu[25] as Sherlock Holmes and Joan Watson. Last but not least, there's *Miss Sherlock* (2018), an-all female version of *Sherlock* set in

---

[25] See Chapter Eleven for a review of *Elementary*'s take on HOUN.

Tokyo, starring the brilliant Yuko Takeuchi[26]. *Sherlock* was such a smash hit that for a while back in the mid twenty tens, Sherlock Holmes was everywhere – it was Sherlockmania, and I delighted in it.

Sherlock: The Hounds of Baskerville, so far as I can ascertain from a delve into *Sherlock* fandom, isn't regarded as the best of the series, nor is it considered to be a failure. I think the fandom has it bang on. There's enough good stuff to make it watchable, but it's overall not the pinnacle of the series. It is, though, absolutely perfect for the Twitter age, so please do go straight to Appendix Three, read the full 'tweetalong' and count along with me the sighs of Martin Freeman.

THE TEN MOST FAMOUS LINES OR QUOTES IN THE SHERLOCK HOLMES STORIES. PROBABLY.

HOUN's Chapter Three picks up from Chapter Two's cliffhanger and the most famous lines in the book (and indeed some of the most famous in literature), as Dr Mortimer explains that the footprints in the muddy ground in the Yew Alley leading away from Baskerville Hall, near to the contorted body of Sir Charles Baskerville, belonged not to a man or a woman:

"Mr Holmes, they were the footprints of a gigantic hound!"

I love that line to bits. It got me thinking about all the famous lines in 'the Canon'[27] that I decided to list them. Obviously, I've done no research, so you'll just have to take my word for it that these are the most

---

[26] Very sadly, Yuko Takeuchi took her own life in September 2020, just as I was starting my HOUN marathon. I watched the whole series of *Miss Sherlock* again in tribute to her. She was amazing and the world misses her.

[27] The 56 short stories and 4 novels written by Arthur Conan Doyle. For Sherlockians, no other subsequent work counts as authentic. Not even my own silly Sherlock Holmes stories. It's a bit like the rules of *Fight Club* (1999): The first rule of Canon is that you don't talk about anything other than the Canon. The second rule of Canon is that Canon must have a capital C, to distinguish it from other uses of the word canon.

famous lines in the Sherlock Holmes stories.

1. "Elementary..." *The Adventure of the Crooked Man*

Never appended with "...my dear Watson"[28], or any other use of his name, despite everyone and their spectral dog believing otherwise. 'Elementary, my dear Watson' has become, ironically erroneously, Holmes's catchphrase because of pastiche use of it in films and television shows. This places it in the Mandela Effect category, alongside *Star Trek*'s "Beam me up, Scotty!"; *Casablanca*'s "Play it again, Sam"; and "I don't think we're in Kansas anymore, Toto," from *The Wizard of Oz* (1939). The origin of the 'elementary' phrase is from a passage in *The Adventure of the Crooked Man*:

> "Excellent!" I cried.

> "Elementary," said he.

No real person ever says it in real life unless they're being a dick.

2. "When you have eliminated the impossible..." *The Sign of Four*

The full quote is:

> "How often have I said to you that when you have eliminated the impossible, whatever remains, however improbable, must be the truth?"

And we don't know the answer to that as this is only the second Sherlock Holmes adventure and Watson hasn't known Holmes long.

---

[28] The phrase "Elementary, my dear Watson!" first appears in print in PG Wodehouse's comic novel *PSmith, Journalist* (1915)

Maybe Holmes says it all the time the way I say, "Oh, for God's sake!" many times a day? Maybe Watson has heard Holmes say the phrase so many times that it's just become white noise to him, and he tunes it out? In any case, it's a snappy line that reduces Holmes's methods to a single process (though this process of extrapolating from facts and applying logic is the cornerstone of his process). He says it again in *The Adventure of the Beryl Coronet* when he's in full 'explaining what happened' flow.

Watson's eye rolling is not recorded.

3.   "Mr Holmes, they were the footprints of a gigantic hound!" *The Hound of the Baskervilles*

The most exciting statement ever uttered[29], this evocative and sinister phrase instantly conjures images of a wild and monstrous dog bounding out of the fog-drenched moor, eyes blazing like fires from Hell, jaws dripping with fresh blood, its savage instinct being the insane desire to kill, and kill, and kill... This is the principal reason I have cats, not a dog[30].

4.   "The game is afoot!" *The Adventure of the Abbey Grange*

"It was on a bitterly cold and frosty morning, towards the end of the winter of '97, that I was awakened by a tugging at my shoulder. It was Holmes. The candle in his hand shone upon his eager, stooping face, and told me at a glance that something was amiss.

"Come, Watson, come!" he cried. "The game is afoot. Not

---

[29] Next to my wife asking if I fancy a takeaway.
[30] Though I'm seriously reconsidering.

a word! Into your clothes and come!'"

Tough luck for poor Watson who is denied a cosy lie-in.

"Is it urgent, Holmes?" I would have asked. "Can't you give me another hour? It's so snug and warm in bed, and I was dreaming of—"

"*Now,* Watson!"

5.   "The curious affair of the dog in the night-time." *The Adventure of Silver Blaze*

This dog-flavoured quote is uttered during an exchange with Inspector Gregory:

"Is there any point to which you would wish to draw my attention?"

"To the curious incident of the dog in the night-time."

"The dog did nothing in the night-time."

"That was the curious incident," remarked Sherlock Holmes.

"Well, why the bloody hell didn't you just say that, instead of being Mr Smarty Pants?" would have been my response.

6.   "You see but you do not observe." *A Scandal in Bohemia*

Newly married, Dr Watson pops into Baker Street. Holmes promptly tells him that he's put on seven pounds and that his housemaid is useless. Instead of punching the detective, Watson laughs and asks Holmes to explain how he knows these things. Holmes insults Watson further by telling his friend that he sees, but he does not observe. Whereas Holmes sees *and* observes.

Seeing and observing was new to the Victorians, but these days we call it mindfulness, and you can get an app for it on your phone. Mine's called ZenBrain and it's full of pictures of squirrels.

7. "The Napoleon of Crime." *The Adventure of the Final Problem*

Professor Moriarty is introduced in *The Final Problem* as a plausible nemesis to Sherlock Holmes. A man of such intellect and such wickedness that he stands as the equal and opposite of Holmes - the yang to Sherlock's yin. The Andrew Ridgely to Holmes's Wham-era George Michael.

Such a formidable opponent could conceivably bring about Holmes's destruction, thus freeing Sir Arthur of the burden of writing more fiddly detective stories – an occupation that was rather getting on his nerves.

The first part of *The Final Problem*, then, is one long info dump of Holmes rhapsodizing about his nemesis, whom nobody has ever heard of, comparing Moriarty to Napoleon, describing him as 'diabolical', 'a genius, a philosopher, an abstract thinker', a malefactor, some deep organizing power which forever stands in the way of the law, and throws its shield over the wrong-doer'. He has 'a brain of the first order'. He 'sits motionless, like a spider in the centre of its web, but that web has a thousand radiations, and he knows well every quiver of each of them,' and so on and on, until poor Watson could be left in no doubt as to what type of villain is being described.

If MS Powerpoint had been invented back in the late nineteenth century, Holmes would have no doubt spent an entire evening displaying photographs of Moriarty:

"Here is the Professor at the corner shop, buying some chalk - I suspect he is planning some audacious and malevolent scheme involving

49

calcium carbonate. Or perhaps it is the number of the chalk sticks in the packet that is of singular interest, for it conceivably be a coded message with each stick of chalk representing— Watson, why are you putting on your hat and coat?"

8. "There's an east wind coming, Watson..." *His Last Bow*

Set on a day in August 1914 – "the most terrible August in the history of the world" – on the eve of the First World War, *His Last Bow* describes the final case for Sherlock Holmes, now in his sixties, as he outwits a German spy. When Holmes has completed his mission for British Intelligence and outfoxed his opponent, he makes his final speech, talking of the terrors that are about to engulf the world, but ending on a hopeful note. After this, he retired from being a detective and settled down in Sussex to keep bees... Until Sir Arthur was offered *yet another* fortune to write even more Sherlock Holmes stories.

9. "You have been to Afghanistan, I perceive." *A Study in Scarlet*

The first words we hear Sherlock Holmes speak (or rather shout) are: "I've found it! I've found it!" Much more interesting are the *next* words he says by way of greeting Dr Watson in their first meeting, as he instantly deduces that the doctor is recently returned from military action in Afghanistan. These words adorn a plaque on a wall in a tiny museum in St Bartholomew's Hospital, London (moved from its original location in the Pathology Department, where the famous meeting took place). Not on a plaque is Watson's reply: "How on earth did you know that?" Presumably because if a plaque was to be erected in every location Watson says such a thing, then the entirety of the British Isles (and parts of Switzerland) would be covered.

I have always wanted to say these words to someone, and for them to react with astonishment at my powers of deductive reasoning. My plan is to stand on the Afgan-Pakistani border and wait until I observe an English-speaking doctor cross over, whereupon I will covertly follow them for a month, then orchestrate a chance meeting with them at a laboratory where I can confidently state that I perceive them to have been in Afghanistan. I will need a million pounds to make this happen, so it's more of a long-term plan, kind of thing.

10. "My mind is like a racing engine..." *The Adventure of Wisteria Lodge.*

A bored Holmes explains to Dr Watson how tedious life is for him without the intellectual stimulus of taking on a taxing problem, preferably one fraught with danger:

> "My mind is like a racing engine, tearing itself to pieces because it is not connected up with the work for which it was built. Life is commonplace, the papers are sterile; audacity and romance seem to have passed forever from the criminal world."

He says pretty much the same thing in *The Adventure of the Devil's Foot*:

> "To let the brain work without sufficient material is like racing an engine. It racks itself to pieces."

Had he been born a century later, Mr Sherlock Holmes would almost certainly wear a "Life sucks!" t-shirt and listen to My Chemical Romance at too loud a volume in his messy bedroom.

ALL IN THE MIND PALACE

Painted gold with wet leaves, the streets of Bristol look like runways to enchanted lands, and my early evening walk to the park takes on an air of unreality as the rains and dark nights of early Lockdown October unclutters the city of its people.

I pass no one as I reach the river. There is no life in the pubs and restaurants in the centre. I half-glimpse hurried figures in doorways and distant avenues, like hunted spies in haunted spaces. Taxis roam the dark lonely streets, looking for fares. Ghostly double-deckers pass by the empty bus stops. Nobody is here. Everybody is home, in the warm, with Netflix and the uncertainty about what will happen to us all in this cold, new world where all hope is for a vaccine.

Back home, I snuggle on the sofa with my wife and a book on silent films, thankful for the warmth and comfort in my life. I have it lucky, and I should never take that for granted. I fall asleep dreaming I'm lost in Benedict Cumberbatch's mind palace and a hound from hell is hunting me down, but I can't run - I can only do a silly walk, accompanied by the theme tune to *Monty Python's Flying Circus.*

CHAPTER FOUR

Pedigree Chum

October 2020

OH CANADA!

HOUN CHAPTER FOUR introduces Canadian Sir Henry Baskerville. We know immediately he's from Canada because, like all Canadians, he says things like: "What in thunder is the meaning of that?" or By thunder, you are right!" and "I appear to have walked right in to the thick of a dime novel. Why in thunder should anyone follow or watch me?"

Henry is thunderously vexed by an anonymous threatening letter which was sent to him at the Northumberland Hotel:

'as you value your life or your reason

keep away from the moor'

What a brilliant fridge magnet this would make! Particularly in cut up newsprint from *The Times*.

I decided that I would spend part of my morning engaged in the task of sending an anonymous threatening letter to a Canadian about keeping away from the moor. I bought a copy of *The Times* and cut up all the words except for 'moor'. Then I went hunting in the house for glue.

After at least an hour's rummaging through drawers, cupboards, and boxes, I finally unearthed an old Pritt stick. Next, I looked for a sheet of plain white paper and, after another hour of searching, I held in my hand a sheet of A4 printer paper.

Unfortunately, when I returned to my desk, I discovered to my great annoyance that the cats had sat on, ripped up, or eaten all my bits of cut up newsprint (and the rest of the newspaper), so I sighed and decided to use fast food delivery service menus instead – we have plenty of them to hand. Finally, after locking out the cats, I had my 'keep away from the moor' letter. Excellent. Now I needed to send it to a Canadian.

Did I know any Canadians? No. At least, none that I was aware of. Canadians could easily pass for Americans - Shatner being a prime example, or Nelly Furtado.

Could I find any Canadians that very morning? Yes, I reasoned: there would be plenty of Canadians at the Canadian Embassy in London. There might even be a Canadian named Henry working there. The Canadian Embassy, I was delighted to discover, even has as its own Twitter account. This made life much easier for me.

I used the camera on my phone to take a photo of the 'keep away from the moor' letter, and then I composed a tweet and attached the photo.

From @VinceStadon

To @CanadianUK

Hi, Canada. By thunder, it's cold, eh? And how about that ice hockey game! As part of a thing I'm doing (looooong story) I need to send you a quick missive about keeping away from the moor. Hope this is OK and that there will be no international diplomacy ramifications.

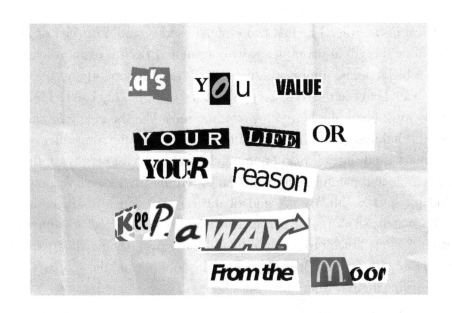

It occurred to me after I had sent it that the tweet wasn't at all anonymous, and I began to worry about retribution from Canada. I made a mental note to be on the lookout for Mounties, in case of sneak attacks.

JEREMY BRETT HAS LOST HIS APPETITE

The Hound of the Baskervilles starring Jeremy Brett (TV movie, UK, 1988)

I'm excited for my next pick from the Deerstalker of Doom! It's always a rush of blood to the head when I dip my hand into the hat, swirl around the slips of paper, and pull out a random selection. What will it be today? Ah, okay.

It's Jeremy Brett.

Hmmm.

I can never make my mind up about Jeremy Brett. I mean, he's *obviously* the best Sherlock Holmes; just perfect casting, genuinely magical in the role. The first two Granada series (and *The Sign of Four* two-hour special) are completely wonderful and Brett is extraordinary in them: high-energy, impish, mesmerising. Arguably, nobody on film has ever been better in the role. Certainly, in my eyes, Jeremy Brett's Holmes is the most believable, the most real, the most like the character on the page. But things go south quickly and drastically, and the remainder of the Granada Brett series is nigh on unwatchable – not least because of the all too visible and painful documentation of Jeremy Brett's declining mental and physical health. By the end of the run, the series had become as subpar as its star's performance. It's heart-breaking. I feel so much for Brett that it's difficult to watch him (and the series) decline. There exists, therefore, two Jeremy Brett Sherlocks: the sublime and the subpar – and reconciling them is where my issues lie.

The brilliant first Granada series was broadcast in 1984 and felt like a gift from God. I was so ready for it. At fourteen, I was a fully-fledged Sherlock Holmes fan, having read all the stories, watched all the wonderfully atmospheric Basil Rathbone movies, and developed a cocaine habit[31]. The year before, I'd even played the Great Detective himself in a school project[32]. So, when, on Tuesday 24th April 1984, I first heard Patrick Gowers' superb theme tune drifting out of the television speakers, announcing with aplomb the arrival of this sumptuous and respectful series of Sherlock Holmes adaptions, I was as hungry as anyone who has ever licked their lips and rubbed their tummies at the promise of something delicious.

Everything about the Granada series was brilliant. It looked and sounded like it was broadcast directly from 1889 – a notion reinforced by

---

[31] This is a joke. I wasn't hooked on cocaine as a schoolkid. I was hooked on curly wurlys (a chocolate bar).
[32] In Mrs Parker's 3rd Year English class, we were tasked with writing/producing/performing a radio play. My friends and I came up with "Sherlock Holmes Meets Fu Manchu Who Meets Dracula". Guess what films we'd been watching that week?

the Sidney Paget illustrations that popped up before and after each commercial break, and the uncanny way the production mimicked several of the more famous illustrations, in a manner not too dissimilar to the sketches of dreamboat Nordic Popstar Morten Harket coming to life to smooch a lovestruck fangirl in the A-ha video *Take on Me*. But four years is a long time and the jump from a fourteen-year-old boy who spends his evenings in the local library to an eighteen-year-old man who whiles away his evenings in the local pub is as huge as the gulf between the quality of the early Granada series and the latter ones.

The Granada HOUN from 1988 is a risible, tedious affair and a chore to sit through. In fact, it took me three attempts to get through it, for the somnambulistic pace and dearth of atmosphere, incident and excitement sent me to sleep several times. And though I knew this version was a disappointment, I still felt bad about sleeping through Brett vs the Hound, because... Well, it's *Jeremy friggin' Brett!* As Sherlock Holmes! Versus the Hound of the Baskervilles! In an ideal universe, it should not get any better than that. It's like Connery Bond vs Blofeld! Batman vs Superman! Blur vs Oasis!

There is one bit of genuine magic and, reassuringly, it's a scene between Jeremy Brett's Sherlock Holmes and Edward Hardwicke's solid Dr Watson. It comes when Watson has tracked down the lair of the mysterious man on the tor, and Holmes is forced to shed his disguise. Watson takes note of the food and other supplies the Great Detective has squirreled away in his hideout, which prompts Holmes to offer his friend a bowl of cold stew he has cooked. "Disgusting" is Watson's quiet verdict on the meal, and Holmes agrees, adding that it would be better hot.

Brett is wonderful in the scene, going from smugly pleased with his culinary efforts to accepting that the food is awful in the blink of an eye. It's a charming moment which perhaps saves this version from being a complete waste of time and effort. All the same, I can't help thinking that it would have been immeasurably better if it had been made in 1984 when the Granada Sherlock Holmes series was the best thing on telly and holds claim to being the best ever Sherlock Holmes adaptations, and I was fourteen and hungry for Holmes.

BLOCKBUSTER!

With both major UK TV channels failing miserably to produce an half-way exciting adaptation of HOUND in the early to mid-1980s – Tom Baker's BBC affair being dull, Jeremy Brett's ITV outing being a crushing disappointment – I venture that guaranteed thrills would have come instead from Hollywood which was pumping out testosterone-fuelled action blockbusters faster than bullets spitting out of an Uzi 9mm, and making unlikely movie stars out of diminutive muscle men with thick European accents. Imagine it: a huge budget *Hound of the Baskervilles*, with an all-star cast, a body count in the hundreds, and more explosions than the Battle of Britain! You could easily pitch it to coked-up studio executives as *Predator* (1987), unintelligible-speaking alien creature hunts a group of heavily-armed men in the jungle, meets *First Blood* (1982), unintelligible-speaking Sylvester Stallone is hunted by a group of heavily-armed men in the woods. Imagine the cast!

Sher 'Lock and Load' Holmes – Arnold Schwarzenegger!

'Doc' Watson – Charles Bronson!

Sir Henry Baskerville – Dolph Lundgren!

Stapleton – Jean-Claude Van Damme!

Beryl Stapleton – Grace Jones!

'Mort' – Carl Weathers!

Inspector Lestrade – Chuck Norris!

Barrymore – Mel Gibson!

Mrs Barrymore – Brigitte Nielsen!

Cartwright – Sylvester Stallone!

Laura Lyons – Sharon Stone!

Frankland – Jackie Chan!

Sir Charles – Steven Seagal!

Mrs Hudson – Linda Hamilton!

Selden – Bruce Willis!

The tagline: "The Dog Fight of the Century! The *Nineteenth* Century!"

Some extracts from the screenplay:

INT. 221B BAKER STREET – DAY

HOLMES aims a revolver at the wall, fires six times. Without looking, he holds out his hand and catches a box of ammunition thrown to him by DR. WATSON. Holmes expertly loads six more bullets, firing. The wall now has the letters 'VR' picked out in bullet holes.

Holmes blows smoke from the barrel of his revolver.

HOLMES

For the Queen. Victoria. My one true love.

WATSON

Her death is not your fault, Holmes. Nobody knew she was CIA.

HOLMES

I should have known.

WATSON

You can't know everything.

HOLMES

I can die trying.

THE WINDOW suddenly explodes, throwing glass everywhere. Holmes and Watson are thrown off their feet. A GAS GRENADE rolls on the floor, exploding with a bang! Gas fills the room.

Holmes pulls down his deerstalker cap, which transforms into a military-style face mask. Watson does the same with his bowler hat. Holmes crawls along the floor. Watson, crouching low, heads to the window, shooting back at the enemy.

WATSON

(to himself)

The Doctor is *in*... Time to face the medicine...

Watson fires more shots, reloads, fires again...

At the fireplace, Holmes pulls on a poker, activating the mechanism for the fireplace to revolve... Revealing the entrance to a SECRET ROOM.

HOLMES

(to himself)

Out of the frying pan... Into the fire.

Holmes signals to Watson, and they both withdraw into the secret room –a fully-stocked ARSENAL.

MRS. HUDSON is waiting for them, holding a welding iron. She wears gunsmiths' gear and goggles. She pulls up the goggles to reveal a sexy, young, beautiful face, covered in soot.

MRS. HUDSON

(sexy)

What took you, boys?

HOLMES

Had a spot of gas. It's cleared up now.

WATSON

I got four of the scumbags, Holmes. Clean head shots. Winged another three. Any idea who they are?

HOLMES

No, but I intend to find out, and kill them all. No mercy.

MRS. HUDSON

(sexy)

Then you'll need this...

Mrs. Hudson produces a 19th Century ROCKET LAUNCHER.

MRS. HUDSON

Because any girl will tell you – size matters.

HOLMES

Fuck, yeah.

EXT. ROOF OF SPEEDING STEAM TRAIN – DAY

Holmes and Watson are running along the roof of a carriage, ducking whenever the train goes under a tunnel. Both men are armed to the teeth.

SIX MEN dressed as ninjas with dog ears and tails are running long the roof of the train towards our heroes. These DOG NINJAS are throwing freaky ninja weapon things at Holmes and Watson.

Holmes is casually shooting the freaky ninja weapon things with a revolver - they explode mid-air. Watson is batting them away with his walking stick, with similarly spectacular effect.

WATSON

I don't understand why we're going to Devonshire, in the west of England, in the United Kingdom, many miles away from our capital city London, Holmes! Howzat!

HOLMES

Elementary, Watson. The gas cannister was marked with the letter 'B'. B for Baskerville!

WATSON

Holmes, you're amazing!

HOLMES

I know.

A dog ninja leaps at Holmes and they engage in impressive, unarmed combat – Holmes using bartitsu; the ninja using karate - as the train goes under a tunnel...

...and speeds out the other side, revealing the dog ninja standing alone, looking puzzled. Where did Holmes go? He's on the bridge – but not for long because he now drops down back onto the roof of the train, several cars behind the dog ninja, right near to Dr Watson, who is fending off several dog ninjas.

HOLMES

Need a hand?

Before Watson can answer, Holmes chops at the dog ninjas, who fall from the train.

WATSON

You took your time.

HOLMES

I stopped for a hand of bridge.

WATSON

What?

HOLMES

Bridge. The card game. And my hand, which I just used lethally to dispose of our attackers. I was making a pun.

WATSON

Contract bridge, bridge whist, or auction bridge?

HOLMES

Not now, Watson. We've still one more dog ninja to dispose of.

Holmes sprints along the roof of the speeding train and soon reaches the dog ninja he had been fighting. The dog ninja remains puzzled. Holmes politely taps him on the shoulder, and when the dog ninja turns round...

HOLMES

Remember me?

Holmes punches him off the train.

HOLMES

It's a dog-eat-dog world, pal.

DOG NINJA

(falling to his death) Arrrrggghhhh! That pun doesn't work because only one of us is dressed as a canine... arrrggggghhhhh!

Hero shot: Holmes on the roof of the speeding train, coat billowing in the wind, fists bunched, eyes narrowed and jaw clenched.

HOLMES

Now, to Dartmoor, where I will solve this thing!

GRAPHIC HORRORS

The morning post brings *Classic Comics Hound of the Baskervilles*, a pared-down to the bone retelling of the story in comic strip form. As I munch on buttered wholewheat toast I can't help but admire the ruthlessness of the adaptor, who gets through ACD's 'Gothic creeper' in a scant 30 pages. Just as notable is the Spanish artist's depiction of

Sherlock Holmes as a square-jawed matinee idol with a towering bouffant, and the Hound as a rather anaemic, oversized ferret. I'd quite like to see both on screen someday.

I have two other graphic novel adaptations of HOUN; both are top notch. The 2009 book published by Self Made Hero has delightfully cartoony art from I.N. J Culbard and a very faithful, chapter-by-chapter script by Ian Edgington. The Hound – a green-glowing muscular mastiff – leaps out of the page with a "GRAAWRRHH!". I always wonder how comic book writers decide on how many R's and H's to use for these onomatopoeia growls, grunts, cries and so on. Probably nothing will ever beat *Dr Who Magazine* picking VWORP! VWORP! for the sound of the TARDIS taking off and landing.

With a "GRRRRRRRAAARRR" (no exclamation mark!), the Hound in Stone Arch Books' 2008 graphic novel flattens Sir Henry, who cries "Noooo!!" in response. Darren Ferran's art leans slightly more to realism, and Martin Powell's script is punchy and uses very little of Doyle's prose. Of the three graphic novels, I think I prefer the cartoony Self Made Hero version, not least because of an appended sketch book filled with charming character designs for Holmes and Watson that had me inspired to pick up a pencil and doodle some of my own. Of course I drew a Hound, giving it a "GRAWWAAGGHHAAACCKKHH!" which I'm sure you'll agree is the only proper spelling of the mournful baying of the Hound of the Baskervilles.

COOKING THE BOOK

The Hound of the Baskervilles, starring Peter Cook (UK comedy feature film, 1979)

From the Deerstalker of Doom emerges the abomination that is the Peter Cook version of HOUN, made in 1978 (but not released until 1979). This was shown on TV a few years after the Tom Baker serial and, as a schoolboy staying up late to watch, I found it hilarious, particularly Dr Mortimer's incessantly weeing dog spraying Dudley Moore's Dr Watson in a continuous stream of urine. I remember giggling about the scene with my best mate Paul Symmons; the two of us inspired to write our own comedy script adaptation of *The Hound of the Baskervilles*. We didn't get more than ten pages into it before abandoning it and instead turning our attentions to making a video filmed version of *Dracula*. Miraculously, I still have the aborted script (and Paul and I are still friends), an excerpt from which I proudly present:

> WATSON: Eight large whiskeys, if you please!
>
> BARTENDER: Coming up, sir. That'll be sixteen thousand guineas.
>
> WATSON: American Express?
>
> BARTENDER: Haven't you got any cash?
>
> WATSON: I was saving it for my Grannie's birthday.
>
> BARTENDER: Sixteen thousand guineas?
>
> WATSON: Yes, she has expensive tastes.

Dreadful. And yet not as dreadful as the Peter Cook/Dudley Moore version, about which no reviewer has managed to find anything much to praise. Kenneth Williams (Sir Henry Baskerville in a terrible wig) records in his diary that Peter Cook became aware that the film wasn't working part way through filming, which greatly disappointed him as he'd initially had high expectations. Director Paul Morrisey's insistence on turning the comedy dial up to eleven at all times results in a film that's almost unwatchable from scene to scene – not helped by Cook inexplicably playing Holmes in a cod Jewish accent. In fact, the HOUN was a dreadful experience all round for Peter Cook. It seemed the only real pleasure he got from it was in reading aloud the scathing reviews it received. According to Williams, "Peter sat smoking fags and gleefully relating the worst notices he'd read".

Aged fifteen, I loved that Peter's HOUN is a riot of undisciplined silliness. I have come to mark the viewing of this film as the moment I became a Peter Cook fan. *Bedazzled* (1967) - Cook's Faustian masterpiece - was shown on TV soon afterwards, cementing my admiration for him. Years later, when I began building a library of Sherlock Holmes reference books, I became all-too painfully aware of the wretched reputation his version of the HOUN held. Not wishing to spoil a pleasant childhood memory or think badly of one of my comedy idols, I steadfastly avoided revisiting the film whenever it popped up on television.

It was with trepidation, then, that I bought a newly restored version of the film in preparation for my marathon viewing, and my heart was heavy as I plopped the disc into the player. To bolster my courage, I had invited my friend Jeremy along to watch it with me. In fact, Jeremy and I make a regular thing of watching bad films together. We're hardy veterans of the unwatchable turkey, having survived through *Crossplot* (1969) in which Roger Moore's eyebrow is raised to maximum smugness by an impenetrable espionage plot in groovy swinging sixties London; *The Wicker Tree* (2011), the incoherent and jaw-droppingly awful 'sequel' to *The Wicker Man* (1973), which features hastily edited-in footage of a very old and very ill Christopher Lee filmed with terrible lighting and sound in someone's kitchen; and *Starsky & Hutch on Voodoo Island* (1977), tedious and inept two-part TV movie in which the Californian cops problematically adopt black face disguises on an Haitian island populated by Playboy beauties, mafia hitmen, voodoo ceremonies, and Joan Collins – nowhere near as fun as it sounds.

But even Jeremy, battle-scarred and hardened from suffering through some of the worst films ever made – *The Tourist!* (2010), *Happy Death Day!* (2017), *Velvet Goldmine!* (1998) – lasted only four minutes before crying, "It's terrible!" and making a dash for the door. I had to agree it is, indeed, terrible. But I wasn't going to let him get away so easily. I pulled him back into the living room, bolted the doors, and readied a cattle prod in case he had more escape plans fermenting in his weary brain. After the credits rolled, we sat in stunned silence for a while before Jeremy gave his verdict:

"Definitely the worst film I've ever seen – there can't be anything worse than this, surely?"

"Don't call me Shirley," I replied, ejecting the disc from the player, wondering how far I could fling it out of the window.

DAS BOOT

Back to HOUN Chapter Four, where Sir Henry Baskerville has another puzzler at the Northumberland Hotel - one of his boots has gone missing. Now this was something I could easily replicate, for I have a neighbour named Henry. I popped my head out of the front door, receiving a blast of wind (autumn had thrown down the gauntlet to winter) and saw that Henry's frosted car was parked outside his home, number 12.

I dressed as if setting off across the Arctic tundra, walked to Henry's house, and knocked on the door. As I waited for him to answer, I realised that I've barely ever spoken to him (I'm a bit of an introvert).

"Hello, yes?" said Henry.

"Hi, um, it's Vince. From down the road." I was wearing a protective mask, so it's possible he didn't recognise me.

"Yes. What do you want?"

"Can I come in?" Technically, he'd be breaking the law if he invited me in, and I'd have to report him to the authorities. Good job I had Special Branch on speed-dial.

"No."

"Oh." I noticed that Henry had a shoe rack very close to the door. It was filled with shoes, but I couldn't see any boots. I wondered if they were upstairs. "Do you have any boots?"

"What?"

"Boots. For your feet."

"No."

"They're not upstairs?"

"No, I don't have any boots."

"It's autumn. You must wear boots in the autumnal and wintry months!"

"What's all this about?"

"WHAT THE HELL IS THAT?!!" I yelled, pointing behind him. Henry turned to look, and while his back was to me, I reached down and grabbed one of his sandals. I hid it behind my back. He faced me again.

"What were you shouting about?"

"Oh, nothing, just thought I saw, um, a moth."

"In autumn?"

"What are you, an expert on moths?"

"No."

"Well then. It was good chatting, but I don't have all day, cheerio."

Back at home, I congratulated myself on a productive morning. I had sent a threatening note to the Canadian Embassy and I had stolen footwear from a man named Henry. I was whistling a happy tune when my wife returned home from a stressful day's work as a teacher. An important job. But my job on *Hounded!* is just as, if not more, important. Over dinner I told her of my day. She nodded and smiled, and I could tell she was impressed at all I had achieved.

"Henry doesn't live at number twelve," said my wife, gulping down some wine. "That's Sam. Henry lives at number eight."

"Sam, the fitness instructor?"

"Yes."

It was a good job I was going away, I mused a little while later, as I packed a bag. For, in the morning, I was leaving Bristol to follow in the footsteps of Dr Watson. I decided I'd mail Sam the sandal from Dartmoor. That way he'd never know it was me who stole it. The game was definitely afoot!

CHAPTER FIVE

Hot Dog

October 2020

WHAT HAPPENED ON DARTMOOR#1: GETTING THERE

DARTMOOR IS ONLY A two and a half-hour drive in good traffic, but I've never personally been there., though my mother's family came from nearby Plymouth and I spent a few formative years there. I remember being thrilled on my very first visit to the cinema to watch a re-release of *Godzilla, King of the Monsters!* (1956). I believe the cinema was on the tiny island of Plymouth Hoe, which happily survived the monster rumpus. But both Exmoor and Dartmoor escaped my attentions.

It was well past time I rectified this, and so on Friday October 16th 2020, I climbed into my friend Chris's car and we drove to the moor. Chris thought it would have been amusing if he hired the dog car from *Dumb and Dumber* (1994), but sadly we had to make do with a Rover. In the car with us were my wife (surprisingly perky after a morning's work) and my friend Tony who had driven all the way south from Runcorn the night before (and was feeling a bit worse for wear after taking one too many beers from my fridge long after the midnight hour had chimed).

Tony is a mysterious man. He often vanishes from our circle of friends for years, only to one day turn up unexpectedly at my door, with a new girlfriend in tow, and no explanation of where the hell he's been or what he's been up to. He's also kind, warm, funny and staggeringly attractive, so everybody loves him – until they get annoyed with him (which admittedly is pretty quickly). For example, Tony had forgotten to bring a sleeping bag. And everything else he would need. We all laughed heartedly as we pictured him freezing to death on the moor.

Chris got us off to an excellent start by driving out of Bristol and back into Bristol again before I fired up Google Maps and directed us towards Dartmoor. I met Chris in a pub 30 years ago and it seems to me that we've never really left that pub – not in spirit, anyway. A tall, big-hearted, passionate and curious man, with a bald head that's always sustaining new injuries, I've had a kind of bromance with him that I'm sure we'll take to the grave (though obviously I'm hoping he'll be the one going to the grave before I do, which seems likely, given his head injuries).

The original plan had been for my wife and me to travel to Dartmoor with my friends, Naomi and Lewis. However, the COVID-19 restrictions meant that households were only allowed to mix with a small number of selected friends and family. Both Naomi and Lewis were exceptionally popular people and I was too low on their list to be included in their 'bubbles'. Chris and Tony, however, are not exceptionally popular people, so travelling with them to stay on Dartmoor was perfectly within the law[33].

In the car, I made myself popular by counting all the dogs I saw out of the window – a count I would continue all through our stay on Dartmoor and the journey home, resulting in a total of 276 pooches of all breeds. I was hoping that a dog-related song would be played on the radio station we were tuned into, having to settle eventually for *Hungry Like the*

---

[33] The UK was under a 'tier system' after coming out of national lockdown, and there were many rules and regulations that were often contradictory or just plain confusing. For instance, you couldn't see your parents a few streets away, but it was perfectly okay to drive 253 miles from London to Barnard Castle, Durham County just to test your eyesight.

Wolf by Duran Duran.

We reached the pretty little town of Ashburton in good time, stocked up on supplies in a high street Co-Op (which, in Chris and Tony's case, meant vast amounts of alcohol and in my wife's case – food, toiletries, gifts, medical supplies, and just about anything else she could think of to drain our bank account). Very soon after, just as the light was beginning to fade, we arrived at Higher Michaelcombe Farm in Holne, in the heart of Dartmoor.

And here I will leave the subject for a while as I will be detailing the madness that happened on Dartmoor throughout this book at appropriate points.

TAXI!

HOUN Chapter Five continues and complexifies the mystery of Sir Henry's missing boot, as the first is mysteriously returned and a second, older boot is stolen, much to the Canadian's irritation. Would I need to steal a second item of footwear from a neighbour, having returned the first one? Perhaps I could nab a sock from someone's washing line? I decided not to risk it. Instead, I wanted to question a cab driver, as Holmes does when he enquires about the cab that followed Sir Henry and Dr Mortimer.

I was thumbing through the Yellow Pages to find a local cab firm when my son approached me and asked me what I intended to cook for dinner. My son is vegan, and I am happy to cook dishes for him that accommodate his millennial tastes as it makes me feel like I'm doing my bit to save the planet without me actually doing anything to save the planet – the Gen X half-arsed way of doing stuff.

"Why are you looking through the Yellow Pages?" asked my son, not glancing up from his phone. In fact, I think it must be several months since I've seen him glance up from his phone and that was when one of the cats fell off the table in its sleep.

"I'm looking for a local cab firm."

"You do know you can just Uber," said my son.

"Of course I know all about the Uber," I replied. I mean, I have actually been in one. I've just never ordered one and have no idea how to do so. "I was just looking through Yellow Pages to find them," I said, in a bit of brilliant improvisation. My son did not respond, and I knew I had once again outwitted him. Unfortunately, Uber are not in the Yellow Pages. I threw the book away, startling a cat.

"They're not in here," I said. "Uber," I added, just so my son understood me fully.

He sighed and beckoned me over to show me his phone. Uber, I now know, is an app, like Solitaire, or the Pedometer that always seems to log at least a thousand steps fewer than I've walked.

"Where do you need to go?" asked my son. This stumped me.

"I don't actually want to go anywhere."

"Then why do you need an Uber?"

"I don't need an Uber. I need to interrogate an Uber driver," I said. "Though thinking about it, it might be good to have the Uber follow someone, preferably a Canadian walking to his hotel, or even better – a Canadian and a doctor walking together to an hotel. Afterwards I would question the driver about who it was who paid him to do such a thing, though obviously he – or she – would identify me as the person who paid them, but I might go incognito, perhaps in disguise in a black beard, and call myself Sherlock Holmes as the villain does when he hires his cab."

But my son had left the room, so I was left talking to a cat who was looking at me like it wanted immediate and ruthless revenge for startling it with a hurled Yellow Pages, so I quickly left the room.

Sir Arthur Conan Doyle's The Hound of the Baskervilles starring Ian Richardson (TV movie, 1983)

I got straight to it. The next pick from the deerstalker was the Ian Richardson-starring version from 1983. I'd seen this a long time ago, and remembered it being quite decent. I hurried out of bed, filled with enthusiasm and purpose. Big mistake. It was a cold and unwelcoming morning. The house was freezing, rain was lashing at the windows, wind was howling through the chimneys. Getting out of bed was clearly a blunder (why do I never learn?) so I made a cup of tea and snuggled back into bed - or at least, I *tried* to snuggle back into bed. My place had been taken by the cats which were very reluctant to move. But while they may have the numbers (there are three of them), I have the brain power.

It took only half an hour's cajoling, a box of treats, and some plasters on the deepest and bloodiest scratches on my legs until I was back under the duvet, cuddled up with my wife. I booted up my laptop, put on my headphones, and tried to ignore the pain as I played the DVD.

Sir Arthur Conan Doyle's The Hound of the Baskerville is the second in an intended series of films by producer Sy Wentraub, who had secured the rights to the Sherlock Holmes stories, *Sir Arthur Conan Doyle's The Sign of Four* being the first film. The third (probably titled something like *Sir Arthur Conan Doyle's Lazy Day at the Beach With His Wife and Some Close Frien*ds) never arrived.

A rather poor Dr Watson prevents this film from being first-rate, but it's a gripping, intelligent adaptation that impresses in many regards – not least Ian Richardson as Holmes, and the visual treat of a beautifully photographed Dartmoor. However (and it's a big however), there's not much anyone can do about Martin Shaw as Sir Henry Baskerville in a Stetson hat. Most of Shaw's lines are overdubbed by American actor

Kerry Shale, though you can hear Shaw's stab at an American accent most prominently in the scene where he meets Beryl Stapleton (it's not too bad). But, even dubbed by a Texan, it's Martin Shaw being Martin Shaw.

I'd better talk a bit about Martin Shaw and how I feel about him. For some years, I've been co-presenting a music podcast[34] with my good friend Jeremy Wall[35] that has a few regular features, one of which is called *The Martin Shaw Sunday Night Vehicle*. This silly segment sees Jeremy and I spinning a wheel to pick out various elements that will make up a proposed new Sunday night drama series, starring Martin Shaw, which I then pitch, via Twitter, to all the UK broadcasters.

Why do we do this? Well, it's because Martin Shaw rather annoys us. He's the star of ludicrous middle-class television dramas where he plays a maverick high court judge, or a maverick police commissioner, or a maverick Ofsted Invigilator, etc. For decades now, Shaw, with his pepper grey hair, weathered face and croaky sexy voice, has been the middle-class male totty of choice for undiscerning viewers. He seems to star in just about any old nonsense, no matter how ludicrously implausible, as long as he can share love scenes with actresses twenty or thirty years his junior, wear a scarf loosely over his tweed jacket (even during the love scenes) and be given a pretentious hobby in an effort to give his shallow characters the veneer of depth: fencing, collecting rare orchids, translating *Beowulf* into Esperanto, etc.

Shaw, we're convinced, has spent forty years trying to pretend he wasn't one of the rugged co-stars of gloriously fun action thriller series *The Professionals*, where he would run around with a gun and kick down

---

[34] *Vince & Jeremy's Overrated Podcast.* Jeremy, knowledgeable about pop music, takes it upon himself to rate every single act in the music industry, while I try to bluff my way into sounding like I know what the hell he's on about. We've rebooted and revamped the show as *Is This Show Overrated?* and added our highly opinionated friend Neil Barret to the line-up, though he only pops up occasionally. So to speak.
[35] Stapleton Cricket Club Player of the Year 1996.

doors and share outrageous sexist banter with his partner Lewis Collins. *The Professionals* was the perfect show for a ten-year-old boy, allowed to watch with his dad[36]. There was nudity, violence, car chases, gun fights, punch ups, violence, more car chases, and even more violence. And the theme tune is awesome. After the series ended, Martin Shaw immediately disowned it, blocking repeat showings (relenting decades later only when Lewis Collins' widow told him she could really do with the money from repeat fees).

The Professionals is the best thing Martin Shaw will ever be in. Except, maybe, one of the shows Jeremy and I develop for him, should a major broadcaster take a chance on us. Until then, he remains an irksome actor who pops up in all sorts of things to remind us all just how irksome he is and always will be. He is a blight on this Hound.

But on the plus side, Denholm Elliot is a splendid Dr Mortimer, and BRIAN BLESSED[37] pops up on screen to much cheering from my cats who love him much more than they love me.

A PATCHY START

That night I dreamed of an old, familiar dog named Patch – a friendly and rather podgy Jack Russell Terrier from my childhood. Dreams and memories of childhood always seem to be bathed in warm, golden sunlight. Patch, when I remember or dream of him, seems to belong to a permanent summer.

It is circa 1983, in this dream, I think: the long and glorious school Summer Holiday when I was thirteen. If there was a radio in this dream,

---

[36] *The Professionals* has not aged well, unsurprisingly. On a revisit to a few episodes, I sighed and winced and rolled my eyes so much that I exhausted myself.

[37] This is the only proper way to write his name. He is no mere 'Brian' and 'Blessed'; he is the mighty, shouty irrepressible God of Awesomeness known to us mere mortals as BRIAN BLESSED!

I have no doubt it would be playing something by Bananarama. I dreamed I was playing with the happy, yappy dog in the house I grew up in, running with him from the kitchen, past my mother who is making blackberry jam on the stove, into the big side garden, Patch rolling around in piles of freshly mown grass. My dad is winding in the long orange cord of the Flymo grass mower, coughing through a roll up. And then Patch is sitting next to me on the steps in the back garden as I read *The Hound of the Baskervilles* to him. Soon, the dog is reading the book to me as I fall asleep.

Patch sounds like Peter Egan. It's weird, but I thought I knew the book very well, as well as I know any book. And yet Patch as Peter Egan is reading aloud passages that are disturbingly and entirely unfamiliar: Dr Watson is writing to Holmes about the cancer treatment he is undergoing at Baskerville Hall. I glance back at the house and see through the window that my mother has vanished from the kitchen. She too is undergoing treatment for cancer. Sherlock Holmes is not reading Dr Watson's letters because he is in the pub, on a bender. I can no longer hear my dad coughing. And of course, continues Patch, the real secret of the Hound is that the monstrous dog never died. It's still on the loose. It could be anywhere. It could be sitting right next to me. Patch laughs and the laugh turns into a bone-chilling howl, and my wife shoves me awake and tells me to stop howling in my sleep.

I got up, leaving my wife to enjoy a lie-in. She works a stressful job on top of having to put up with me. She deserves a sleepy morning.

Ice had formed on the windows as the savagely cold autumn continued its attack on my comfort. I put the heating on and fed the cats. The cats were not happy with the food; they yowled at me. They craved, I knew, the plate of cold meats in the fridge that I was keeping for a sandwich. I wasn't going to let them have it, no matter how much yowling (though it was a little unnerving to have them all yowling at me at once). Usually, the cats are wary and hostile with each other. But now they had become a united front of wariness and hostility against me. I stared them down. They would not win this war.

I wondered why I was having nightmares. I don't normally have nightmares. But the Patch dream was so vivid and awful. I wondered if I was being haunted by a dog who died a long time ago, as well as my next-door neighbour's phantom pooch. At any rate, I decided to never again listen to Peter Egan. I switched audiobook narrators to Stephen Fry. Good old Stephen Fry, dependable, cuddly, loveable old Stephen Fry. He wasn't going to give me nightmares.

I gave the cats the cold meat from the fridge, took some paracetamol for the headache and the pain from the fresh scratches on my legs, and reached for my deerstalker.

THE HAMMER OF THE BLOODY BASKERVILLES

The Hound of the Baskervilles, starring Peter Cushing (Technicolour film, 1959)

I bloody love Hammer films. They are a series of films that, like Bond, provide a kind of cultural scaffolding to my appreciation of cinema; a gateway drug into 'film'. I think the best of them are as good as anything British cinema has to offer, standing proud with David Lean and Ealing and Merchant Ivory, and so on. I would also argue that Peter Cushing might be the single most underrated movie star of all time – he is never anything less than superb, whether he's stitching together body parts, bossing around Darth Vader or hunting down the Hound of the Baskervilles. Needless to say, he is a delight as Sherlock Holmes. And Hammer absolutely nails it.

As with all Hammer adaptations of Gothic horror classics, the narrative is pared right down to the gristle and bone, and the spookiness is turned up to eleven. Thunder booms, lightning flashes the night, as something monstrous stalks the land. The blood runs thick and red[38] as Peter Cushing strides into an ornately furnished room, stands near a welcoming open fire, removes one of his gloves, holds up one of his fingers like a stern lecturer, and reprimands everybody in the room for not following his strict instructions to ward off Evil – and that's evil with a capital E, mind you. The Hammer film throws a villain with webbed fingers, ritual mutilation, a mine shaft collapsing, and a tarantula crawling up Christopher Lee's[39] arm into the mix. Frankly, this is my kind of drug. You could hook me up to an IV and pump 5,000 millilitres of Peter Cushing combatting Gothic Evil into my veins and I'll be happy for the rest of my life, thanks.

Hammer's Hound was screened on BBC2 as part of the legendary Horror Film Double-Bills from the late 1970s/early 1980s, which had thousands of ten- and eleven-year-old kids in the UK begging their parents to please let them stay up late on Saturday nights to watch all these brilliant horror films... And, consequently, have weeks or months of nightmares

---

[38] This fake blood is known as Kensington Gore. It's made from golden syrup, water, corn starch, and a mix of red, yellow, and blue food colouring, much like my home-baked cupcakes. The cheaper film used in these low budget horror movies exaggerated the red colouring, especially when the films were processed with Eastmancolour, a forerunner to Technicolour. This formula was also used in *The Shining's* infamous elevator scene.

[39] Christopher Lee makes an excellent, if very English, Sir Henry. Lee was also brilliant as Mycroft Holmes in *The Private Life of Sherlock Holmes* (1971), a passable if rather stiff Sherlock in *Sherlock Holmes and the Deadly Necklace* (a very odd Italian-West German-French co-production that has Sherlock sporting throughout a terrible and unnecessary prosthetic nose), and a sleepy Sherlock in a couple of dreary made-for-TV films about an aged Holmes, *Sherlock Holmes: The Golden Years* (1991), co-starring Patrick Macnee as a dreary Watson. My favourite anecdote about the brilliant Christopher Lee comes from his friend Roger Moore: the two men were on location in Thailand shooting Moore's sophomore Bond outing *The Man with the Golden Gun* (1974), when a flock of bats flew out from a cave and ruined the take. Roger turned to Lee and said, "They are yours to command, Master!" Reports vary as to what Lee's response was but given how famously irascible he was. I lean towards him being not remotely amused. A few years later Roger Moore played an eyebrow-raised Sherlock Holmes in a dreary made-for-TV movie, *Sherlock Holmes in New York* (1976), co-starring Patrick Macnee as a dreary Watson.

afterwards.

I missed the 1979 season of Horror Double-Bills where the Hammer Hound prowled the desolate moor, but I joined in the scary fun the next year – the 1980 collection, which ran from late June till late August when the school holidays started. It kicked off with 1957's *Night of the Demon* (a superb version of M R James's *The Casting of the Runes*) and concluded with 1974's *The Beast Must Die* (a barmy, funky fusion of werewolves, whodunnits, and blaxploitation action films, featuring, of course, Peter Cushing).

Peter Cushing pops up in four other horror films from the vintage 80 season, but though the great man is benched for the next two years, he makes a resounding comeback when the Horror Double-Bills are revived by a resurgent BBC2 in the early 1990s, putting in a record seven appearances in all manner of horrors. The celebrated Mr C was, in fact, barely off my TV screen growing up, as he battled *The Avengers* and *The New Avengers* (the second time as a Nazi), foiled not one but two Dalek masterplans, visited Moonbase Alpha in the baffling *Space: 1999*, got embroiled in one of those *Tales of the Unexpected,* popped up in a *Hammer House of Horror* TV episode as (another) Nazi, and donned the Deerstalker and Inverness Cape for a final time in 1984's rather plodding Sherlock Holmes TV serial, *The Masks of Death.*

So often was Cushing on my telly (and in so many of the books on horror films I read) that I began to regard him as part of the family, or the furniture. I'm happy to say that Peter Cushing *is* actually part of my furniture these days – at least one of the soft furnishings. For I have a Peter Cushing cushion! Yes, a plush and lovely Cushing cushion, part of a range of merchandising I created when I started my YouTube channel and uploaded the first (and so far, only) two segments of *Peter Cushing Opens Another Coffin* – my exhaustive catalogue of every coffin opened by Peter Cushing on screen. I'll get to making some more videos someday. Maybe.

"What's up with you?"

"I've got a problem."

"Just the one?"

"Well, more of a conundrum. Or a vexation. I've pulled the late 60's BBC Peter Cushing Hound out of the Deerstalker of Doom."

"Didn't you watch the Peter Cushing one last night?"

"Exactly! I watched the first Peter Cushing Hammer Hound last night, and today I've pulled the *second* version, made just shy of a decade later by the BBC."

"So?"

"So nobody's going to believe that! *I* wouldn't believe it if someone told me! It's too much of a coincidence that I would pick the two Cushings back-to-back, especially in chronological order! I mean, come on! Everyone will think I've cheated. And if they question the honesty of my selections, they'll be questioning everything else about the book."

"Who? Who will be questioning?"

"My readers."

My wife laughed long and hard. I walked away, grumbling to myself. She may doubt that anybody will ever buy a copy of this book, but that doesn't assuage my concerns over consecutive Cushings. As ACD might have put it if he was in my predicament: It may not be impossible to pull consecutive Cushings (in fact, it clearly wasn't). It was, however, certainly *improbable*.

I lost all my worries when I watched both episodes back-to-back and thoroughly enjoyed myself. Part of the fun was recognising a cast of British character actors famous for other things, such as Ballard Berkeley (or is it Berkeley Ballard?), the Major from *Fawlty Towers*, making an excellent troubled Sir Charles Baskerville, and Gary Raymond (or is it Raymond Gary?), the terrifying doppelgänger dad from *The Two Faces of Evil* episode of *Hammer House of Horror,* as a rather meek Sir Henry with a rubbish American accent.

Weirdly, the director has cast two actors who look almost identical as Dr Mortimer and Stapleton – they're even dressed in identical posh clobber when we are initially introduced to them. Given that the entire plot of HOUN revolves around Stapleton secretly being in line to inherit the Baskerville title and fortune once he's done away with everyone in his way, it seems odd to have Dr Mortimer and Jack Stapleton look like twin brothers. Stapleton is played splendidly by Philip Bond, looking like Peter Cook's relaxed and cool Satan in *Bedazzled,* and he's one of my favourite versions of the villain.

Hilariously, the sound effect used for the Hound is the famous wolf howling SFX from BBC Records's rather wonderful LP *Sound Effects No. 13 - Death & Horror.* My school friend Paul had this very album, which we recorded to tape, and used not only in our own Sherlock Holmes audio plays, but also just in a general mucking about sense: on some evenings, we hid behind bushes in residential areas, turned the volume up full blast, and played Band 1: *Execution and Torture,* which includes *Neck Twisted and Broken, Stake Driven Through Heart, Branding Iron on Flesh* and *Red Hot Poker into Eye.* God knows how these sound effects were made, but, as mischievous thirteen-year-olds, we were delighted we could play them to our neighbours.

The sound effect used for this second Cushing Hound of the Baskervilles (or Hound 2, if you like) is called *Wolf Howling,* and you've no doubt heard it many times, from many sources. It's the go-to wolf howling sound effect, piped into every ghost train ride, Halloween party, and spooky pop video. Indeed, the only comparable famous sound effect is the Wilhelm Scream[40] which you've almost certainly also heard countless times. I cheered when I heard that familiar wolf howl as Sir Charles runs for his life. So lovely to hear it again.

Elsewhere, there is Peter Cushing as Sherlock Holmes, dependably brilliant as always. The direction really favours him, with many close-up shots of Cushing's Holmes in profile, smoking a pipe, and a really striking shot of him filmed from a low angle, standing on the platform at the train station as Watson and Sir H speed off to Devonshire.

Quite why the travellers disembark at Dawlish[41] is a mystery, though it does lead to a charming sequence of the three men straining to push their carriage – laden with all their heavy luggage – up a steep Dartmoor lane.

Nigel Stock as Dr Watson seems to occasionally fluff his lines, which lends him a Nigel Bruce quality. There's a lovely shot of him[42] strolling along the moor, dressed in a cloth cap and long tan-coloured coat, in walking socks and shoes, swinging his impromptu walking stick, that makes him look uncannily from Clegg (Peter Sallis[43]) from 'sexist-old-codgers-mucking-about-on-the-Yorkshire-Dales' perennial BBC1 sitcom *The Last of the Summer Wine*. I half expected Ronnie Hazlehurst's melancholic theme tune to kick in, and to see Dr Mortimer speed by downhill in a bath with wheels, chased by an irate Mrs Barrymore brandishing a rolling pin for tediously contrived plot reasons. And that

---

[40] A man's 'falling-to-his-death' scream. There are countless YouTube videos explaining all about it and listing every usage on screen.
[41] I've been to Dawlish. My wife and I have walked along the long path and beach wall next to the railway line to Dawlish Warren – it was raining, and I had a panic attack on the walk as my fear of heights kicked in. My wife had to get me down off the hight stone wall and safely onto the beach. She's wonderful. At any rate, Dr Watson, Sir Henry and Dr Mortimer would have actually taken the train to Buckfastleigh, rather than to Dawlish (which is many miles east of Dartmoor).
[42] Insert your own 'Stock footage' joke here.
[43] Sallis was famous as the voice of Wallace from Wallace & Gromit. He also played Dr Watson onstage in *Baker Street*, a short-lived Sherlock Holmes Broadway musical.

(and the Major from *Fawlty Towers*) got me thinking about a sitcom version of HOUN. I jotted down a few ideas to pitch to major broadcasters, via Twitter:

From: @VinceStadon

To: @Channel4 @bbccomedy @ITV @Netflix

Hi, I have 2 pitches for potential smash-hit sitcoms based on Arthur Conan Doyle's 1902 'Victorian Creeper' *The Hound of the Baskervilles*. I know you must get 100s of tweets pitching sitcoms about *Hound of the Baskervilles*, but mine are gold:

AFTER SIR HENRY Newlyweds Sir Henry and Lady Baskerville (Geoffrey Palmer, Penelope Keith) move into their Devonshire manor house and have to continually fight off various terrifying spectral animals that come after Sir H - with hilarious consequences!

OPEN ALL HOUNDS After leaving Baskerville Hall, butler Barrymore (Geoffrey Palmer) and his housekeeper wife Anna (Penelope Keith) run a B&B on the moor. But Anna's criminal family keep escaping from the nearby prison and hiding in the B&B - with hilarious consequences!

At the time of publication, no broadcaster has responded.

SHRINKING FEELING

George Shrinks / Season 2 / Episode 13 / *Hound of the Bath-ervilles* (TV kids cartoon, 2001)

Fifteen minutes into this cartoon I realised that, aside from the title, it has absolutely nothing whatsoever to do with *The Hound of the Baskervilles*. At that point, I could have stopped watching and pulled another HOUN from the hat, but I was enjoying the episode so I kept watching till the very end. I made only one note: 'terrible pun dad towel drying a duck's head'. Make of that what you will. I go into these cartoons not knowing anything about them, and I must quickly pick up the premise and figure out the tone of the show, and it can be a disorientating experience.

But *George Shrinks* is basic stuff: helpful kid is shrunk to the size of a chess piece and gets into scrapes with his sister and parents. In this episode, George and his Sister decide to clean all the neighbourhood pets. That's it. Even my puny brain could understand this. And that's probably why I enjoyed it. So there. Go watch *George Shrinks* – you'll not be confused, not even a tiny bit.

CHAPTER SIX

Old Dog, New Tricks

November 2020

No Place Like Holmes

HOUN CHAPTER SIX, titled *Baskerville Hall*, finally gets us to, well, Baskerville Hall.

"My word, it isn't a cheerful place," says Sir Henry, having spent less than three hours in his new home.

But before we get there, our gang is at Paddington Station where Holmes asks Watson if he's packed his service revolver, telling him to "keep your revolver near you night and day and never relax your precautions." - a phrase I've taken to using as the signature in my email.

It strikes me that Holmes sometimes treats his friend and colleague like a trusted soldier, and packs him off to do battle with the forces of evil. Perhaps it's because Watson is a military man who has survived fields of combat, or perhaps it's Holmes just being a complete git.

Loveable Watson spends the train journey to Devonshire chatting with Sir Henry and Dr Mortimer and playing with the latter man's spaniel.

How lovely is that? It made me immediately want to take a train to Devonshire with a spaniel just so I could spend the journey telling the dog what a good girl (or boy) it is. But then the men arrive in Devonshire and head onto the moor where they soon get their first glimpse of Baskerville Hall, described by ACD in some of his most evocative prose:

> Over the grass squares of the fields and the low curve of a wood there rose in the distance a grey, melancholy hill, with a strange jagged summit, dim and vague in the distance, like some fantastic landscape in a dream.

Gorgeous.

WHAT HAPPENED ON DARTMOOR #2: FORCES OF DARKNESS

We weren't staying at Baskerville Hall, sadly. Instead, we had booked two shepherds huts on a farm. Originally, I had wanted to go camping, but Chris and Tony were not keen on freezing to death on the moor - not even for my book all about *The Hound of the Baskervilles* - so a compromise was met by hiring the huts.

On arrival, we found that the hut I'd booked for me and my wife was perfunctory, tiny, and a little shabby (and tricky to get through, as you had to cross a stream by jumping from rock to rock). Conversely, the hut I'd booked for Chris and Tony was a spacious, fully-furnished, heated palace, with four beds, a shower, and an outdoor dining area. Obviously my wife wanted to stay in that one instead. Tony and Chris knew better than to argue with her.

We walked two miles to a nearby village pub, called the Church House Inn, where we enjoyed an enjoyable evening meal. It was pitch black and freezing cold when we left the cosy pub, an hour's walk before us. There was a bright moon in the clear night sky, and away from the pollution of the city the starry night was breath-taking.

Suddenly, a howl rang out. I froze.

But it was only Tony, who had stumbled and stubbed his toe. My nerves were shredded, and my senses were on high alert because we were on the moor. I remembered, with dread, the warning laid down in the Curse of the Baskervilles to forbear from crossing the moor in those dark hours when the powers of evil are exalted. I said as much to my companions whose senses were dulled and spirits raised by their willingness to try just about everything on the drinks menu at the Church House Inn.

"How will we know," asked my wife, "when the forces of darkness are excited?"

"You mean, 'how will we know when the powers of evil are *exalted*?'" I corrected her. It's important to get these things right.

"Yeah," she conceded, "that."

"Tuesdays are evil, in my experience," said Chris.

"That may be, but that's way too vague. The curse doesn't forbear Baskervilles from crossing the moor in those dark hours when the powers of evil are exalted on Tuesdays."

"Good point. We need to know when the forces of evil are expected so we can avoid crossing the moor and, instead, *zigzag* the moor."

"*Exalted*, not expected, but I think you might be on to something. What we need is some way of detecting precisely when the forces of darkness are exalted."

"We could build some sort of portable device," offered Tony. "A gadget calibrated to indicate the passing of day and when darkness falls, maybe something you can wear for ease of use."

"You mean a watch?" I said.

But Tony's idiocy had got me thinking in another direction – we couldn't measure when the forces of darkness were exalted because what constitutes the forces of evil is nebulous and open to interpretation (Chris's lethal homebrew, for instance, might well be categorized as evil). But we *could* determine, with little effort and with a high degree of accuracy, when the rock band The Darkness were at their peak of commercial popularity, thus exaltation. I mean, *darkness* equates to *evil*, doesn't it? It's a synonym, I'm sure. And, it's probable that ACD only employed the word 'evil' because he'd earlier used 'dark' in the sentence – those dark hours when evil is exalted. You could swap them round with no fuss: those evil hours when the dark (ness) is exalted. Therefore, it would follow logically that the rock band named The Darkness could represent 'Evil' in all its forms – particularly those which exalt. All we'd need was an internet connection and Google.

Back at our luxury hut, in the warm, I soon learned that on the 17th February 2004 at 20:04, Justin Hawkins, lead singer of The Darkness, held aloft the Best Group Award at the Brit Awards, having moments earlier nabbed Best Album and Best Rock Group gongs – all in the wake of The Darkness's smash hit album, *Permission to Land*[44] which had spawned a UK number 1 hit single (and a second single peaked at number 2), sold 1.5 million copies, and led to them being rock festival headliners. I can therefore confidently record that the forces of The Darkness were exalted at four minutes past eight on Tuesday February 17th 2004.

---

[44] Contains the song *Black Shuck*, based on local folklore about a ghost dog. Coincidence? I think not! (As an aside I have to say that The Darkness really aren't my cup of tea, sorry.)

Chris had been right, damn it – Tuesdays really *are* evil!

How To aggravate Stuffy Sherlockians

Matt Frewer as Sherlock Holmes in *The Hound of the Baskervilles* (TV movie, 2000)

Like an evil Florence Nightingale, The Deerstalker of Doom shows no mercy. Day after day after day, I plunge my hand into the upturned cloth hat and pull out a Hound of the Baskerville – and frankly (and aptly for a garment of clothing), it's wearing me down.

Sometimes I dread the Deerstalker of Doom, knowing that contained within its comfy depths lurk some bloody awful versions of this great novel. Like the dying days of the month when the only vaguely appetising things left in the fridge are any foodstuffs that don't have a green fuzzy mould over them, or video rental stores from the 80s and 90s that hadn't updated their catalogue for weeks so the only films left to rent were terrible *Basic Instinct* knock-off erotic thrillers starring mediocre actors from *Beverly Hills 92010* and *Baywatch* who wanted to be overnight sex symbols. Which brings me to today, as I write this. For somehow, I just knew that today would be the day when I must watch the Matt Frewer version of The Hound – considered by many to be amongst the very worst.

Today of all days when I have a blinding headache and I'm in a terrible mood. I don't want to watch a terrible film when I'm in a terrible mood. I only like watching terrible films when I'm in a good mood and someone else is watching it with me and *they* have a terrible time – it's a kind of film sadism, I suppose.

I ask my wife if she wants to watch a version of *The Hound of the Baskervilles* with me. She tells me that she must sadly decline my invitation. (I'm paraphrasing, obviously, and removing all the expletives.)

I ask my son and my daughter and receive similarly colourful rejections.

Then I hit upon the idea of inviting Jeremy over – my friend, had after all thrown down the gauntlet when he had grimly proclaimed the Peter Cook version of HOUN to be the worst film ever made and that there couldn't possibly be a worst one. And then I remember that he's coming over anyway, specifically to watch this version of HOUN, because I'd planned this a week ago, and then forgotten all about it.

If all this sounds confusing, then that's because it *is* confusing, and accurately describes my mental state. For one thing, the world is wrapped in a dark shroud of anxiety as we deal with a pandemic on top of all our other 21ˢᵗ century problems. Writing this book is supposed to be a kind of valve release for me (and it mostly is); like chronic insomnia or pain, sometimes things get a bit overwhelming and it's the tiny things that break you. You thought there was a chocolate digestive biscuit left in the box, but it's gone. You wanted to go for a nice walk, but it hasn't stopped raining all day. The socks you were certain were in your sock drawer – the ones with little doggies on them that you got for a birthday – inexplicably aren't there. Little things.

And thus it was with the Matt Frewer HOUN. I'd forgotten I'd arranged to watch it with my friend Jeremy. I could not understand why I had put the slip of paper, with the Matt Frewer HOUN neatly printed on it, *back* in the Deerstalker of Doom. I couldn't believe that I had again fished it out of the Deerstalker of Doom on the very day I had no patience whatsoever for a terrible version of HOUN. I was irked three times over (irked cubed?).

It wasn't as bad as I was expecting. Things usually aren't as bad as we fear. For one thing, this film boasts a quite terrific Dr Watson – namely Kenneth Walsh. He's engaging, intelligent and quite a delight. He carries the entire film. The rest of the cast are also good, and there's some nice photography and a reasonably effective Hound.

Where the film sinks into the Great Grimpen Mire, however, is in the casting of its leading man. Matt Frewer is awful. I mean, a complete failure on every front. Not a single bit of anything approaching good survives his risible performance. I suppose I ought to cut the fellow some slack as by all accounts he was a last-minute replacement for Charles Dance, but nah. Frewer stinks in the role.

"Fruity of diction and flighty of mood," writes Alan Barnes in *Sherlock Holmes on Screen*, "there is much about Frewer's Holmes to aggravate stuffier Sherlockians, from his playful over-gesticulation to his amusingly idiosyncratic choices of loungewear." I'm anything but a stuffy Sherlockian, but I was certainly aggravated.

Nicko Vaughn, in *Cut to Baker Street*, writes that "With Watson remaining the focus of the investigation, one critic wondered if Frewer's rubber-faced overacting was a ploy to make the most of his time on screen, 'He didn't just go over the top, but took a running jump over the top with a boost from a springboard!'"

It may be poor form to go scouring the internet for more scathing reviews of Frewer's performance (and I admit that I really ought to be more charitable), but I couldn't help but laugh at a customer review from someone who had bought the DVD on Amazon: "May I kindly ask Canada to leave Holmes alone? Whichever (not so) bright spark had the idea of casting Matt Frewer as Holmes needs medical attention. This man is about as far from Sherlock Holmes as Danny DeVito." I think Danny DeVito would have been better as Sherlock Holmes than Matt Frewer, but point taken, reviewer, point taken.

Perhaps the most accurate, and certainly the most succinct, verdict on Frewer's Holmes came from my friend Jeremy, aghast at what he was seeing on my 40-inch flatscreen, "What the fuck is he *doing!?*[45]"

Frewer's casting got me thinking about Elvis. I think Elvis should have played Sherlock Holmes in a series of dreadful 60s movies set in Vegas. I mean, he was already in a series of career-killing dreadful 60s movies anyway, so why not add Sherlock Holmes to the mix to add some interest? Think about it – Elvis, in his white Vegas jumpsuit, blue suede shoes and Deerstalker Hat (adjusted to fit his might quiff), serenading Irene Adler (Ann-Margaret) with *Always on My Mind*, karate kicking Professor Moriarty (Jerry Lewis) into a fountain in front of a gaudy casino. He'd have help from a bunch of detectives who also form his backing group called The Suspicious Minds, a grouchy Officer Lestrade from the L.A.P.D (Burgess Meredith), and his Dr Watson would be a different love interest co-star every film (Mary Tyler-Moore, Angela Lansbury, etc). And, of course, he'd get to track down the Hound Dog of the Baskervilles –not on the moor, but in the ghetto. Come on, it would have been brilliant! Certainly it would have been better than Matt Frewer.

But then, that's a low bar to jump.

THE GHOST-DOG NEXT DOOR

My next-door neighbour has a mysterious new dog. I've never seen this dog. Others have seen it and spoken of it to me, but their reports have been perplexing and contradictory. According to one report, it's a cute little bull mastiff puppy— No, it's a quite adorable little red setter, insists another witness. Nonsense retorts a third: the pooch is a winsome chihuahua.

I don't know why everyone is lying to me. I don't know what monster roams my neighbour's high walled garden, howling and snarling

---

[45] Inexplicably, there followed three more Sherlock Holmes films starring Matt Frewer! I'm sorely tempted to watch them all, just because I feel guilty about giving such a kicking to the rubber-faced actor.

in the evil night when the forces of darkness are exalted. The hair-raising howls and snarls and growls and barks are the only tangible indication that this ghostly beast exists, though it's quite possible that it's my neighbour, himself, making these noises, or that they come from his extensive record collection (he's in the music industry).

But I'm on to him.

I'm determined to find the truth.

REMEMBER TO LIKE AND SUBSCRIBE!

Ah, YouTube, mankind's message to the universe that we've stopped pretending we ever had any standards. I watch an awful lot of YouTube (most of it awful), mainly as background noise as I wind down at night. Nothing relaxes me more than a YouTuber failing disastrously to replicate a Bob Ross painting.

There are quite a few HOUN related YouTube videos, including *Selden*, a Russian film from 2019, which amusingly and ingeniously centres completely around escaped convict Selden as he tries to survive on the moor. Shot in broad summer daylight somewhere in a marshy field resembling the Florida Everglades more than desolate, fog-drenched Devonshire moorland (not least because of the incessant chirping of crickets and croaking of frogs), in a bizarre fusion of surreality, fake beards and slapstick (it's like Mr Bean/Jaques Tati on a Ray Mears-style survival weekend), this arty amateur movie beguiles and irritates in equal measure. And I found myself rather charmed. It's certainly leagues ahead of the amateur film I was involved in back in my school days...

In 1983, my best friend Paul Symmons and I somehow charmed the headmaster of Lockleaze Comprehensive School into letting us skip lessons and, instead, use school equipment to star in and film our own version of *Dracula*. God knows why he agreed to let us do this. Perhaps I had underestimated my hypnotic powers.

96

Over several weeks, we set to work filming our masterpiece. I played the Count, because I already had the cloak and the fangs (and the magnetic sexual prowess). We had no script and no real idea of what we were doing, but we did have a director – Mr Voss. And a coffin, made by Mr Gerrard. We also had use of the castle set on the school stage that had been created for the school pantomime, as well as free reign of the local woods[46].

Paul was (and is) great at coming up with ideas, framing shots, making special effects, and generally being excellent at all things. Mr Voss, we discovered, was rubbish at coming up with ideas, framing shots and everything else he did as director. So we fired him. Our second director was Mr Miller – ceramics teacher who was much more on our wavelength, not just because he bore a resemblance to David Dixon[47].

Ian Miller (cheekily, we were on first name terms) had striking ideas for our version of *Dracula*. Firstly, he fired me as the Count and cast Paul since he is tall and good-looking (and a far better actor) – the Christopher Lee to my Max Shreck. This left me to scribble down rubbish dialogue and suggest we swap out Professor Van Helsing for Mr Sherlock Holmes, and also to maybe reveal that Count Dracula, in shape-shifted canine-form, is actually a kind of werewolf Hound of the Baskervilles. (Both ideas that we never developed, but which I'm sure would be a winner if Netflix wants to pick up on it.)

We took the coffin down into the woods and shot moody footage of it shrouded in mist (we crumpled up torn pages from school exercise books and lit a small fire). Our good friend, Jeremy Wall[48] played a victim/acolyte of the Count, and he was filmed (by both directors, oddly enough) running through the woods in fear of his life – or at least in

---

[46] Where, coincidentally, scenes from *Robin of Sherwood* (1984-86) would be filmed.
[47] Actor who played Ford Prefect in the wonderful 1981 BBC TV version of *The Hitchhiker's Guide to the Galaxy*
[48] Stapleton Cricket Club Player of the Year 1996. Yes, I know.

trepidation of tripping over and grazing a knee. A key scene saw Jeremy approaching through a stone tunnel deep in the woods, drinking blood (red paint purloined from the art department) from a chalice (with hokey dialogue using the phrase "I do anoint thee"), and gingerly stepping over someone's pet rat. Miller decided to sex things up a bit and persuaded one of the more gorgeous schoolgirls to dress up as a Victorian lady, sit at the school piano and pretend to play it (presumably setting the scene for Paul's vampire Count to prey on her later), whilst another teacher – Miss Grainger, English – strapped on a bonnet and played her tone-death mother.

God knows what any of this nonsense had to do with Bram Stoker, but it got us out of tedious lessons, so we were prepared to do just about anything. Unfortunately, we carelessly left the coffin to rot in the woods over the summer holidays. Upon our return, the furious teaching staff shut the project down, thus *Dracula* went unfinished. And sadly, no footage survives for me to upload to YouTube. But you never know – perhaps one day it will be found, and the world will get to see me as a scrawny Count Dracula with long straw-blonde hair, plastic fangs, and high cheekbones, emerging from a rubbish coffin with all the terrifying power of a kitten with a ball of wool.

VOICES IN MY HEAD

To give my weary eyes a rest, I'm listening to various audiobook readings of HOUN, switching between them chapter by chapter. There are far too many audiobook readings of this book to list (yet alone listen to), so I am limiting myself to readings by Hugh Burden (an actor I only know from playing the lead villain Auton in Jon Pertwee's debut *Dr Who* story from 1970), Tony Britton (smooth), Peter Egan (smooth and sexy), Stephen Fry (arch and fruity), Derek Jacobi (comfy), and Freddie Jones (arch, fruity and comfy).

I've been wondering about actors with voices suited for narrating *The Hound of the Baskervilles*, and I have come to think that the actor who would have been perfect for it was Sir Richard Attenborough – that grandfatherly, slightly husky, friendly voice is perfect for Watson. On the other hand, the actor I think would be disastrously unsuited for the job is the great Samuel L Jackson – not that I, for one, wouldn't pay good money to lock Mr Jackson into a recording studio with a copy of *The Hound of the Mother-Fucking Baskervilles*.

I read some of the Sherlock Holmes stories to my children, back when they were very young, but they didn't make for good bedtime stories, sadly – too wordy, too intricately plotted, too much. *The Very Hungry Caterpillar* was much more their thing. But I recall how difficult it was to read aloud the stories. I've an okay speaking voice, but you need to be much more than just 'okay' to narrate Sherlock Holmes. And you really need to bring your A Game when tackling *The Hound of the Baskervilles*. Arch, fruity, comfy Freddie Jones is my pick for the best of the narrators I've heard. I recommend his version.

UNLIMITED FUN

Dr Watson is so (understandably) fascinated and perplexed by Sherlock Holmes that, a scant few weeks after he first rooms with the detective at Baker Street, he picks up a pencil and compiles a list of what he perceives to be Holmes's intellectual limits, like some sort of obsessive schoolteacher who can't resist applying his occupational methods to every single part of his personal life. I've always wondered if Watson made similar lists about Mrs Hudson (Knowledge of Gastronomy – feeble), or his dog (Knowledge of Walkies – exceptional).

There are twelve items on Watson's list of Sherlock Holmes's 'Limits' – Knowledge of Literature (nil); Philosophy (nil); Astronomy (nil); Politics (feeble); Botany (variable); Geology (practical, but limited); Chemistry (profound); Anatomy (accurate but unsystematic); Sensational literature (immense); plays the violin well; is an expert singlestick player, swordsman and boxer; has a good, practical knowledge of British Law.

Having jotted down this list, Watson immediately throws the paper into the open fire, having considered on reflection that exercise was a pointless waste of time. Which is where I come in, for I love a pointless waste of time, and actively seek out such things to do.

I decided I would follow in Dr Watson's footsteps and compile my own list of a person's limits! And then I'd throw the list into the open fire in my study because it would help in some small part to heat this old, cold house. But my problem was immediate – a list of whom? Not my wife – that would be exceptionally stupid and dangerous[49]. My children were also out of the question. The cats? No, that way led to madness. My brothers? I barely really knew them, sadly. My friend Jeremy (Knowledge of Pop Music – exceptional) was an option, but then I had an inspired idea – the list should be about *me*! What exactly *are* my limits? Indeed, do I actually have any?

Immediately I had another inspired idea – I would ask my wife to compile the list! She is, after all, the person I room with, and who is most fascinated and perplexed by me.

My wife took to the idea with glee, but that might be because she was on her second glass of Bailey's Irish Cream. I present below her list (which only took her about ten minutes), which she texted to me. I have removed numbers 1, 2 & 3, as they were very rude.

4. Knowledge of The Washing Machine – nil. Utterly useless! Never put reds in with the whites!

---

[49] I made a list anyway – a loving and flattering list of my wife's many qualities which I put in an envelope, sealed with a wax crest, and sent to my solicitor to be opened after my death. Unless my death is suspicious and my wife is questioned by the police, in which case the envelope must remain forever sealed.

5. Bed Making – abysmal! How many times have I shown you how to put on a duvet cover???!

6. Romantic gestures – feeble. A night in front of the telly watching a silent German film version of *The Hound of the Baskervilles* is not, repeat NOT, how to show your wife you love her.

7. DIY – abysmal! Remember the herb garden wooden box you made? LMFAO! And you still haven't finished the bathroom ceiling!

8. Languages – abysmal! But v. funny to see you attempt to order coffee in Paris!

9. Sensible Pet Care – Useless! Don't feed them from the table! Don't buy them treats every time we go shopping! Don't let them eat from your plate!

10. Grumpiness – Exceptional.

11. Knowledge of Obscure Film Facts – Exceptional, but useless.

12. Cake-making – brilliant. Can you please bake me some cupcakes? Now? As in right away? Ta.

The next morning, my wife had no memory of making this list. It took me showing her the text she sent me, and the batch of freshly baked cupcakes, to convince her that she had done so. The cupcakes were, of course, delicious.

MOON DOG

Sherlock Holmes in the 22nd Century / Episode 4 / *The Hounds of the Baskervilles* (TV animated series, 1999)

Arthur Ignatius Conan Doyle was exactly my age (fifty-one) when he believed he saw faeries. He wrote an article for the *Strand*, published Christmas 1920, in which he proselytized the existence of supernatural creatures that he was convinced had been captured in a series of photographs[50]. This was Sir Arthur at the height of his credulity, having been a founding member of the Hampshire Society for Psychical Research, attended seances and experiments in telepathy, and had a spectacular public falling out with his friend – the famed illusionist and escapologist, Harry Houdini. As you do.

But even *this* Conan Doyle – with his imagination blazing and his scepticism dampened – could never have conceived of a portly cyborg Dr Watson (with monocle) riding the Hound of the Baskervilles into a space control room on the moon, banging his head on a low metal ceiling, thus allowing a cloned version of Professor Moriarty to evade capture in an escape pod. Unlike ACD, the writers[51] of episode three of *Sherlock Holmes in the 22nd Century* have no such limitations on their fantasies.

Someone, somewhere, has watched every episode of this Fox Kids animated series, which follows the adventures of no-nonsense 22nd century cop Beth Lestrade. She has, for complicated reasons, overseen the revival of Sherlock Holmes's body[52], who had been preserved in honey since the 1890s, so that they might pair up and investigate crimes and take down a clone of Professor Moriarty... And I would very much like to know what drugs they're on.

---

[50] The famous Cottingley Fairies, a subject so compelling and fascinating that I spent three days down the rabbit hole of research, just to write this sentence. Doyle's *Strand* article, *Faeries Photographed*, can be found in full on the superb and invaluable website, The Arthur Conan Doyle Encyclopedia.

[51] Mysteriously, the writer is credited as Martha Moran (daughter of Colonel Sebastian Moran, villain of *The Empty House*?) who astonishingly has a slew of writing credits for US animated series like *RoboCop, X-Men, Super Mario Bros*, plus one oddity: a 1978 live action adaptation of the celebrated ghost story, *The Monkey's Paw*. Hmmm. Colour me intrigued.

[52] I was surprised to learn that Holmes is voiced by Jason Gray Stanford, who is the amusing Lieutenant Randy Disher in the wonderful US detective comedy-drama *Monk*.

Garfield and Friends / Season 3 Episode 9a / *The Hound of the Arbuckles* (TV kids cartoon pastiche, 1990)

I've never liked Garfield. I find the cartoon cat to be obnoxious, smug, and contrived. It's as if Jim Davis had created him to be offputtingly irksome, like those square-shaped Princes' Corned Beef tins that you have to open with a key, or the post-*Professionals* acting career of Martin Shaw. I wasn't looking forward to watching *The Hound of the Arbuckles*, but I came away not too annoyed, for in its favour is a) it's short (around five mins), and b) it does the *Without a Clue*[53] 'Watson-is-really-the-smart-one-and-Holmes-is-an-idiot' thing really well. Garfield makes a surprisingly good Dr Watson.

My loathing of Garfield, in fact, once inspired me to create my own newspaper strip character. Back in the early 1990s, I was a penniless art student still living with my parents and was desperate in every sense. I read the daily newspapers free in the college refectory. From there, my hatred of Garfield grew and grew – this bloody cat had conquered the world and made its creator a fortune! Surely I could create an equally popular smug, obnoxious and contrived newspaper strip character? After all, I could draw, I could write, and I was smug, obnoxious and contrived (and desperate in every sense), with absolutely nothing better to do with my life.

I set to it, and created a character named Oxford – a pretentious and snooty parrot in a cage in an (unseen) Oxford Professor's rooms. He alternately wore the two pieces of headwear that immediately symbolise intelligence – the mortar board and the deerstalker. Indeed, I based him in part on Basil Rathbone's Sherlock Holmes, crossed with Tony

---

[53] 1988 British comedy feature film starring Michael Caine as an idiotic, alcoholic actor pretending to be Sherlock Holmes at the employ of Ben Kingsley's super smart detective Dr Watson. I love it.

Hancock[54]. I couldn't help but pepper the strips with Holmes references, not least by having the Professor's dog named Baskerville.

I showed my draft scripts and artwork to a friend, my old school English teacher, who saw potential in the character and asked if he might co-write some of the strips. Pretty soon we had amassed enough material (and art) to start submitting it to newspapers. We tried all the half-reputable UK tabloids – *The Daily Mirror, The Daily Mail, The Daily Express*, and then the broadsheets, and then the gutter press, and over the course of a year the sad little rejection letters arrived one by one. Then, my friend and I had a spectacular and permanent falling out over a woman, my mental health took a dive off a cliff, and I ended up in hospital after a stupid suicide attempt (gosh, this got dark quickly, didn't it? Told you I hated Garfield!). Oxford was shelved forever, perhaps for the best.

According to Wikipedia, Garfield is syndicated in 2,580 newspapers and is read by approximately 300 million readers every day. But is Jim Davis as happy as me, sat here in my lonely study, scoffing down bourbon creams and writing about my life experiences with *The Hound of the Baskervilles?*

Yes. Yes, of course he's much happier! Bastard.

---

[54] See *Hancock's Half Hour*

CHAPTER SEVEN

Outside of a Dog, a Book is Man's Best Friend.
And Inside of a Dog, it's Too Dark to Read

November 2020

FOR THE BIRDS

I DON'T THINK I would be at all useful to Mr Sherlock Holmes. I simply don't have the get up-and-go that he requires from a faithful companion. Dr Watson, for instance, spends all of Chapter Seven busying himself with all manner of things, from instantly deducing that it is Mrs Barrymore who cries in the night, to irritating a postmaster with his dogged questions about whether a telegram sent by Holmes for Barrymore was actually put in the hand of Barrymore or if it was left for him, or if anybody saw the butler when the telegram was delivered to him, and so on. I mean, I think I could handle the 'irritating people with dogged questioning' bit rather well, but Watson walks at least four miles over the moor, four miles back, and meets and questions people, then writes it all down in exhaustive detail to send back to Baker Street. Quite frankly, I'm knackered from just reading all that.

Also in Chapter Seven, we meet the villain of the piece, cheerily wearing a straw hat and chasing a butterfly, though within minutes he's witnessing a pit pony sink to its death in the Grimpen Mire, so, you know, foreshadowing and all that. And most crucially, Watson gets to hear the Hound of the Baskervilles:

> A long, low moan, indescribably sad, swept over the moor. It filled the whole air, and yet it was impossible to say whence it came. From a dull murmur it swelled into a deep roar, and then sank back into a melancholy, throbbing murmur once again.

Watson is obviously a little unnerved, but Stapleton pretends to dismiss all notion of a legendary hell hound and instead tries to pin the sound on:

a) mud settling
b) water rising
c) the boom cry of the last of the bitterns, a near-extinct bird[55]

Dr Watson doesn't have a smart phone with him, so alas the good doctor can't fire up his YouTube app to watch a video of a bittern booming... But I can and I can tell you, here and now, what Dr Watson could not there and then: bitterns don't sound anything remotely like the mournful baying of a hound. You wouldn't in a million years ever confuse the two sounds – they're as distinct from each other as, say, the faint, gentle tinkling of a tiny little fairy bell atop an attractively decorated Victorian Christmas Tree, and Tom Cruise whooping in toothy delight into his US Airforce comms unit as his state-of-the-art jet fighter thunders through the stratosphere, accompanied by a jubilantly patriotic Hans Zimmer score, during an especially obnoxious bit of *Top Gun*. If I were in Watson's place, on the moor, listening to that deep roar filling the air, I'd have told Stapleton he must be a complete fruit loop to even consider the possibility

---

[55] Having become extinct in the late 1800s as a result of drainage and hunting (according to the RSPB), as of 2016 there are 160 booming bitterns in the UK.

that it was the boom of a bittern. Bittern? More like 'bite me', I'd have said.

WHAT HAPPENED ON DARTMOOR #3: WISH YOU WERE HERE

Princetown is apparently one of the highest places in England. I was certainly high on life as I walked through it, delighting at sight of the prison, the High Moorland Visitor's Centre (once the Duchy Hotel, where ACD had stayed on 2nd June 1901), the post office, the very air itself. In the Visitor's Centre, I posed for a photo near the exhibition featuring ACD, his writing desk, and a Sherlock Holmes mannequin, and I felt a kinship to Sir Arthur and his greatest detective. Sadly I couldn't enter into the exhibition itself, as it was closed due to Covid-19.

While there, I daydreamed that this book would be one of the most successful books of the twenty-first century and that a mannequin of me would one day takes its place beside these two great men. Though I'd hope the artist would sculpt me thinner, taller, with darker hair. And perhaps with a sword, so that I look less nerdy, a dead Hound at my feet as if I had slayed the beast between writing best-selling books that change the world.

I bought postcards and trinkets and I couldn't resist – how could anyone? – buying another copy of *The Hound of the Baskervilles*. It was an attractive Penguin Classics paperback edition with an introduction by Christopher Frayling[56], as well as a hand-coloured Sidney Paget illustration on the cover depicting Holmes shooting the Hound as it mauls at a prone Sir Henry, Watson racing to help in the background. I also bought a new deerstalker.

---

[56] More of him later when I tackle all the HOUN documentaries.

Well, I say *I* bought these things, but before we left for Dartmoor, I'd had to cancel our bank card after I stupidly left it in our local Tesco's, so it's more accurate to say that *Chris* bought all these things for me, and my wife paid him back later.

I wrote a message on the postcard, addressed it to Sherlock Holmes at 221b Baker Street, London, bought a stamp in the Princetown post office and popped it in the post box. The message read:

"Holmes,

Have arrived safely at Baskerville Hall. I think Stapleton is the villain 'cause I think he's a long lost Baskerville relative who wants to inherit. The Hound is just some big dog half-starved and daubed with phosphate. That's my guess anyway, but hey, you're the detective.

Love to Mrs H, see you back at Baker Street, unless you're secretly hiding on the moor or something!

Your faithful companion,

--JH Watson"

I can't wait to pay another visit the Sherlock Holmes Museum at Baker Street to see if they've put my postcard on display. And, of course, if they're stocking this book.

THE ADVENTURE OF THE UNREVIEWED CHIPMUNKS

Chip 'n Dale Rescue Rangers / Season 1, Episode 8 / *Pound of the Baskervilles* (TV cartoon, 1989)

Has anyone on Earth ever reviewed an episode of *Chip 'n Dale Rescue Rangers*? The internet's a big place, populated with the most arcane and strange things, but I don't think anyone's ever sat down and reviewed an episode of this lively kid's TV cartoon series.

I liked this episode with its bizarre plot involving Rodger Baskerville, a hidden Will, a villain with a dog allergy, and the Hound itself being a loveable old English Sheepdog with a Liverpudlian accent. Once I got used to the chimpunks' helium voices (are they chipmunks? I really should do some research on this[57]), I was amused by the constant references to other 'Sherlock Jones' cases, all of which had bizarre titles[58].

Throughout the sixty Sherlock Holmes stories written by ACD, there is a sprinkling of cryptic references to other cases – perhaps the most famous ones being 'the giant rat of Sumatra', 'the colossal schemes of Baron Maupertuis', and 'the politician, the lighthouse, and the trained cormorant'. Indeed, in HOUN Holmes tells Sir Henry that it would be impossible for him to journey to Baskerville Hall because "at the present instant one of the most revered names in England is being besmirched by a blackmailer, and only I can stop a disastrous scandal." This might be a whopping great fib, of course. It's difficult to tell with any certainty if Sir Arthur was being playful, or if he simply jotted down whatever occurred to him at the moment, much like I do when compiling shopping lists. These weird cases have formed the basis of hundreds of pastiche stories across all media.

I thought it might be a hoot to take inspiration from ACD on this, and to begin referring to things in my past in a similar way. That time a curry disagreed with my digestive system on a tube train could be 'the Brick Lane Horror'. And the time in my early twenties, when me and my friends dropped LSD in a cinema whilst watching the newly released

---

[57] They are indeed 'anthropomorphic chipmunk brothers' according to ten seconds of Googling. Now I know.

[58] *Zero Effect,* a wonderful film by Jake Kadsan, is a loose reworking of *A Scandal in Bohemia* set in contemporary Los Angeles, featuring a wonderfully rude and eccentric consulting detective named Daryl Zero (played by the superb Bill Pullman) who gives his cases the most amusingly prosaic titles possible, such as 'The Case of the Man Who Lost His Keys But Found Them Again'. *Zero Effect* is one of my favourite movies.

Oliver Stone biopic of *The Doors* (1991), got kicked out for causing a disturbance, drank a gallon of homemade beer and ended up lying in the middle of the road at sunrise, would be 'The Case of the Hallucinogenic, the Usherette, and the Home Brew'. The writing of this book, I'm sure, will be known by future old man-me as either 'The Hound, the Book, and the Colossal Fame and Fortune that resulted from it' (extremely optimistic version), or, 'The Wife, the Hound, and the Seeds of Divorce Proceedings' (more realistic version).

TAKING A BATH

The Hound of the Baskervilles - stage production by The Rondo Theatre Company[59].

Stuck indoors and feeling miserable, I remember a year ago when I popped over to the Heritage City of Bath to watch a stage performance of *The Hound of the Baskervilles.*

Bristol and Bath are sister cities, being only fifteen miles apart. Even so, it took me an hour and a half to get to the Rondo Theatre. Traffic was appalling because there were disruptive Climate Change demonstrations in Bristol City Centre (I can never complain about them because I'm fully on their side; nonetheless I wished they'd chosen another night). Bath, in turn, was hosting an important Rugby match on the same evening the Christmas market was opening. And, when I finally got there with only minutes to spare, it was bloody freezing. The temperature had dropped a few degrees in the already chilly evening. I had wrapped up warm, but I was chilled to the bone by the time I took my seat in the tiny 100-seater theatre.

There was in fact a small problem with my seat (which had cost me £13.50) – it was already occupied by an elderly lady. I politely

---

[59] This performance was on Saturday 29th November 2019. The adaptor/director was Louise Wallace.

explained how she had stolen my seat and I was relieved to discover that she was fact charming and apologetic and made for good company throughout the production - not least because she insisted on applauding at the end of every scene, confusing the cast and most of the audience, most of whom, I couldn't help but notice, were wearing Bath Rugby scarves. I wondered why they were not at the match (kick off was the same time as curtain rise) and if they were here because this was a second choice when they couldn't get tickets to the Rugby. I also wondered if Dr Watson supported a Rugby team[60], but I was told to shut up because the curtain was rising.

It was a spirited, clever and engaging stage version of HOUN, with many ingenious pieces of staging and a very good cast, including a splendid, shouty Sir Henry, whose accent had never been anywhere near Canada, and a brilliantly camp and sinister Stapleton who almost had the engrossed audience booing him. I was charmed to count how many times Richard Chivers' Watson took off his coat and hat, only to almost immediately put them back on (seventeen times, by my reckoning). Robert Finlay was an excellent, energetic Holmes, commanding the stage and radiating intelligent charisma. To my mind, he looked not too dissimilar to Tony Hadley, the lead singer of 80s New Romantic pop group Spandau Ballet, and I half expected him to say, "Watson, I know this much is true...".

Dry ice flooded the room (the Rondo is a black box theatre, with no raised stage) at exciting moments, though the room was so cold that it might have just been our breath misting up. The sound effects, props, costumes, and music were great – with some sly touches, such as the portraits of Sir Arthur Conan Doyle adorning the Baker Street set (and a portrait of Jeremy Brett, I fancied, standing in for one of the dastardly

---

[60] According to *The Adventure of Charles Augustus Milverton*, Dr Watson had played for Blackheath FC, a team from south-east London. I reckon he'd have been a prop forward, whatever that is.

111

Baskervilles). Patrick Gowers' wonderful theme music to the Brett series was played over a scene transition and – most amusingly – a muzak version of Gerry Rafferty's *Baker Street* played in the intermission. I left the theatre to stretch my legs and wondered if I could buy a programme or playbill.

"Excuse me," I asked a man by the front desk, who was warming his frozen fingers on a steaming hot mug of tea. "Could I buy a programme?"

"You probably could," he replied, "but not from me, 'cause I don't work here."

"Ah. It's just…"

"What?"

"You're by the front desk, so naturally I assumed you were manning it."

"I'm not *behind* the front desk, though. I'm just standing by it."

"Even so…"

He scowled at me, so I went back inside and took my seat. The nice old lady next to me was reading her programme.

"Where did you get your programme?" I asked her.

"Oh, a nice young man at the front desk."

"Oh really? How interesting."

"Yes, it cost me £1.50."

"Was the man who sold you it *behind* the front desk, or just stood *by* the front desk?"

"I'm not sure…"

"Think! Remember back!"

"I'm trying..."

"Either he was behind the desk, or he was standing by the desk - which was it?!"

But before the old lady could answer, the curtain raised for Act 2, more dry ice flooded the room, and soon I forgot all about the man by the front desk as I was delighted by the splendid production - Act 2 being even better than the first, and the finale on the moor – grippingly realised. A real triumph of a show that earned warm applause from the audience.

As soon as I got home, I emailed the Rondo Theatre. I congratulated them on a wonderful show. I added a P.S to my email, enquiring if their front of house staff were contractually obliged to serve customers whether they were stood by the front desk or behind the front desk.

I also emailed Alan, my botanist friend, just to annoy him.

BOOK CASES

Sherlock Holmes was Wrong: Re-opening the Case of the Hound of the Baskervilles (non-fiction book by Pierre Bayard, 2008)

The Moor (mystery novel by Laurie R King, 1998)

Hounds of the Baskervilles: From Devil Dogs to Sherlock Holmes (Collected essays and stories, edited by Timothy Green Beckley and William Kern, 2012)

Mark of the Baskerville Hound (pastiche novel by Wilfred Hueffel, 2011)

The Baskerville Legacy (novel by John O'Connell, 2011)

The Hound of the Baskervilles According to Spike Milligan (comedy novel by Spike Milligan, 1997)

Professor Moriarty: The Hound of the D'Urbervilles (pastiche novel by Kim Newman, 2011)

Ken Ludwig's Baskerville: A Sherlock Holmes Mystery (2015)

My eyesight is not what it used to be. These days I need spectacles and a magnifying glass to read heating instructions on the packaging of Findus Cottage Pies or to see the little white L and R printed on my earbuds. It is, therefore, heart-breaking for me to admit that my reading has slowed considerably over the past decade, to the point where I now read around a book a month. I was a voracious reader in my teens and twenties and would often read several books a week. At the rate I'm deteriorating, I'm expecting to read a book a year in my sixties and a single book throughout my seventies, should I be lucky to live that long. If I make it into my eighties, I can only guarantee reading a single word per year.

For my HOUN marathon, however, I adhered to a strict training regime for my eyes. Like Rocky Balboa rising at dawn, punching the crap out of meat carcasses, and running up the steps of Philadelphia Town Hall, I got up at eleven, read the crap out of the Mr Men books and went back to bed again. The result is I trained my eyesight to withstand long reading periods, meaning I could step up my game and subsequently, I have been engrossed in all manner of Baskerville literary shenanigans.

I don't like to boast, but I fancy I may have read more books based on *The Hound of the Baskervilles* than anyone. Certainly, I've passed the threshold for 'genially exploring an interest' and stepped into the Grimpen Mire of 'obsessively consuming a load of nonsense'. I'm grouping all the books here, in one easily digestible section. Try not to hear Bill Conti's classic *Rocky* (1976) theme in your head as you read this.

Sherlock Holmes was Wrong: Re-opening the Case of the Hound of the Baskervilles is an amusing and ingenious takedown of the shonky plot mechanics of HOUN, and serves as a kind of literary equivalent of giving Sir Arthur a wedgie. In particular, author Pierre Bayard explores the delightful notion that the Hound itself may be innocent and, instead, presents an entirely plausible retelling of events that points the finger at a different villain. Bayard has written on Agatha Christie's *The Murder of Roger Akroyd*, a book my wife holds dear, so I am very much tempted to buy her a copy of that. I'm also tempted to write a book titled *Pierre Bayard was Wrong: Re-Opening the Case of Sherlock Holmes was Wrong: Re-opening the Case of the Hound of the Baskervilles*, in which I take Bayard's book apart with tongue-in-cheek forensic detail, presenting an entirely new solution instead.

Every now and again readers discover a new author who delights them and it's like forming a new, exciting friendship. Such a thing happened to me when I started reading Laurie R King's *The Moor*: a quite brilliant, absorbing pastiche novel that has Sherlock Holmes return to Dartmoor (and Baskerville Hall), with Dr Watson swapped out for Holmes's young wife, Mary Russell. Having not read any other books in the series, it was quite a shock for me to discover that Holmes was married, and that faithful old Dr Watson was out of the picture, but Mary Russell is such a terrific character and engaging narrator that I was swiftly taken with her and I scarcely missed Watson. But it is with her evocative depictions of the moor, and the people who live there, that Laurie R King earned my most admiration. There's a chapter detailing Mary having a most peculiar pub singalong that's one of the more striking passages of fiction I've ever had the pleasure to read. *The Moor* gives a supporting role to the remarkable Sabine Baring-Gould, the real-life Reverend of Lew Trenchard (the manor being a likely inspiration for Baskerville Hall), a prolific writer and collector of folk songs, amongst many other things[61], and inspired me to read a biography of the man. I enjoyed *The Moor* so much that I bought all the other Mary Russell and Sherlock Holmes mystery books. I also tweeted Laurie R King (I've a long history of shamelessly brownnosing writers and I encourage all readers to follow suit, especially readers of this book). I received this charming reply:

To @VinceStadon

From @mary_russell

How Kind. I'm pleased you enjoyed reading about our time on Dartmoor.

The essays and stories in *Hounds of the Baskervilles: From Devil Dogs to Sherlock Holmes* are a mixed bunch, to say the least (weirdly, it contains the entire text of HOUN), with my favourite being an amusingly melodramatic and thoroughly comprehensive essay on spectral dogs from UK folklore, full with eyewitness reports faithfully transcribed in all their nutty glory. I love the non-story of Sally Armstrong, a retired auctioneer who, one early morning in 1987, "was witness to a monstrous black-hued dog with wild staring eyes" which she these days "concedes that there was nothing definitely supernatural or paranormal about the fiend-dog she saw more than a quarter of a century ago." So, it *wasn't* a fiend-dog, then? Cheers for that, Sally. I'm reminded of the 'It Happened to Me' subforum on the delightful *Fortean Times* message board. I used to visit the board often, particularly if I was struggling for ideas for a project. The board is populated with (supposed) eyewitness accounts of people seeing ghosts or poltergeist activity or being abducted by UFOs or having out of body experiences, and the like. There was one story that's stayed with me because it made me laugh so much: the writer, a man in his twenties

---

[61] He wrote *Onward Christian Soldiers*, among many other hymns. And his *A Book of Dartmoor* almost certainly influenced ACD in the writing of HOUN.

named Dave, was at a friend's house, relaxing with a beer, watching television. His friend gets up to go to the bathroom, leaving Dave alone with his friend's big, friendly Alsatian. The dog looks at Dave, Dave looks back at the dog. "Alright, Dave?" says the dog. It is a few paragraphs later before Dave mentions that certain chemical substances had been taken, washed down with their beers. Okay then. Cheers for that, Dave.

In *The Mark of the Dartmoor Hound* by Wilfred Huettel, a retired New York cop who, by 1982 has become a world expert on the text of *The Hound of the Baskervilles* (as New York cops are wont to do), visits a priest and relates a story about the time he was abroad on Dartmoor years ago and got wrapped up in a mystery and a romance. It's an excellent premise and I liked it well enough. The New York cop thing lodged in my head. Because my cultural references are invariably of the low-brow kind, I kept picturing Telly Savalas' NYCPD Detective Lieutenant Theo Kojak as the central character. I read every line of dialogue in that distinct "Who loves you, baby?" voice and couldn't help but imagine him in black trilby and massive sunglasses, sucking a lollipop as he saunters across the moor. Then I remembered that Telly Savalas had once recorded a hit record called *If*[62] that my mum had loved (she had an eclectic taste in pop music) and I pictured Telly Savalas on the moor, speak-singing to the Hound:

> "If the world should stop revolving, spinning slowly down to die, I'd spend the end with you."

I'm quite sure this is all far removed from anything Wilfred Huettel had in mind, but if you're reading this, William, then I know I speak for everyone when I say that, for *Mark of the Dartmoor Hound 2:*

---

[62] A spoken word cover version of the hit song by ultra-smooth Californian soft rock band Bread which inexplicably got to number 1 in the UK Singles Chart in early 1975, and stayed there for two weeks because the charts in the 70s were completely nuts. The B-side to *If* is a cover version of *You've Lost That Loving Feeling*. God knows what that's like.

This Time It's Personal, you owe it to us all to find a way to get Telly Savalas on the moor.

The Baskerville Legacy by John O'Connell is a quite extraordinary novel that zooms in on the difficult friendship between Bertram Fletcher Robinson and Arthur Conan Doyle and gets into the detail of inspiration for and the writing of *The Hound of the Baskervilles*. Narrated by Robinson, who is earnest and secretive and insecure (not to mention half addicted to laudanum and sex workers), the narrative gets darker as the two men holiday on Dartmoor and rivalries emerge, leading to a falling out. Conan Doyle is portrayed as robust and curious (and slightly wounded by the war he's returned from with enteric fever, as well as the bruising he's taken in a failed political career), but with darker waters running deep within him. *The Baskerville Legacy* is an unsettling book, dreamlike in places, but compelling and memorable – I couldn't stop thinking about it for days after finishing it. Not quite a mystery novel, not quite a biography, not quite a snapshot of a friendship blighted by the Hound, *The Baskerville Legacy* is something else, more than all these things – it is living, breathing, beautiful literature. I loved it.

You wouldn't describe *The Hound of the Baskervilles According to Spike Milligan* as literature, but then, nothing in literature is as funny as Spike Milligan. *According To...* is pretty much what you'd hope for from Spike, meaning it's a gloriously unhinged and often surreal retelling of HOUN – the one-legged Hound is a genius idea that still has me giggling. In some regards, this is the comedy version Peter Cook was hankering after (or at least, the Derek and Clive[63] HOUN, for this book might be the only version of Conan Doyle's most famous novel that has the 'c word'!). There are so many jokes that the hit rate is about half and half, though

---

[63] Exceptionally crude, rude and offensive alter-egos of Cook and Moore who released several legendary filthy audio recordings in the mid- to late 70s.

when Spike does get it right, he makes me laugh like a drain. Take this bit:

> "I could even quote a passage from your letter. It ran, 'Please, please, as you are a gentleman, burn this letter, and be at the gate by ten o'clock with your cheque book'".

> I thought that she had fainted, but she recovered herself with a supreme effort by doing a backward somersault into the upright position.

> "Do you think a woman could go alone at that hour to a bachelor's house? I never got there."

> "Why not?"

> "Something intervened to prevent my going."

> "What was that?"

> "An elephant fell on me."

It's like Arthur Conan Doyle on an acid trip at a vaudeville show where every character is played by Spike Milligan. Who wouldn't want to read that? The book is graced by Rob Seabury's line drawings, which are as silly and engaging as Spike's prose. I have the drawing from Chapter Eleven on my wall. It depicts Holmes and Watson, who had just shot himself in the foot, walking across the moor as a dog pulls at Watson's bandaged foot. It makes me smile every time I look at it.

I've been a fan of Kim Newman for years. He has the kind of career that makes me envious – writing film reviews and guides to horror cinema, appearing as a cultural expert in various documentaries, writing novels based on his favourite creations (Dr Who, Count Dracula, Sherlock Holmes). Back in the mid-80s, he and I had a shared interest in

119

'video nasties[64]' and the fan publications that talked about them. I never had the courage to contribute, but Kim Newman did. After reading his reviews, I quickly considered his to be an authoritative, yet approachable voice and I was always pleased to see him whenever he popped up on TV as a pundit. His novel, *Anno Dracula,* is such an entertaining read that I've returned to it (and the equally good sequels) many times. *Professor Moriarty and the Hound of the D'Urbervilles* is in the same rich and bloody vein as *Anno Dracula* – a celebration of all things Newman loves mixed in a heady genre-splicing brew. This book is more a collection of short stories rather than a novel (my favourite being *A Shambles in Belgravia*) and it positions Professor Moriarty and Colonel 'Basher' Moran as a delightfully perverse anti-Holmes and Watson pairing, the two villains running London's criminal network in the opposing way that Holmes and Watson investigate it. As always, there are so many references to other works and characters that it often reads as a fan love letter to everything Newman admires, but clearly, I'm all for that sort of thing 'cause, well, I'm writing this book, which has even more obscure references in it than Newman's entire ouvre. Witty, bloody, and very clever – that's Kim Newman. He deserves his brilliant career.

I've never seen a performance of Ken Ludwig's *Baskerville: A Sherlock Holmes Mystery* (2015), but as it's perhaps the most staged Sherlock Holmes play of modern times, I'm very keen to experience it. My friend, the actor/writer/director/producer/all-round nice man, Kyle Borcz, was in a production of the play in Indiana. He tells me he had an absolute whale of a time and that it went down a storm, which perked my

---

[64] Surprisingly, my sweet and gentle mum was into grim 'feminist revenge horror' exploitation films like *I Spit on Your Grave* (1978) and *Last House on the Left* (1972) which were released on home video in the early 80s alongside a raft of other films with equally schlocky titles, including a whole abattoir's worth of unpleasant, low-budget Italian cannibal films or zombie films (or cannibal-zombie films). I watched a fair few of them all; hardly any deserve a rewatch.

interest further[65]. A copy of the Samuel French edition plopped onto my doormat, and I was so eager to read it, I let my buttered breakfast kippers get cold and the cats ate them instead. *Baskerville* starts out sober enough, but soon descends into brilliant farce, with the spine of Doyle's narrative intact but a whole host of amusing new characters added, and comedy incidents thrown in – my favourite bit being between Watson, a nurse, and a very tactile Sherlock Holmes. As a neurotic, struggling, bitter comedy writer who has dabbled often in this field, I confess shamefully that I wanted to dislike this play – all successful things to me are like daggers in my talentless, withered heart. But it's so good that my envy lost out to admiration and appreciation for making me laugh so much. I intend to seek out Ludwig's other plays in the expectation of further amusement. If my eyesight is up to it.

LADIES MAN

Back to HOUN Chapter Seven, where I've been musing on Dr Watson's effect on women. He's only really stepped foot on the moor before he's had two married women react to him in very odd ways: Mrs Barrymore tells him a pack of fibs about not crying in the night, while Beryl Stapleton mistakes him for Sir Henry and warns him to get the hell off Dartmoor. Before he's even met Beryl Stapleton, thirsty[66] Watson is keen to meet her, or indeed it would seem *any* woman. As he muses on whether to decline Stapleton's invitation to come to Merripit House to meet his sister – Watson is tired and knows he should get back to check

---

[65] "It was one of the most difficult plays I've done, but so much fun," says Kyle, "27 costume changes! Each of the three "actors" had a dedicated costume person backstage. It's not in the script, I played Lestrade in the last scene just for the fun of it; by that time, the moustache the actor used had been stuck on and re-stuck I usually couldn't keep it on my face. One time, it flew off during one of my lines and I caught it in mid-air and stuffed it in my pocket!"

[66] 'Thirsty' = 'horny' in Millennial-speak, according to my daughter, after a long, awkward and baffling conversation.

on Sir Henry – the doctor reasons that Holmes's instructions were to meet every neighbour and report back, so he accepts the invite. I mean, he's only doing his job, right? So what if Beryl is drop dead gorgeous? Pure coincidence, eh, Watson, you old devil!

I wonder if Watson's description of Beryl – he notes her 'sensitive mouth', 'beautiful, dark eager eyes', and her 'perfect figure' – made it into his report to Holmes, and whether, on reading it, Holmes had sighed and rolled his eyes. Good old Watson. Never could resist the ladies.

CHAPTER EIGHT

Gives You Paws

December 2020

WATSON & I

FOR HOUN CHAPTER EIGHT, I'm swapping my Oxford University Press edition for the beautiful *New Annotated Sherlock Holmes – The Novels: The Hound of the Baskervilles*, written by Leslie S Klinger. This gorgeous book is a work of art in itself and flicking through its pages gives me a gentle thrill. I haven't mentioned Sidney Paget's original illustrations for HOUN because I've been saving them for now, when I'm in control of my superlatives.

Paget's art is one of my very favourite things in the world. The artist produced 60 superb illustrations for HOUN, all of them faithfully reproduced in this beautiful book, which also collects fine pen and ink illustrations from the German artist, Richard Gutschmidt. I love looking at these illustrations. I have several prints adorning the walls of my house: Paget's drawing of Holmes stood by the fire as Watson relaxes into a comfy chair[67] adorns the wall above the fireplace in my study.

---

[67] From *A Scandal in Bohemia*. The other prints I have are from *The Speckled Band* and *The Final Problem*. I purchased them from the Sherlock Holmes Museum at 221b Baker Street.

Chapter Eight is one very long letter from Watson to Holmes. I've gotten out of the habit of writing letters to friends, but even when I was writing them, none of them were of the length and detail that the good doctor sets down. It must take him hours and hours! It took me half an hour to type the above two lines; not only are they not especially good sentences, they're the result of quite a bit of fussy editing on my word processing package. Watson writes beautifully, by hand, in one draft. What a man! Of course, he's been faithfully chronicling his adventures with Sherlock Holmes for many years, and is no doubt making a tidy packet from his publisher, whereas I haven't written anything other than shopping lists and begging emails to my bank manager... We're so different, Watson and me.

Anyway, of note is Watson vs the telegram to Barrymore, round 2. You may remember that, back in Chapter Five, Sir Henry was being followed by a man with a black beard. Dr Mortimer had volunteered Barrymore as sporting such a beard, at which point Holmes had sent a telegram to him at Baskerville Hall, to be delivered by hand so that the detective might ascertain if Barrymore really was in Devonshire and not sneakily in London stealing boots, sending threatening notes to Canadians, and following Sir Henry around in a cab.

Then, in Chapter Seven, Watson gets up bright and early, walks to the local post office and irritates the heck out of the postmaster and his young messenger boy with his insistent questioning regarding whether the telegram was actually placed into Barrymore's hand. (Watson is acting like an especially craven sub-team leader on *The Apprentice* who is covering his arse in case the team fails the task so that he can smugly tell Sir Alan that he's in no way responsible for the team losing because as sub-team leader he followed the project manager's instructions to the letter and made triple sure that the business with the telegram to Barrymore was sorted out; in Watson's view, Sir Alan should fire Holmes, because Holmes lied to his team.)

Round 2 of the Barrymore Telegram has Watson enlisting Sir Henry to give Barrymore a morning grilling on the matter, with Watson - presumably playing Good Cop to Sir Henry's Bad Cop - opting to keep out of the tête-à-tête altogether. This puzzling interrogation clearly upsets the sensitive Barrymore, who stews on it all day. In the evening, he plucks up the courage to approach his master and raise the thorny matter with him. That's when a contrite Sir Henry is forced to drop the Bad Cop approach in order to give his manservant assurances that all is good between them and further sweetens the situation by gifting Barrymore a considerable part of his old wardrobe (I'm assuming clothing, rather than the furniture). Watson, who has now irritated four people over the Barrymore telegram, drops the subject altogether, his job done. Atta boy, Doc! I can only admire his work and wonder if I'd have handled things differently or if, perhaps, we are not so different after all, Watson and I.

WHOSE HOUND IS IT ANYWAY?

Arthur Wotner as Sherlock Holmes in *Silver Blaze (Murder at the Baskervilles)*, 1937

Well, this is a hoot: a wild crime thriller that grafts onto an adaptation of *Silver Blaze* Sir Henry Baskerville and Baskerville Hall, Professor Moriarty, a secret hideout under a disused Tube Station, and an explosive car chase shootout sequence at night - all to create a kind of mutant super-Holmes film. It stars a laid back, genial middle-aged Holmes who strolls through the whole thing like he's merely enjoying a change of pace. The car chase is bags of fun: on a road winding through Dartmoor, after leaving Sir Henry at Baskerville Hall with his daughter's fiancé, who Holmes has just cleared of the theft of Silver Blaze, the Great Detective, Watson and Inspector Lestrade are fired upon by Colonel Sebastian Moran and Professor Moriarty. The hail of bullets - from a custom-made gas-powered machine gun! - sends Holmes's car careening off the road to overturn on the wild moor.

I found myself gripped and charmed by this batty movie (the second HOUN-related feature film made in 1937!), and very much taken with the 'throw-everything-into-the-pot-and-see-how-it-tastes' approach. Indeed, I decided that this mix and match method of plot ingredients would make for a great little game and might even prove inspiring for writers working on new Holmes fictions.

Here's how it works: I cut out three large cardboard circles and divided the circles into eight segments. In each segment is a different category, depending on the circle.

Circle A has eight Sherlock Holmes story titles (the seven most famous[68], plus *The Adventure of the Golden Pince-Nez* – the one everybody forgets about – thrown in for the lols).

Circle B has eight characters: Queen Victoria, Jack the Ripper, Professor Moriarty, Irene Adler, Mycroft Holmes, Inspector Lestrade, and Count Dracula.

Circle C has eight exciting incidents:

1. Boat chase down the Thames;
2. Scotland Yard is blown up;
3. Holmes & Watson are attacked by bears;
4. Hot air balloon chase over the Reichenbach Falls;
5. Ninjas;
6. Some kind of giant stompy robot-thing;
7. An experimental submarine disguised as the Loch Ness Monster;
8. A fist fight to the death on the top of a speeding train.

I made a small hole in the middle of the cardboard circle, pushing one of those weird small pencils you get in the Bookies through (I always

---

[68] These are, I'm guessing, *A Study in Scarlet; The Sign of The Four; A Scandal in Bohemia; The Final Problem; Silver Blaze; The Dancing Men; The Speckled Band.* Fight me.

126

grab a handful when I make my one and only annual visit on Grand National Day). I now spin each circle, making a note of the segment which touches the tabletop when it comes to a complete stop.

With *The Hound of the Baskervilles* as the default starting point (obvs!), I can now jot down all the elements for an exciting new Sherlock Holmes adventure! My first three goes ran thus:

1. HOUN + The Speckled Band + Jack the Ripper + Scotland Yard is blown up = Sherlock Holmes and the Terror of the London Snake Killer of the Baskervilles!

2. HOUN + A Study in Scarlet + Queen Victoria + Holmes and Watson are attacked by bears = Sherlock Holmes and the Royal Revenge Bears of the Baskervilles!

3. HOUN + A Scandal in Bohemia + Count Dracula + Ninjas = Sherlock Holmes and the Undead Warrior Seductress of the Baskervilles!

You get the idea. Fun for all the family! And of course, you can create even more circles with new categories (Watson's Wives; Mrs Hudson's Breakfasts; Countries at War with England, etc.) to further complicate and develop the game. I'm calling it *Whose HOUND Is It Anyway?*

DEERSTALKER & INVERNESS CAPE	PLAYS THE VIOLIN	SMOKES A MEERSCHAUM PIPE	"ELEMENTARY, MY DEAR WATSON!"	MRS HUDSON
PROFESSOR MORIARTY	INSPECTOR LESTRADE	MYCROFT HOLMES	IRENE ADLER	QUEEN VICTORIA
MARY MORSTAN/ WATSON	7% SOLUTION OF COCAINE		221B BAKER STREET	THE REICHENBACH FALLS
GIANT RAT OF SUMATRA	STEAM TRAIN	HANSOM CAB	FOG	BIG BEN / THE THAMES
JACK THE RIPPER	CLIENT NAMED VIOLET	GOVERNMENT CONSPIRACY	BAKER STREET IRREGULARS	THE STRAND MAGAZINE

WHAT HAPPENED ON DARTMOOR #4: MAN ON THE MOOR

Before we had left Bristol, my wife had installed the What3Words app on her phone, because she does not trust my sense of direction (having managed to get us lost in Rome, Berlin, Paris, and even our home city) and did not want to die from hypothermia on the freezing moor. The app essentially points to a very specific location, its developers having divided the world into 57 trillion squares, each having a unique, randomly assigned three-word address. Thankfully, I'll never know the three words assigned to the stretch of the moor we were exploring that day as we didn't get lost, didn't have to call the emergency services and did not need to be rescued, but I very much hope the words are Amazing Lover Vince, or even Hound Mystery Baskervilles.

It was a crisp, though quite sunny, Saturday morning when we set off on our hike across the moor. Tony wanted the walk to be over and done with by 3pm so that he could find a pub to watch the Liverpool v Everton derby[69], and Chris just wanted to find a pub. I, on the other hand,

---

[69] It was, apparently, a 2 – 2 draw. I don't follow sport, so unless a spectral Hound invaded the pitch and started eating the players, I'm not interested.

was happy to follow in the footsteps of Dr Watson, and my wife was happy to be with me.

There is a stillness to the moor and an absence of sound that's a little unnerving. It is so vast, it is like its own country. I could not help but remember Watson's perfect description of the place as 'the melancholy moor,' for I don't think there is a more concise picture to be painted.

I was pleased to find that the ground was soft and that, near to a path, there were the distinct footprints of a gigantic hound, plus something even more extraordinary – dry white dog poo, long-since disappeared from England's fields, parks and footpaths[70], which had the four of us cheering. Our walk took us to Fox Tor where we could see the Fox Tor Mires, the inspiration for the Grimpen Mire. I kept an ear out for bitterns. We were following *The Hound of the Baskervilles* Trail which led past Nun's Cross to the forlorn-looking farmhouse, as mapped out by the Dartmoor Tourist Board in an attractive booklet. We trailed a tricky path beside a leat[71], where Tony discovered magic mushrooms and gathered as many as he could see, presumably so that later he might ingest them, better to suffer through yet another dismal Liverpool FC Performance.

We saw the old abandoned tin mine where, I assume, a caretaker in disguise as a spectral hound is scaring away visitors, having unearthed a seam of gold that he has no rights to and would see him doing serious jail time if caught by the authorities. The needlessly convoluted scheme would have worked perfectly if not for the meddling investigations of Mystery Inc.

---

[70] We stopped feeding cooked bones to dogs, meaning dog poo isn't full of bone powder, which stays around for ages. Obviously, a Princetown dog owner didn't get the message, but hey, they're just following in the (gigantic) footprints of villainous Princetown pooch owners.
[71] An artificial watercourse dug into the ground; there are many on Dartmoor, feeding into the tin mines.

The map in the booklet could do with some refining in regards of clarity of the route, for somewhere along the leat, as we looked out for (but failed to identify) a small prehistoric burial site, my wife and Chris discovered they had conflicting ideas of which track we should be following. Somehow, we found ourselves off course. Around us, the moor in the hazy autumn sunlight felt to me to be pushing us away as if we were intruding on mystical land that was not meant to be trespassed by devilishly handsome writers and their misfit companions. The wind picked up and the temperature dropped. I shuddered, glad that I had packed a rain cape to protect me from the bitter wind.

We found a clear path and followed it until we drew level with South Hessary Tor. Some wild sound rang out across the moor, something alive but inhuman. I felt the hairs on the back of my neck stand on end, and my heart skip a beat. Could it be the Hound, baying on the tor? No. It was only Tony, who was singing to himself as he skipped on ahead; he was using his data allowance to check on the footie and apparently Liverpool FC had just scored a very unlikely goal. We trudged on along the winding Royal Tor Lane, aware that every step was taking us out of the wilderness and back to civilization – or, as Chris calls it, the pub.

We made it back to Princetown unscathed (though there was a dicey moment with some very big and very skittish cows crossing the road, herded by a young farmer on an off-road buggy), donned protective masks and piled thankfully into the spacious Plume of Feathers Inn. We found a table near a roaring fire and a perfectly acceptable menu.

I looked out of the window which had a view of the carpark and, beyond it, the path that led to the *Hound of the Baskervilles Trail*. I thought I saw a man looking back at me. A tall, thin man in a cape and deerstalker hat. I turned to my wife to tell her, but when we looked out of the window he was gone. Then Tony burped very loudly and the moment was gone forever, like a forgotten dream. Amazingly, Liverpool won the match.

PROG DOG

The Hound of the Baskervilles (Prog Rock concept album by Clive Nolan and Oliver Wakeman, 2002)

The Hound of the Baskervilles (Prog Rock concept album by Looking-Glass Lantern, 2014)

Believe it or not, there is not one, but two prog rock concept album versions of HOUN! Clearly something about this particular novel appeals to prog rock fans like no other; while there are other 19th Century books that have inspired a noodlesome prog epic (*Dracula, Frankenstein, The War of the Worlds*, etc), you'll search in vain for prog rock concept albums based on 20th Century blockbusters like *Fifty Shades of Gray* or *Clifford the Big Red Dog - Colouring Book.*

It will come as a surprise to absolutely no one that, being a bookish, white, introverted Cis middle-aged bloke, I am into prog rock. Since it's undoubtedly the least sexy or cool genre of music, it is therefore a perfect fit for me, the least sexy and cool man in my neighbourhood. You can't boogie on down to *The Dark Side of the Moon*, and no babies were conceived by couples "getting jiggy with it" during Marillion's *Script for a Jester's Tear.*

Jeff Wayne's Musical Version of H G Wells' The War of the Worlds (to give it its full, unwieldy title) is in fact one of my favourite albums. I was around twelve years old and my friend Paul Symmons played it to me after he purloined it from his dad's record collection. It's stayed with me ever since. Indeed, I play the whole thing every year on the Twelfth of August (the date given in book and album when came the first missiles that were to bring so much calamity to Earth)[72]. The narrator's wife, in Jeff Wayne's version, is named Carrie, and frustratingly, she doesn't get to utter even a single word: she is swept up in events and taken away from the narrator. *The War of the Worlds* would definitely fail the Bechdel Test[73]. I often wonder about Carrie. How old was she? What did she do? What would she have had to say about the Martian invasion of Earth? I remembered her when, in 2010 I came to write *The Misadventures of Sherlock Holmes: The Stalking Death* (a five-episode silly epic involving Irish terrorists, Annie Oakley, killer scorpions, and trifles). I thought it might be amusing to have her once more swept up in events and taken away from her husband. She survived the Martians. But would she survive Sherlock Holmes?

Of the two HOUN concept albums, I prefer the version by Looking-Glass Lantern which, according to the description on their website, "fuses 'classic' progressive rock with the atmosphere of Victorian England". It's a charming sound and I enjoyed walking around the house during lockdown, attending to chores with headphones on, listening to the album and occasionally singing along to bits like: "He was running so that he burst his heeeaaarrrt, oh-oh, his heeaaart!" and "Don't go alone! Take my friend! He'll see you through!" My wife is used to hearing me tunelessly belt out prog rock lyrics (especially if I've had a few beers), so from her perspective, it was pretty much business as normal in Lockdown Chez Stadon.

The other prog rock album version of HOUN is an altogether less

---

[72] Being a bit of a geek, there are a few 'fannish' things I do each and every year: I watch *Groundhog Day* (1993) every Groundhog Day, I watch *Groundhog Day* (1993) every Groundhog Day (see what I did there?), I play the Marillion song *Easter* on Easter Sunday, I watch *The Wicker Man* (1973) on May Day, I watch John Carpenter's *Halloween* (1978) every Halloween, I read or watch *V for Vendetta* (2005) every Bonfire Night, and I watch *On Her Majesty's Secret Service* (1969) every Christmas.

[73] I became familiar with the Bechdel Test – a useful indicator of bellwether a work is treating female characters with any respect or attention – when I was producer of *The Sitcom Trials*, a competition to find new sitcoms.

enjoyable affair, despite it being graced by an excellent narration by the wonderful Robert Powell (an actor who had played Holmes on stage in two different productions – including a musical! – and on radio). Without trying to be unkind, this prog version is dreadful, a real struggle to get through. I know you shouldn't judge a book by its cover, but even the album cover is awful, featuring a painting of Baskerville Hall surrounded by bats, stone dragons, and what appears to be an anorexic greyhound wearing a diamond studded collar. The lyrics to this album are sometimes hard to make out as they're sung by someone who sounds like a mumbling Meatloaf. Astonishingly, no one has updated Lyricfinder.org, but occasionally I'll make out certain phrases like: "Death by the Hound that was sent out from Hell!" and "Why do I feel so weak? How can I find my feet?", and break out into giggles.

One of the key criticisms of prog rock – especially from proponents of the perfect three-minute pop song – is that it just goes on and on and on. And on. There's a famous story of Rick Wakeman – grumpy keyboardist from uber-proggers Yes (and father of Oliver Wakeman, who is one of the key creatives of this dreary HOUN concept album) whose frustration and boredom with his bandmates playing on and on and on while he waited for his cues culminated in him eating a curry on stage during a show in Manchester. With this in mind, I decided to write the lyrics to a three-minute pop song that succinctly and movingly captures the spirit of HOUN. I've sent it to Beyonce's management.

When a bloody big dog

Bounds out of the fog

On the Moor, eh.

And a Canadian boos

"By thunder, my shoes

Are on the Moor, eh?"

Sir Henry, hurry!

The Hound scents your curry!

It's way oversalted

And evil's exalted

You shoulda had Chicken Tika

Like they have in Costa Rica

Though I'm unsure that's what they'll feed ya

So I'd better check Wikipedia

And no, I was wrong, they have altogether different dishes there, sorry.

Stick a dance beat underneath, sample bits from the Rathbone film and call it *Baskerville Beat Comin' At Ya* – it's got hit single written all over it.

SHHHHHHHHH!

I miss going to libraries. I miss going anywhere – in lockdown, a trip to take out the recycling is a calendar event, while going to the park is like jetting off to Bermuda: you pack for it, get your shots (or at least you use hand sanitiser and wear a mask), get neighbours to look out for your house while you're out, and leave a note on the door for Amazon couriers arriving with yet more versions of HOUN.

But I especially miss going to libraries, or even to a café, to sit, read, and be amongst people quietly going about their day. I desperately want to read a chapter of HOUN in Bristol's awesome Central Library, housed in a beautiful old stone building right next to cloisters and Bristol Cathedral (where they once filmed scenes from the 1978 psychological thriller *The Medusa Touch*, starring Richard Burton's intense, alcoholic, staring eyes).

I love libraries. I spent a great deal of my teenage years in them; my elder brothers were tearaways, and my home life wasn't especially harmonious, so I took sanctuary amongst books. There was a library just up the road from the family home, another library near Jeremy's home, one on the main shopping high street, another opposite a cheap flea pit that used to show movies on Mondays for only £1. And, of course, there was the school library and the great Central Library.

These libraries became like points on a compass marking places of sanctuary. My friend Paul and I knew which ones had all the best books, and though we could each borrow up to seven books at one time, we never seemed to have enough. All the libraries stacked various Sherlock Holmes books and I sometimes indulge my nostalgia by Googling the cover art for old editions of *The Adventures of Sherlock Holmes*, or *His Last Bow* (which seemed to be the two most popular titles with Bristol's libraries). Seeing those familiar dust jackets instantly takes me back to when I was fourteen, on a school night, sat at a desk in the library, absorbed in the world of Sherlock Holmes. For even though I had the book at home in my bedroom, I still felt the need to sit in a library and read it. And it wasn't just Sherlock Holmes books. I would read just about everything and anything – particularly if it had vampires, robots or spies in it. Sadly, there isn't a Sherlock Holmes story featuring vampires, robots and spies, so I may have to put writing such a story on my ever-growing 'To Do' list.

I was always late returning books. I don't know why – the loan period was three weeks, which is ample time to read them. I'm always organized and on time in every other area of my life. Late books incur fees and sometimes these fees would add up to so much money that I, perpetually penniless, could not afford to pay them[74]. This would pray heavily on my mind as I lay in bed at night, unable to sleep. I would feel awful about the situation and try to think of quick money-making schemes I could put into operation to raise the library fees.

One time I felt so desperate that I planned to break into the library, return the books and retrieve my library card, and break out again. That way, they would have their books, my record would be clean, and everybody would be happy. I even thought about starting a piggy bank so that, over time, I could collect enough money to pay the late fees which I would somehow anonymously donate to the library. I had no idea how to break into a public building without setting off alarms, so I mused on the problem for a few days and came up with a revised version.

My new plan was to hide in the library at 7:30pm closing time and exit the library when it opened at 9am the next morning. Overnight, I would complete my mission, then spend the remainder of the time reading as many books as took my fancy. I was thirteen. Of course, I never went through with it (and have still never broken into a public building, or indeed, any building, on a book-related mission), but I still remember the thrill of planning it and the name I came up with: Operation Moriarty. I was clearly a criminal mastermind.

---

[74] Pocket money would inevitably be spent on *Doctor Who Monthly, House of Hammer Magazine*, and Sea Monkeys. Remember them? What was that all about?

CHAPTER NINE

Puppy Love

December 2020

STAPLETON QU'EST-CE QUE C'EST

D R WATSON FINDS HIMSELF with much to report to Holmes in Chapter Nine of HOUN.

First, there's the burgeoning romance 'twix Sir Henry and Beryl Stapleton which has the besotted baronet sneaking out at every opportunity to be with the Costa Rican beauty who reciprocates the attraction. One night Watson spies Stapleton spying on Henry and Beryl. I've no doubt Barrymore was spying on Watson spying on Stapleton spying on Henry and Beryl, and Mrs Barrymore was spying on Barrymore spying on Watson spying on Stapleton spying on Beryl and the Baronet. Stapleton can't control his temper and Watson sees him incandescent with rage, shouting at Sir Henry and Beryl, dragging his sister away from the Canadian lothario. The next morning, Stapleton visits Sir Henry and is all sweetness and light, grovelingly apologetic for his outburst, begging forgiveness. Just about everything Stapleton says and does gives off massive danger signals – the man is so obviously a psychopath that had he been played on stage by Ted Bundy, you'd think him overacting.

Sir Arthur introduced Stapleton by having him enter the novel holding a butterfly net, but I think he should have been waving several red flags. Anyway, Stapleton says that he reacted so badly because he doesn't want to lose his sister and asks Henry to stop making eyes at her for three months. After that, he can go to town. Inexplicably, Henry doesn't find this unreasonable. I mean, what?! Why three months? That's a very specific number. How did Stapleton arrive at it? Had he made some calculation that would give him enough time to bump off Sir Henry? Why did Henry agree to it? It remains a mystery.

Watson indulges in more spying as he follows Barrymore creeping about the Hall at night, to stand by a window with a candle, obviously signalling to someone on the moor. It is Mrs Barrymore who confesses the truth – Selden, the Notting Hill Murderer, is her brother, and the Barrymores have been providing the escapee with food and warm clothing. And that's fair enough, the man was going to need both, but I think it's a little mean of the Barrymores to stop there. Why not provide Selden with some entertainment by making a candlelit puppet show to jolly away his long cold lonely nights on the moor? If it were one of my brothers out there (and I wouldn't ever reject the possibility that one day it might well be), I'd certainly be throwing in some shadow puppetry with the grub and the clobber.

WHAT HAPPENED ON DARTMOOR # 5: SIGNAL TO NOISE

I had come to Dartmoor with a list of things I wanted to do, beyond tracing Watson's footsteps and exploring the beauty of the moor. The list included:

1. Watch a film version of *The Hound of the Baskervilles*
2. Play a recording of the Hound baying on the moor
3. Buy a new copy of HOUN; read a few chapters on the moor itself
4. Mimic Barrymore signalling to Selden on the moor

I achieved number one on the first night – I had a Galaxy tablet onto which I had downloaded my copy of the Rathbone/Bruce film. My wife fell asleep to it, but I was thrilled to be watching this wonderful movie, snuggled up warm in bed, in our hut on the moor. I can't tell you how happy that made me. I had also downloaded a sound effect of a hound baying to my phone, and I played it at full volume as I stood outdoors by the firepit with my wife and our friends. I don't think anybody heard it, sadly, so next time I'm there I'm going to come with a PA System.

The Selden-signalling scheme provided some problems. First, I couldn't send a signal from within the hut because a) the hut was only one floor and had no view of the moor, and b) had no windows. This also meant, of course, that I couldn't receive a visual signal from the moor. My idea of the hut standing in for Baskerville Hall was completely scuppered.

The logical thing, I reasoned, was to send a signal outside on the moor to someone further away. I conscripted Chris to help me in this plan because he is as mad as I am. I had come equipped with a pack of 100 Wilko's unscented tea lights ("Light up your room!" declares the packaging, "Burn time 3.5hrs!") and a box of extra-long matches. Unfortunately, as Chris discovered, trudging off into the distance, the tea lights give barely any flame (certainly not enough for me to see half a mile away back at the hut) and the wind extinguished them so often that we burned through an entire box of matches. Arse!

Chris and I sat at the table by the pit, considering our options. We had phones equipped with torches, but they were on alarmingly low battery power, and I wanted them charged up because I get anxious when I see phones with battery levels below 20%. It's just another one of my hang-ups, I guess. I mean, I know some people lead exciting lives and like to live on the edge, but letting your battery drop below 20% is just asking for trouble. Be sensible, people, and keep your phones charged at all times! At any rate, rejecting tea lights and phone torches meant that one avenue had been closed off, and as visual signals were completely ruled out, we needed to seriously think again.

"Owl sounds. How about owl sounds?" asked Chris after a gulp of gin and tonic.

"What about owl sounds?"

"We could make owl sounds. Like in films like *Where Eagles Dare* (1968)[75] when commando forces need to signal each other."

"Can you make owl sounds?"

"No. Can you?"

"No. I can do a chimpanzee!"

"Great," said Chris. "Why don't you walk half a mile onto the moor and make chimpanzee sounds, and I'll try to decode the message you're sending."

"I don't know how to send a message in the language of chimpanzees, though," I confessed. "I only know how to make random chimpanzee noises."

"Why don't you play a musical instrument?" suggested Tony as he joined us at the table with a steaming hot plate of vegetarian pasta he'd just cooked.

"Good idea," I said, hungrily eyeing his plate of food. "Did you bring any musical instruments?"

"No of course not," said Tony through mouthfuls of penne. "Why would I bring a musical instrument to Dartmoor?"

I wanted to throttle him and then eat all his pasta, but I was being polite and keeping it together.

---

[75] It's just occurred to me to wonder why the commandos in *Where Eagles Dare* don't make eagle sounds, rather than owl sounds, just to keep things tidy. Otherwise, why not call it *Where Owls Dare*?

"Hang on a minute, wait there," said Chris, hurrying to his car. He returned a few minutes later with a shoe box. It was filled with brightly coloured plastic objects.

"What," I asked Chris, "am I looking at?"

"Kazoos," said Chris. "That's 100 kazoos. I forgot I had them in the car."

"Why do you have 100 kazoos in a shoe box in your car?"

"Because I ordered them for a gig on Lundy Island[76]. The idea was to hand them out to the audience so they could join in with the band[77]. Trouble is, I ordered 50 when I was drunk, but they didn't turn up in time for the gig, by which point I'd ordered another 50."

I nodded. I had no idea what madness he was babbling on about, but that was par for the course with Chris (and/or Tony). The main thing was to determine if they might be used to send a signal on the moor, as the Notting Hill Murderer had done. I picked up a bright green kazoo and blew into it.

"It sounds like a duck having a stroke," said Tony, mopping up the remainder of his tomato sauce with a wedge of bread.

"It'll have to do." I trudged into the pitch-black wilderness. When I had reached a suitable distance, I played a tune on the kazoo. It was a tune everybody knew, so my companions should have had no difficulty at all in identifying it. It wasn't Selden with a candle signalling to Baskerville Hall, but it was the best I was going to get.

"Well?" I said, on my return.

"No idea," said Chris.

---

[76] A small rocky island off the north coast of Devon, dotted with hotels and holiday houses.
[77] Chris has been in dozens of bands over the years, and I've followed his career with amusement.

141

"It sounded like Kermit the Frog having sex," piped in my wife who had joined us at the table and who I couldn't help but notice also had a plate of pasta.

I sighed. They hadn't identified *How Much is That Doggie in the Window*. I tried again, with Elvis's *Hound Dog*, and a third time with Led Zeppelin's *Black Dog*, with no success. My companions took pity on me and helped me out by taking turns to trudge out onto the moor and play a kazoo.

Eventually, after much frustration and failure, a tune was correctly identified. I was the musician and *Bad Moon Rising* by Credence Clearwater Revival was the tune. Hooray! I had signalled on the moor! Another life goal achieved. Unhappily, by the time I had accomplished my task all the pasta was gone so I had to make do with bread and cheese which later gave me nightmares about a *Muppet Show* version of HOUN – Kermit the Frog as Sherlock Holmes, Fozzie Bear as Dr Watson, The Great Gonzo as Stapleton, etc - where the Hound eats all the muppets on Lundy Island.

FULL STEAM AHEAD

For my birthday, I am gifted *The Hound of the Baskervilles* PC game. After my son sarcastically sets it up on my laptop and explains what Steam is and how to use it (it's some kind of games platform, apparently), I set to work playing it.

It's not what I expected, to be honest. Granted, my limited experience in playing computer games extended to a couple of Lara Croft games on the Playstation and some James Bond games on the PS2, and my favourite bits were when I could hide up somewhere high and take-out bad guys with a crossbow or sniper rifle.

I had kinda hoped that this game would have me playing as Dr Watson on the roof of Baskerville Hall, surveying the moor with a high-powered laser-sighted rifle, picking out Selden and taking him down with a head shot. Instead, this is one of those 'go-into-a-room-to-find-an-object-to-gain-entrance-to-another-room-where-you'll-need-to-solve-a-puzzle-to-be-rewarded-with-an-object' type johnnies. Only with time travel, werewolves, and magic powers. I'm not enjoying the gameplay much 'cause I'm impatient and rubbish at puzzles and I'd rather be scanning the fog-drenched moor with a surface-to-air missile launcher. But I'll persevere. Or I'll give up. One of the two.

DOG-UMENTARY EVIDENCE

Castle Secrets & Legends / Season 1 Episode 3 / *The Hound of the Baskervilles* (TV documentary, 2014)

Nightmare: Birth of Horror / Series 1 Episode 4 / *The Hound of the Baskervilles* (TV documentary, 1996)

On the Scent of the Baskerville Hound (TV documentary, 1989)

Great Books - The Hound of the Baskervilles (TV documentary, 2002)

Dartmoor, Devil Dogs and Conan Doyle (TV documentary, 2001)

Periodically, I've been watching HOUN documentaries, so I'm lumping them all together here in one big meaty HOUN documentary broth, with lumps of facts and floaty morsels of opinion stirred in. There is another documentary – *Great Books: The Hound of the Baskervilles* (2002) that would nicely help flavour this broth (to torture this metaphor), but I couldn't track down a copy, so I have no idea what it tastes like.

I started with the rather overwrought *Castle Secrets & Legends – The Hound of the Baskervilles*, from 2014, because it was the first to be pulled from the Deerstalker of Doom. A camera lingers lovingly over the flint stonework and crenelations of a beautiful three-story Tudor Gothic manor house as Voice Over Guy growls that, "This sprawling estate is home to a chilling tale of murder, revenge, and literary genius." Voice

Over Guy probably does this sort of thing all the time, wherever he is.

Buying cat litter for the kitten: 'This innocent bag of litter will soon be violated by all manner of horror by a creature that can't control itself."

Seducing someone who's caught his eye: "This innocent and unsuspecting beauty does not know the power they have over the hearts of men."

Anyway, here in this very short documentary Voice Over Guy is describing Cromer Hall, a major inspiration on Arthur Conan Doyle who first heard stories of spectral black dogs (or Black Shucks, as they're known) when he stayed there with his friend Fletcher Robinson in 1901. Doyle's description of Baskerville Hall certainly matches that of Cromer Hall, as Matthew Sweet points out in the documentary. Sweet is a journalist, author and Cultural Historian who I have a lot of time for, not least because I've actually met him at a wonderful free outdoor screening of *Flash Gordon* (1980), introduced by journalist Samira Ahmed and director Mike Hodges, at Bristol's M-Shed on the Harbourside. I'm not too keen on *Flash Gordon*, but my wife loves the film, and we both got agreeably sloshed in the summer night, and a great time was had by all.

I've never been to Cromer Hall[78], but it's on my list of places to visit. In fact, that part of England - Suffolk and Norfolk - seems really appealing to me as it's where the great M.R. James set many of his ghost stories (including two of his most famous - *Oh Whistle and I'll come to You, My Lad,* and *A Warning to the Curious*). I'd love to stay in a spooky B&B in Aldeburgh (which M.R. James took as inspiration for Seaburgh) and write a ghost story, before travelling north to Cromer to wander the grounds of the real Baskerville Hall.

---

[78] Indeed I've never been to Cromer, and only know of it from a deadpan remark made by *Dr Who*'s Brigadier Lethbridge-Stewart when his Top Secret military base has been transported to an anti-matter universe – an idea the Brig dismisses as nonsense, as he's pretty sure the view outside the window is of Cromer.

"If ever there really was a model for Baskerville Hall," says the brilliant Professor Christopher Frayling, striding towards a house that looks exactly like Baskerville Hall, "this was it: Lew Trenchard Manor House, the remote Dartmoor home of the Reverend Sabine Baring Gould." I confess that at these words a shudder passed through me. So it's *not* the one in Cromer, then? Oh. Okay. And Mr Trenchard was the name of Head of French at the secondary school I went to, so now I'm wondering if his first name was Lew. Regardless, Lew Trenchard Manor House is Baskerville Hall, according to Christopher Frayling, and I friggin' love him and his superb documentaries, so that's good enough for me.

Nightmare - Birth of Horror: The Hound of the Baskervilles is an all-round superb documentary, quite possibly the best made about Sherlock Holmes. The other three in the series – *Frankenstein, Dr Jekyll and Mr Hyde,* and *Dracula* – are equally as good. I remember being engrossed by them on their first BBC broadcast, back in the dying days of the millennium, and they've only improved with age. Professor Frayling looks like my wife's dad (who looks like a cross between Lech Wałęsa and Super Mario, meaning that Professor Christopher Frayling resembles a fusion of my father-in-law, Lech Wałęsa and Super Mario), which makes him all the more loveable to me. Frayling globetrots from the Reichenbach Falls to Cromer (where he plays golf), to the Welsh border, and finally to Dartmoor where he breaks into the tomb of a vampire guarded by a devil dog[79], explores the Great Grimpen Mire and the old tin

---

[79] This is at Cabell Mausoleum, in the graveyard of Holy Trinity Church, Buckfastleigh. Richard Cabell, who is entombed here, is almost certainly the inspiration for Sir Hugo Baskerville, the wicked squire killed by a huge dog. Professor Frayling explains that so wicked was 'Dirty Dick' Cabell (he sold his soul to the Devil, and then murdered his wife, Elizabeth, and was then savaged to death by her loyal hound) that nobody took any chances when they buried him, and so a metal spike was hammered through his heart, just in case he was a vampire and had designs on rising from his grave to drink the blood of virgins. As you do. A ghostly pack of fire-breathing black hunting dogs bounded out of the moor to surround the tomb, baying through the night. And of course, the ghost of the murderous Squire Cabell leads a pack of ghost dogs to hunt

mines, finds Baskerville Hall, and seems to be living the life I would love to have.

Inevitably things take a darker turn as Professor Frayling concludes his documentary series on the Fields of Flanders. Walking through fields of the dead, the Professor laments how the coming East Wind would bring so much real horror to the world. The candle-lit monsters from the great Gothic fantasies of English Literature, he says, would retreat in shame and dismay.

Posh-speaking elderly Sherlock Holmes Society members genially contradict each other as to which Devonshire pile is the true Baskerville Hall in *On The Scent of the Hound of the Baskervilles*. Clearly they haven't consulted Sir Christopher Frayling who is right about everything. Also popping up in this documentary is the remarkable Jean Conan Doyle, Sir Arthur's daughter, who is a joy to listen to.

Air Commandant Dame Lena Annette Jean Conan Doyle, Lady Bromet, DBE, AE, ADC (to give Jean her full title and alphabet of awards) was seventy-seven when she appeared in this documentary, and she looked in better shape than me, sitting here munching on Mary Berry's fork biscuits, typing this. And come to think of it, there's more than a touch of Mary Berry about Jean Conan Doyle, so it wouldn't surprise me at all if she baked better fork biscuits than I do.

Another participant in the documentary is a dog handler named Ruth Murray who speaks eloquently and persuasively of how the legend of the Hound might have its foundation in hunting dogs baying all around the tors and hills, and police dogs hunting and killing escaped criminals from Princetown. Just as Ruth paused dramatically, there came inevitably a dog barking in the night – I assume the mystery pooch from next door – that froze my blood and made the hairs of the back of my neck stand

---

across the moor, on the anniversary of his death, 5th July, 1677. This is exactly what I want for my death, entombment, and spectral afterlife.

on end. You've got to give it to spectral hounds – they have excellent timing.

More Sherlockians prowl Dartmoor looking for Baskerville Hall in *West Country Tales: Dartmoor, Devil Dogs and Conan Doyle*, which was made in 2001 – a century after the publication of HOUN. I can't remember what I was doing in 2001 (aside from that tragic day in September when I went to the pub with friends to sit in shock), though I'm sure I would have marked the centenary of HOUN by reading the book. I'm certain I did the same, four years earlier, for the hundredth anniversary of Bram Stoker's *Dracula*.

For these aimable Sherlockians, though, 2001 was the opportunity to dress up as Victorians and take a steam train to Buckfastleigh, tracing the journey made by Dr Watson, Sir Henry and Dr Mortimer. I felt a pang of envy, watching these fans immerse themselves in such a delightful pastime. They come in all sizes from around the world, these members of the Hounds of Dartmoor Sherlock Holmes Society, and they seem to have enormous fun. It struck me that I might join a Sherlock Holmes fan club society thing. Yes, that sounded appealing – to be in a fraternity that obsessed about the things I obsess about, and to occasionally undertake steam train journeys dressed as Sherlock Holmes! That's so me! The only society thing I've ever been a member of is the Dennis the Menace[80] and Gnasher[81] Fan Club when I was ten. You got two badges (the Gnasher one had googly eyes) and a membership card, and I think that was it. I wonder if the fan club is still running? I wonder if I could join two clubs – a Sherlockian one and the Dennis the Menace and Gnasher fan club?

---

[80] The 'star' character from anarchic UK kids comic *The Beano* (my good friend, the artist Kev F Sutherland, worked on *The Beano*, amongst many other publications) not to be confused with the US character of the same name.

[81] Dennis's irritable and very bitey dog, who looks exactly like Dennis. The breed is unknown.

The Dennis the Menace Fan Club is no more. Damn. According to a BBC News report (it made the BBC news!), "The Dennis the Menace club started in 1976. It cost only 75p to join and membership peaked at 1.25 million members. It ran for 22 years." Ah well.

A quick Google search, however, gave me much better news about The Sherlock Holmes Society of London (there doesn't appear to be a Sherlock Holmes Society of Bristol), which advertises itself as "a literary and social Society for study of the life and works of Sherlock Holmes and Doctor Watson." I presume this means that the Society plays what is known as 'the game' – an exercise which takes Conan Doyle out of the equation and treats every word written by Dr Watson as gospel; the 'game', as my understanding has it, is to find inventive ways to reconcile all the sloppy errors in the stories that contradict other stories (Sir Arthur was notoriously lackadaisical in his approach to continuity). *Dr Who* fans do this kind of thing all the time (except for the bits of stories they don't like, confusingly), and I do it with everything my wife says. So, I'm all for it, especially because it's completely barmy.

I created an account, after proving I'm not a robot (and having had a window pop up to inform me that I have 32 compromised passwords), and clicked on the button beneath a photograph of a shifty-looking Douglas Wilmer as Sherlock Holmes. Having closed yet another pop-up window that notified me that this time I have 46 compromised passwords (What is going on here? Has the Sherlock Holmes Society of London been compromised by Russian bots?), I paid the £23 annual membership fee and, finally, went to bed happy, cuddling up with my wife and the cats – or at least hoping to cuddle my wife and cats, but they cuddled each other and hogged all the duvet, leaving me shivering and alone. And then I realised that, when setting up an account with the SHSL, I'd typed in the wrong postcode. Oops! I'm always typing in the wrong postcode, which is mildly ironic because once I was briefly a postman.

Happily, a very nice person from the SHSL assured me that they will send my membership goodies to the correct address, though obviously I can't be sure if this was yet another ruse by Russian bots. I'm aware that I might be becoming paranoid, but only because a mysterious dog is haunting my dreams and Russian Intelligence Agencies have hacked my Iceland Groceries Delivery Account.

ZOINKS!

The New Scooby and Scrappy-Doo Show / Season 1 Episode 3 / *The Hound of the Scoobyvilles* (TV kids cartoon pastiche, 1983)

If you could rely on anything in this mixed-up, crazy world, it would surely be that the team behind Scooby-Doo would get round to *The Hound of the Baskervilles*. Is there a more famous dog than the Hound? No. But I'd bet all my cats that Scooby (and Snoopy) would be in everybody's Top Ten Famous Fictional Dogs (and probably in the Top 3), along with Lassie, Gromit, Digby the Biggest Dog in the World, K-9 from *Dr Who*, and Clifford the Big Red Dog. A meeting of the two dogs, then, seems inevitable, and perfectly fitting. If any dog was going to be a match for the Hound it would be Scooby-Doo.

And I loved Scooby-Doo as a kid. The theme tune! The animation! Velma, being sexy in a way my pubescent brain couldn't quite understand! The Scooby Snacks, the disused mines or abandoned old houses 'haunted' by obviously villainous caretakers in hugely elaborate costumes to scare away people who might discover the true wealth hidden there, or something! The "I would have gotten away with it if it wasn't for you meddling kids!" dodgy confession that any half-decent defence council would laugh out of court! *Scooby-Doo, Where are You!*[82] was a classic.

---

[82] Yeah, that exclamation mark really should be a question mark. But it was the 60s, man! They didn't follow our square rules, man, you dig?

The New Scooby and Scrappy-Doo Show, however, is awful. For one thing, it's got Scrappy-Doo in it. I can safely say, without fear of exaggeration, that Scrappy-Doo is the single worst idea in the history of the creative arts. Every single second he's on screen, I want to gouge my eyes out with a red-hot poker (as in the famous BBC Sound Effect), rip my ears off with my teeth, somehow, and scrub the wretched, hateful memory of him from my brain with industrial strength detergent and absolutely massive amounts of psychotropic drugs. And there isn't a single reader of this book[83] who doesn't feel the same way. For another thing, Scrappy-Doo seems to have been put in place as a replacement for the lovely Velma and the blonde dude who I can never remember[84], meaning that the Mystery Inc. team consists of Shaggy, Scooby, Daphne and Scrappy, a 50/50 human/anthropomorphic dog split that throws the show disconcertingly off balance. I mean, why Daphne and not Velma? What happened to the missing team members? Had they left in protest at having to work with Scrappy-Doo? It's all too much of a mystery for me.

In *The Hound of the Scoobyvilles*, Scooby gets framed for being the Hound that is menacing sheep on the estate of Barkerville Hall (why not name the episode *The Hound of the Barkervilles*? Madness!). Obviously, it's the caretaker, Bentley, who, dressed as a kind of werewolf, is using the legend of the Curse of the Barkervilles for nefarious purposes. It's *always* the caretaker. In fact, I wouldn't be at all surprised if the Caretakers Guild took the animation studio to court over their continual, unwarranted, and unfair defamation of cartoon caretakers. I reckon such a case has got more of a chance of standing up in a court of law than any of the flimsy cases brought in by Scoob and the gang.

Anyway, the episode has all the requisite "Zoinks!" and "Like run, Scoob!", as well as Shaggy thinking he's talking to Scooby but, zounds!

---

[83] "Stop the sentence here for accuracy," quips my wife.
[84] Fred, apparently. I still don't think I know him. He's an enigma to me. Also, there exists online a resource called Scoobypedia, which goes into forensic detail on all things Scooby. I'm delighted by this.

He's actually talking to the Hound of the Barkervilles. It's dull and uninspired and annoying, and at only eleven minutes, it outstayed its welcome. I paid £1.89 on Amazon Prime to watch it and was so annoyed by Scrappy-Doo that I didn't watch the second episode it comes packaged with (*The Dinosaur Deception*, which sounds rather cool), meaning I effectively threw away 90p, the price of a Greggs medium-sized sausage roll[85] (at the time of writing). Zoinks!

THE SILENCE OF THE HOUNDS

Alwin Neuss as Sherlock Holmes in *Der Hund von Baskerville* (Silent film serial, 1914-1920)

Note: Throughout the book, I tend to employ the English titles for foreign language films, but I'm making an exception for the German and Bengali films, for arbitrary reasons that you'll just have to accept 'cause it's my book and I make the rules.

As a kid growing up in the 70s and 80s, it wasn't unusual for me to be found watching silent films as part of my TV diet, for BBC2 would often screen short slapstick films by Laurel and Hardy, Charlie Chaplin, Buster Keaton, Harold Lloyd and the like; indeed, BBC2 would run entire seasons of silent comedies, scheduled for after school. I always enjoyed watching these shorts, delighting at the actors' physical comedy skills and the ingenuity of their escapades.

Every now and then, BBC2 would screen classic silent feature films, and naturally the horror films interested me most – the likes of *Nosferatu* or *The Cabinet of Dr Caligari* or *The Phantom of the Opera*, and these movies felt to me to be strange and unnerving in a way that talkies weren't. They seemed to come from a place and time that was alien to the modern world as I experienced it – the monsters just looked and

---

[85] I had been ~~commanded~~ persuaded to cancel the order for the expensive DVD boxed set from the Ukraine, as mentioned in Chapter One.

moved in ways that felt inhuman. And the human characters, with their pale faces and black ringed eyes, looked almost as strange. Reading the intertitles only added to the weirdness of the experience. And yet for all their strangeness, Silents became as familiar to me as things like cartoons, or cop dramas, or the News.

Silents were all part of the TV mix. I would happily watch Harold Lloyd, then a Tom and Jerry cartoon, then World Championship Snooker (Snooker seemed to be never off the telly), then a silly game show like *Blankety Blank*, then an adult drama like *Tales of the Unexpected* (which my mum loved), then a Saturday Night movie like *Bullet* (my dad's pick). It was quite the mix.

When I became a dad, however, the television landscape had changed so drastically that despite the millions of channels available, no mainstream broadcaster scheduled silent films; my kids never got to see Chaplin or Keaton when they were growing up, and though the digital age has quite wonderfully made so much material available to be watched at any time, I know from conversations I've had with my kids and with friends that they would never decide to watch a silent film. I can understand why, but I can't help but feel a tiny bit disappointed, like an old and grumpy English teacher who feels a little bit dead inside every time he comes across a misplaced apostrophe in the signage of a shop owned by a favourite former pupil. I was, I confess, very much looking forward to reacquainting myself with silent films as part of this HOUN binge, as I, too, had fallen into bad viewing habits, having eschewed great works of cinema in favour of the mindless comfort of whole seasons of needlessly confrontational talent competition shows like *Project Runway* or *Ink Master: Grudge Match – Cleen vs. Christian*.

This German film is a quite remarkable thing. It was such a hit that it spawned a series of further instalments (or 'reels') in the Stapleton/Baskerville/Sherlock Holmes saga, released over a six-year period (and which recasts Holmes for the final two chapters). On its own, it stands as a milestone: the first film adaptation of HOUN. And what a good one it is, too! Completely nuts, but in a most appealing and engaging way. I watched with either a grin or a baffled expression and was so entertained and perplexed that I immediately watched it again, just so I could be baffled all over again.

Apparently, the script was adapted from a stage play of HOUN which relocated the action away from Dartmoor and into the Scottish Highlands, and adds a dash of Edgar Allen Poe into the mix for good measure, but what it really feels like to me is an episode of *Columbo*. Because just as in the 'Just one more thing...' US classic crime drama, *Der Hund von Baskerville* spends the entirety of its first third following the villain – in this case, Stapleton – as he goes about his villainous business, before introducing the detective who takes him down. And Stapleton is quite something – with his enormous sideburns, long cadaverous face and mad staring eyes, actor Friedrich Kühne resembles the monsters from German Expressionist Horror and he embraces the role of dastardly villain with such tenacity and aplomb that this is the only version of HOUN where I found myself rooting for Stapleton to win.

There's a wonderful sequence where Stapleton reveals his villainous plan by writing it all down in a diary, then going outside to pull up a square hatch, hidden in the grass, that opens a secret underground hideout where he's keeping the Hound – a very friendly looking white Great Dane with black spots that's more Disney dalmatian than a hound of hell.

This Stapleton is also a bit of a pyromaniac, as he's addicted to blowing things up. Delightfully, he prevents a letter penned by Sir Henry Baskerville from reaching Sherlock Holmes, the former hoping to engage the services of the latter, by the simple and ingenious method of blowing up the pillar box it had been placed in. But best of all, Stapleton then disguises himself and pretends to be Sherlock Holmes so that he might freely 'investigate' the case!

I was laughing into my Heinz beef and tomato cupasoup when the real Sherlock Holmes (Alwin Neuss, who had played the part before in *The Stolen Million Bond,* a Danish silent film from 1911[86]) reads in a newspaper report that Sherlock Holmes is apparently investigating the case of the Hound of the Baskervilles... This prompts him to head for Baskerville Castle where, for perplexing reasons, Holmes disguises himself as Stapleton! There's a marvelous sequence soon after where, as Sir Henry holds a swanky soirée, Stapleton climbs the outside wall of Baskerville Castle to gain entry unseen to an upstairs room where he plants a bomb in a chandelier, only for Holmes, having witnessed Stapleton leaping down from a balcony, nonchalantly deduces there's a bomb, informs Sir Henry that in twenty seconds the Castle will blow up, asks for a light of his cigarette, and, on not receiving one (Sir Henry naturally being too terrified), promptly pulls a revolver from his pocket and shoots the fuse of the bomb, which drops to the floor, still lit, disarming the explosive and providing a light for his cigarette! Bravo! A strikingly photographed earlier scene shows Stapleton, in silhouette, ordering the Hound to attack Sir Henry Baskerville. This film is Stapleton's show, and I'm all for it.

Dr Watson is briefly in this film[87]. There is a bizarre sequence of Holmes in Baker Street, sending an electronic message to Watson, who appears to be living in the flat beneath Holmes's apartment (221a Baker

---

[86] Alwin Neuss appeared in a couple of other Danish silent Sherlock Holmes films, though not as Holmes; it's possible, though unconfirmed, that he made a few appearances as Dr Watson. If so, that puts him in a small category of actors who have played both Holmes *and* Watson – Jeremy Brett being the most striking example, having played Watson to (of all people) Charlton Heston's Holmes in an LA stage production of *The Crucifer of Blood,* based on *The Sign of the Four.*

[87] This film has only recently been made publicly available, after being lost for nearly a century. It was a bit of mystery to compilers of reference books as to if Dr Watson was actually in this film, with many books opting quite understandably to omit him from the list of characters. My own paltry research efforts have failed to identify the name of the actor who plays this most bizarre Watson. Perhaps it's a German relative of Michael Evis?

Street?). The message – "KOMME ZU MIR WATSON" - is displayed on a screen made up of yellow dots. This version of Dr Watson is a bald old man with a weird beard, looking vaguely Amish, like Michael Eavis, dairy farmer co-founder of the Glastonbury Music Festival. Watson then gets into a weird elevator device and heads up to see Sherlock Holmes. The sequence has an air of surreality about it, as if this is *The Hound of the Baskervilles* directed by David Lynch in his *Eraserhead* phase – only in German and with no sound.

CHAPTER TEN

Give a Dog a Bone

December 2020

SNOOZETIME

Deadtime Stories / Episode 5 / *The Beast of Baskerville* (US Kids TV drama, 2013)

I ALWAYS GET A LITTLE bit excited when the Deerstalker of Doom presents me with a short kids TV programme because I can watch it in half an hour as I peel potatoes or fold laundry or – as is becoming increasingly more likely – search Amazon for Sherlock Holmes thermal-lined socks, slippers or Inverness Capes. I've never owned an Inverness Cape, and it's about time I did, especially in this weather, where my weather app's continual update that it "feels like -4°" is the depressing new reality of life in freezing lockdown. An Inverness Cape would certainly jolly things up and give me a whole new look.

Anyway, the point is that quick and easy kids TV stuff demands very little of me, allowing me to multi-task. Reader, I fell asleep watching *Deadtime Stories*. Three times! I put the show on the TV and soon found myself snoozing on the sofa, with a cat on my lap and a colander of half-peeled Maris Pipers, jolting awake when the wood in the fire makes a loud crack. Then I'd set to peeling the startled cat claw-by-bloody-claw from my head. Then peeling the remaining spuds. And after a fourth attempt, I finally finished this and have absolutely nothing to say about it because it has nothing to do with *The Hound of the Baskervilles.*

I mean, it's fine. The kid actors are okay, the script is okay, there are gags, the thing has charm. The 'telling kids a spooky and funny story in a tent at night by torchlight' set up is really rather excellent. I used to tell my kids spooky and scary stories. My daughter particularly loved 'the spooky', as she would term all things Halloweeny. Though, after failing with some Sherlock Holmes short stories, as I mentioned earlier, I never told my young ones the story of HOUN, which I now regret. If my wife and I are to be blessed with grandchildren, I'm counting down the days till they're old enough to be told the tale. Four years old, do you think? Five? I wonder if there's a preschool picture book edition in the same manner of *The Very Hungry Caterpillar.*

Once upon a time, there lived a grumpy man who had a grumpy dog. They lived together on the moor and the grumpy man kept the grumpy dog a secret.

"Why do you hide me away?" asked the grumpy dog. "It makes me grumpy when you hide me away."

"Because I want to use you to murder my way into inheriting the Baskerville fortune, title and estate," said the grumpy man. "Now be quiet and cover yourself in phosphorus to make yourself look like a spectral demon from ancient legends as I gaslight my wife into believing it's in her best interests to pretend to be my sister so that she might sexually entice Sir Henry Baskerville."

LIVING MEMORY

Reading HOUN in the run up to Christmas makes me feel cosy and happy and safe – as if I'm a child again. I've always loved Christmas, especially the exciting and magical build up to the day itself. Even though this particular festive season is the most stressful and extraordinary of my lifetime (or perhaps because of it), I find myself associating *The Hound of the Baskervilles* with innocent, happy times, as if opening the pages of the book is like stepping into a Christmassy Victorian wonderland of howling ghost dogs and men having panic attacks as they run for their lives. It's weird. Surely such things should be having the *opposite* effect on me? Perhaps, this Christmas, I've discovered that HOUN is actually my safe space, and that the Hound itself is my comfort animal?

In contrast to my cosy state, Chapter Ten finds Dr Watson in a low mood. It's mid-October and continually pissing down with rain. He's got nothing to do other than to write letters to Holmes or entries in his diary, and he's having no truck with ghost dogs:

"If I have one quality upon earth," writes our no-nonsense doctor, "it is common sense, and nothing will persuade me to believe in such a thing." And quite right, too.

One of my favourite things about Conan Doyle is that, though he himself was a firm believer in all manner of supernatural manifestations, he instilled in his most famous creations an arch rationalism which made Holmes and Watson the perfect debunkers of supposed unnatural events.

Watson also reveals himself to be concerned for the nation's finances, as he readily agrees to keep schtum about Selden and the Barrymores as long as the convict gets the hell out of England on a ship to South America, thus saving the British tax payer from having to pay for Selden's capture/incarceration, etc. In return for his silence, Watson is given new info from Barrymore: on the night of Sir Charles's death, he received a letter from a woman who signed herself LL, requesting Sir Charles meet her at the gate at the far end of the Yew Alley at midnight. How does Barrymore know this? He saw the remains of the letter in the fireplace, but it disintegrated when he tried to fish it out. What a memory Barrymore possesses! Sir Charles died on the 14th of May[88]. Mid-October,

---

[88] Though it might be May 4th – there's a discrepancy in the text. ACD was notoriously sloppy at this sort of thing, for which I can only admire him.

Barrymore can recall word-for-word lines from a letter he only glanced at the morning after the death of his master. Elsewhere in *Hounded!* I discuss fourteen-year-old Cartwright's sensational memory tricks; here, we have fully grown adult Barrymore demonstrating similar miracles of memory.

Was *everyone* in the nineteenth century blessed with such amazing powers of recollection? Have we twenty-first century people devolved intellectually? Why can I never remember my wife's birthday or the prolonged pain I am made to suffer in consequence? How can I forget that which is important, yet find myself without difficulty able to accurately quote whole chunks of *Monty Python and the Holy Grail*? Ni!

LOST DOG

By far the most upsetting part of HOUN Chapter Ten – and the most upsetting bit of the novel for me – is Dr Mortimer's missing spaniel. We'd been introduced to this loveable pooch way back in Chapter One, and Watson had spent an entire train journey fussing over the dog. I'd grown to love the animal as much as I love my cats. I am as invested in Dr M's doggie as I am any other character in this book. It is heart-breaking to discover, then, that the scampy spaniel is nowhere to be found, and Watson gloomily predicts the poor mutt has perished in the Grimpen Mire. Don't do it to me, Sir Arthur! I can't bear the idea of animals being hurt (aside from Scrappy-Doo, of course: *that* little runt can get stuffed), and though I've read this book many times and I know by heart the spaniel's unhappy fate, a part of me wishes that this time – *this time* – the dog will survive.

I wonder if my neighbour's phantom dog is a spaniel. Perhaps the ghost of Dr Mortimer's spaniel. Am I being haunted by a fictitious ghost dog that isn't even the most famous fictitious ghost dog in the book it originates from? Am I so unworthy that I'm being haunted by a second-rate fictional ghost dog?

O'TOOLE IF YOU THINK IT'S OVER

Peter O'Toole as (the voice of) Sherlock Holmes in *Sherlock Holmes and the Baskerville Curse* (1983)

I was looking forward to this, but it turned out to be another disappointment. The animation is as basic as it comes. The character design couldn't be blander – though I quite like the obese Dr Watson, and a villainous Stapleton who looks more like the long-lost brother of The Hooded Claw from *The Perils of Penelope Pitstop* than the long-presumed dead sibling of Sir Charles Baskerville. He also sounds like smarmy brainbox computer Orac from *Blake's 7*.

The Baskerville Curse is clearly a cheap production without any inspiration or creativity, made worse by a clearly bored-to-death vocal performance by Peter O' Toole, an actor who was born to play Sherlock Holmes[89]. This is the second in a series of animated Holmes novels by this team, after *A Study in Scarlet*, so I'm tempted to give the next two a listen just to hear how increasingly bored O'Toole sounds. What a shame our only screen document of O'Toole as Sherlock Holmes is this bland cartoon version. Ah well.

As always with animation, the backgrounds are great, so there's that. I always wanted to paint backgrounds for animated movies and cartoons, and loved seeing background art collected in books – I remember being particularly awestruck by the backgrounds for *The Jungle Book* (1967) and *Akira* (1988). When I was a kid, I used to be gifted colouring books for Christmas, and I always enjoyed working on the ones with detailed backgrounds, like jungles or Dickensian street scenes.

---

[89] Peter O'Toole did get to play Holmes (and other detectives) on stage, and he was nearly cast as Holmes by Billy Wilder for *The Private Life of Sherlock Holmes* (1970), and by Bob Clark for *Murder by Decree* (1979).

And I would enjoy drawing my own backgrounds: usually very weird rocky landscapes inspired by Chuck Jones *Road Runner* cartoons. In fact, there are some backgrounds in *Sherlock Holmes and the Baskerville Curse* that make the moor look like Death Valley; surprisingly, it works. There's also a really good sepia-tinted flashback sequence to Sir Hugo that succeeds artistically, in stark contrast to the rest of the film.

I was amused by the ruthlessness of the adaptor, who gets this story rattling along as fast as he can, like he's a coked-up city executive from the 80s demanding his staff to hustle, hustle, hustle 'cause time is money, baby. There's a brilliant sequence with Watson and Henry arriving at Baskerville Hall, Watson asking Barrymore to please take the suitcases inside because he, Watson, wants to stretch his legs after the train journey from London. Immediately as he explores the moor, the super-rotund doctor bumps into Stapleton, who couldn't be more obviously villainous if he were twirling his evil moustache whilst gloating melodramatically over a damsel in distress tied to a railway line as a steam train speeds towards her. I half expected him to turn round and reveal a sign pinned to his back saying PROUD TO REPRESENT VILLIANY! Watson then meets Beryl, then hears the Hound of the Baskervilles, then meets Frankland and then Laura Lyons, and then returns to Baskerville Hall where Barrymore is waiting with the suitcases. Every major character is introduced in under five minutes. I felt like applauding. But I didn't, I suffered through the rest of this poor adaptation and wondered if there are Sherlock Holmes colouring books[90].

Imagine, though, a really brilliant animated movie version of HOUN! Something as good as *The Jungle Book*, something that would delight viewers of all ages, smash the box office, and win a shedload of Oscars. Imagine *The Hound of the Baskervilles* done by Bristol's Aardman

---

[90] There *is* a Sherlock Holmes colouring book, but disappointingly for me it's for the Cumberbatch *Sherlock* rather than the Sidney Paget illustrations or the backgrounds in *Sherlock Holmes and the Baskerville Curse.*

Animation. In 1983, when this dismal film was released, Aardman were just getting started and would soon be making ground-breaking pop videos for Peter Gabriel and Nina Simone as they worked on their first Wallace and Gromit short. And I was there, with my friend Paul, who was gifted in modelmaking. In fact, Paul got an apprenticeship with a model-making SFX team who worked closely with Aardman, and one day when he was having a toilet break, he bumped into none other than George Harrison in the gents – George being there to have a full body cast made for his nostalgic *When We Was Fab* hit single. Paul and I were given a tour of Aardman by co-founder Dave Sproxton, and we watched in awe as a second's footage of the first Wallace and Gromit movie was filmed by future Oscar-winner Nick Park.

A Wallace and Gromit *Hound of the Baskervilles...* Gosh, how much I would give to see this! Cracking case, Sherlock!

Pet(aluma) Sounds

In the build up to Christmas I find myself yearning to be back in *any* year other than the one we are all suffering through. Get me out of here!

As we decorate the Christmas tree and give stern warnings to the cats to leave it the hell alone this year or there'll be no treats over the festive season, I realise that it's been three years that The Petaluma Radio Players staged, live performances of my silly radio plays to packed audiences at Hotel Petaluma over three nights and one afternoon. How extraordinarily happy I was, on the debut night, listening to the simulcast live broadcast on California radio at 4am in the morning (there's an eight-hour time difference between the UK and Pacific Standard Time).

As the performers took their bows to an appreciative audience five-thousand two-hundred and sixty miles away, I took my bows to two of my cats, but they were asleep and had no idea what I was doing up at such a godforsaken hour. I did wonder how on earth the production had staged my silly playlet of HOUN, with a seriously irked Watson re-writing events so that a cowardly Holmes flees in terror at the sight of the Hound, leaving Watson alone on the fog-drenched moor to heroically slay the mighty spectral beast... But perhaps these things are left to the imagination.

A few months earlier I'd never heard of Petaluma[91]. If someone had asked me if I knew what it was, I'd probably have guessed that it was a type of butter, or a moon buggy. That changed when I received an email out of the blue from **Ralph Scott** and **Kendra Murray**, introducing themselves as producers for the PRP, telling me they'd just recorded one of my *Misadventures of Sherlock Holmes* radio plays. I had no idea who they were or why they'd want to record my daft plays. In fact, I had told my wife that nobody on earth would ever want to record my nonsensical Sherlock Holmes radio plays, and it was ridiculous to offer the collected volume of scripts I'd just put together for sale. I'd only collected them into a book because I was cleaning my study of the mountains of piled documents and scripts I'd amassed; self-publishing a handy little book with all the MOSH scripts seemed like a lovely solution. I'd never dreamed that anyone would actually buy copies of the book (my wife had told me I'd literally nothing to lose by offering them for sale), yet alone perform and record them. And yet, they were indeed buying and recording them.

MOSH had begun ten years earlier on a whim. I was involved with a bunch of fun and talented Americans, spread across all States, who created amateur audio drama and comedy. I somehow lucked into casting retired Chicago theatre actor **Jeff Niles** as Sherlock Holmes and New York voice actor **Elie Hirschman** as Dr Watson. This pair was so good

---

[91] I've recently become a fan of the wonderful true crime/comedy podcast, *My Favorite Murder,* and was delighted to discover that co-host Karen Kilgariff comes from Petaluma. She mentions it often, with fondness, and I almost feel like I know the place now.

that they more than made up for the deficiencies in scripting.

The scripts afforded me an indulgence in exploring the detail of the Sherlock Holmes stories – Holmes's monographs were used as inspiration for a series of murders; the flat at 221a Baker Street is rented by a pair of con artists who pretend to be Holmes and Watson and fleece their potential clients; serial husband Watson accidentally gets married to Professor Moriarty. One meandering five-part epic folded in killer scorpions, a plot to assassinate Queen Victoria, a bomb in Big Ben, and Holmes's long forgotten girlfriend. Jeff Niles loved playing Holmes so much that he became the driving inspiration for doing more and more of them. Jeff took over producing duties, directed the actors, and even set up his own amateur audio group, which then branched out into dozens of other shows. The man was a dynamo, and such a wonderful person to know.

Jeff died in February, just before the pandemic hit the world. I still can't believe he's gone[92].

My memory returns to three years ago, to that Christmas run of shows in Petaluma, and how happy I was. I made a promise to myself to visit Petaluma one day soon – it looks to be a very pretty, welcoming city. I've always wanted to visit San Francisco, too (Petaluma is a little north of San Francisco), especially the Haight-Ashbury area, the Hippie mecca. And I had promised I'd one day take a trip to Illinois to see my good friend Jeff, but that will never happen now. I'm reminded that life is short and precious, and we must live it to the full right now, rather than tomorrow, because tomorrow is not guaranteed. In that spirit, I wolfed down several cream cakes just for the hell of it. It's Christmas!

After the Christmas stage shows, the PRP partnered with Downpour

---

[92] You can read the obituary I wrote for Jeff at
https://the4077th.blogspot.com/2020/02/jeff-niles-rip.html

to release a gorgeous box set of four MOSH stories[93]. At exactly the same time, I learned that another, *completely different* Californian theatre group were *also* staging several MOSH stories! This was The Baker Street Players, from Jackson CA, who were staging a week's run of *The Misadventure of the Impossible Magician* and *The Misadventure of the Disobliging Cadaver* at Baker Street West. Astonishing! What the hell was going on in California? (Christmas 2018 also saw *another* Californian staging of a MOSH play, this time by an amateur theatre group of senior citizens! And a theatre group in Ireland, at a newly opened drama school[94], also staged some MOSH plays in Christmas 2018.)

Clearly, I need to head to the west coast as soon as funds are available, and Covid-19 is under control. This will probably be a while. Sadly, the brilliant actor Paul Reffel, who played Watson in the Petaluma productions, opposite Iain Morris as Sherlock Holmes, also passed this year. The year 2020 is an absolute horrorshow.

For the Christmas Petaluma shows back in 2017, I found myself on a Skype call to a reporter for a Petaluma newspaper, being interviewed about the plays. I remember telling the reporter that news of the production was the best news from the US I'd heard in years, receiving a very pointed silence in return[95]. Why am I so rubbish at interviews? At any rate, I had thought that this stilted long-distance interview experience was peak MOSH madness, but I was wrong...

In the spring of 2018, Ralph and Kendra emailed me asking if I'd write them a special MOSH play to be performed on their wedding day

---

[93] Available as a download and CD at bargain prices! A must for every home! https://www.downpour.com/the-misadventures-of-sherlock-holmes-boxed-set
[94] Apparently, the patron of the school is none other than the amazing US actor Danny Glover, famous for the *Lethal Weapon* films (amongst many other celebrated performances).
[95] The full interview is online here: https://legacy.petaluma360.com/entertainment/7752213-180/stepping-out-holmes-for-the

in the early autumn. In fact, they wanted me to write a scene into the play where two characters get married and, when they performed the scene, Ralph and Kendra would step in for the actors and get married for real, right there and then! The audience wouldn't have any idea of what was about to happen, neither would the cast. And it was going to be staged in The Petaluma Historical Library and Museum, which was exhibiting the "I Do" collection - vintage wedding dresses from the Petaluma Museum's exquisite and extensive textile collection, including wedding gowns. And it was all to be broadcast live on Petaluma public radio! Completely bonkers, and delightfully romantic.

I said yes before I'd finished reading the email. I'm quite confident in saying that nobody in history has ever received a commission quite like it. I remember being completely thrilled (and charmed, and grateful!). The resulting play - *The Misadventure of the Beleaguered Bridegroom* (Kendra's suggested title) - folds in Professor Moriarty, *Twelfth Night*, a singalong in Covent Garden, a naked Dr Watson, a thinly-disguised Meghan Markle, a remarkable housemaid, Herr Fledermaus and his Amazing Performing Mice Squeaky Squeaky, and a fiancée for Dr Watson who, he comes to learn to his dismay, is strikingly like Sherlock Holmes. It is, I think, my favourite MOSH script. Here's a brief extract:

ELSIE THE MAID Telegram from Dr Mortimer at Baskerville Hall, sir.

WATSON Good heavens! Baskerville Hall! I always meant to go back there some day, see how Sir Henry is getting on now that the spectral Hound is slain and he is safe!

ELSIE THE MAID Message reads: "Mr Holmes, please come at once to Baskerville Hall. Sir Henry in grave danger!"

HOLMES Throw it on the fire, Elsie, I fear Dr Mortimer has been on the sherry again.

WATSON What?

HOLMES He periodically drinks himself insensible, Watson, and childishly thinks it would be an amusing wheeze to summon me on false pretences to the most desolate and remote mires of Dartmoor, foolishly wasting all my time and energies hunting down a fictitious spectral animal. Last month he got hammered on Chianti and telegrammed me that Sir Henry was being menaced by a giant ghostly squirrel.

ELSIE THE MAID (giggles) The Squirrel of the Baskervilles!

WATSON Oh. Shame. That sounded quite promising. Do they even have squirrels on Dartmoor?

HOLMES No.

A KICK IN THE GÜTTNER

Bruno Güttner as Sherlock Holmes in *Der Hund von Baskerville* (B&W film, 1937)

My next selection from the Deerstalker of Doom was the second German pick. I'm a big fan of German cinema (and indeed, Germany), so I was excited to see this. I poured myself a glass of pilsner lager and fired up YouTube.

Der Hund von Baskerville is the first talkie version of HOUN filmed in a foreign language. It's a small budget and rather eccentric film from a production company formed by a famous Czech actress and her filmmaker husband. Notoriously, a print of this film was found in Adolf Hitler's bunker after his death[96].

This is a bizarre film. The tone is all over the place, veering from slapstick to melodrama in the same scene. If I ever die in a bunker, you won't find a copy of this film amidst my belongings.

It starts very well, with a tremendous prologue framed as a fairy tale set in a wild Castle Baskerville in the mid-Seventeenth Century, but sadly this promising opening is then followed by at least twenty minutes of interminable scenes at twentieth century Castle Baskerville, featuring a Stapleton who is prone to misogynistic rants (he even shows a pistol to Sir Charles, and says it's the best way to get rid of a woman. Shudder!)[97].

Sherlock Holmes, when he eventually turns up, is played by Bruno Güttner, aged 30, about 6'1", lean, with a chiselled face, big beaky nose, and a highly dramatic widow's peak. In a black roll neck jumper, breeches and jodhpurs, he looks like a cool and saturnine beat poet who listens to obscure jazz when he's out horse riding. His voice is dubbed throughout by actor Siegfried Schürenberg, and to the best of my knowledge, no footage survives of Güttner speaking in his own voice – he appeared in two other films, both of which are lost to time. I like to imagine Güttner sounding like a German William Shatner; the director[98] having decided that a German William Shatner-sounding cool and saturnine beat poet, who listens to obscure jazz when he's out horse riding, was exactly what Sir Arthur Conan Doyle had in mind when he created

---

[96] The other film was *Der Mann, der Sherlock Holmes war (The Man Who Was Sherlock Holmes)*, a German comedy-mystery from 1937.
[97] Stapleton is played by Erich Ponto, but really he should have been played once more by the remarkable Fritz Rasp (Stapleton in the vastly superior '29 German version).
[98] Kael Lamac (oftentimes credited as Carl Lamac), who made dozens of films, among them the excellent *Honeymoon* (1936).

Sherlock Holmes. Take *that*, Sidney Paget!

The geography in this film is mind bending. Charing Cross seems to be only two miles from 'Castle' Baskerville, which is on a moor in London. Are there any moors in London? There's Moorgate, of course, and Moorfields (next to Moorgate), an area of marshy fields that could well substitute for the great Grimpen Mire, I suppose.

I like to imagine Bruno returning to Baker Street, cool and stylish, after a night in an underground jazz club. I picture Bruno's Holmes facing off against Professor Moriarty at the Reichenbach Falls. The Professor is incandescent with malevolent rage, but Bruno's Holmes is chillaxed, cool, maybe smoking funny jazz cigarettes, telling his arch nemesis to mellow out and not stress about anything, man. And of course I imagine that Bruno Holmes is overdubbed with the voice of William Shatner, perhaps from his spaced-out recording artist phase when he put down on tape a bizarre spoken-word version of *Lucy in the Sky With Diamonds*. Wouldn't that be worth seeing?

CHAPTER ELEVEN

Bad Woof

December 2020

LL COOL J

HOUN CHAPTER ELEVEN sees the return of Sherlock Holmes, who gets to speak one line at the end of the chapter. The great detective has been missing from his most famous and celebrated case for seventy pages of my Oxford University Press Edition! We last caught glimpse of him looking moody at Paddington Station, way back at the start of Chapter Six, but at long last he's back – even if it's only to say nineteen words of snark to Watson.

The bulk of the chapter, though, deals with Watson's prickly interrogation of LL – Laura Lyons, a typist in Coombe Tracey. She is the elderly local crank Frankland's estranged daughter. Frankland enjoys suing people and spying on the moor through his telescope. He's Doyle's third red herring character in this plot (after Barrymore and Selden) and the most amusing; he's such a larger-than-life creation that he feels Dickensian. But back to Watson and Laura who, if HOUN was a trashy reality TV show[99], would bring all the drama. I'm here for it.

---

[99] *The Real Housewives of Dartmoor*, perhaps, starring feisty Costa Rican Beauty Queen Beryl 'the Peril' Stapleton, weepy housekeeper and secret sister to escaped

Watson begins his verbal tussle with LL by describing her beauty. Of course he does, because he's Dr Watson, and we wouldn't expect anything less from him. "Her eyes and hair were of the same rich hazel colour, and her cheeks, though considerably freckled, were flushed with the exquisite bloom of the brunette, the dainty pink which lurks at the heart of the sulphur rose," rhapsodizes our narrator before souring the picture by adding that "there was something subtly wrong with the face, some coarseness of expression, some hardness, perhaps, of eye, some looseness of lip which marred its perfect beauty." Well, yeah, Watson – you've just accurately described the face of a woman who's royally pissed off with you.

How bad does this 'long and inconclusive' interview get? Well, Watson has only asked a single question before he notes the "angry gleam in her hazel eyes." Then Laura "flushes with anger", then goes so pale that Watson describes "a deathly face before me". Then Laura nearly faints and very soon after she's sobbing her eyes out. Good job, Watson! I think the good doctor ought to be sent on a training course where he might learn strategies and techniques to manage difficult behaviour and producing positive outcomes, not least so that he might never have to come away from an interview feeling "baffled and disheartened" (I wonder if the UK journalist and broadcaster Jeremy Paxman was influenced by this scene and used it to underpin his notoriously fiery interview technique?[100]).

At any rate, Watson does learn one crucial piece of information – Laura has been given help not just from the late Sir Charles, but also from Jack Stapleton. Armed with this knowledge, Watson goes hunting for the

madman Eliza 'Incisor' Barrymore, and the alliteratively named, abandoned-by-all-the-scoundrel-men-in-her-life secretary, Laura 'Lucky' Lyons.

[100] The most famous example of 'Paxo''s abrasive interviewing style was his dogged questioning of the then Home Secretary Michael 'Something of the Night' Howard, on an edition of BBC2's *Newsnight* in May, 1997. Dragging Howard through hot coals over a scandal involving prisons Paxo asked Howard the question, "Did you threaten to overrule him (the Head of Prisons)?" fourteen times in a row... *And still didn't receive a straight answer.*

Man on the Tor and finds himself reunited with Sherlock Holmes as the narrative heads into the final act...

THE BEST BRAIN IN NEW YORK CITY

Hounded, episode 16 of Season 4 of the US television drama *Elementary,* starring Jonny Lee Miller.

Another cold December day, another pick from the Deerstalker of Doom, another scramble to find a copy of the Hound I've picked from my disorganised DVD collection. I really ought to alphabetize them. And put them on shelves instead of in teetering piles mixed with books. And dust them and clean them of cat hairs. The cats enjoy climbing all over my book/DVD towers and I enjoy throwing balled up pieces of notepaper at them to see if I can train them to bat them away with their paws. But these cats are too lazy, too stubborn to be trained.

My pick for today is *Hounded.* Yay, it's the title of this book! It's also the title of an episode of *Elementary,* the hit US TV drama. I wonder why the producers had decided on 'Elementary' for the name of their Sherlock Holmes show. It's not a terribly exciting or interesting thing to call a hit television drama featuring all manner of gruesome deaths. I mean, yeah, it was almost certainly picked as a title because it's the most famous word associated with Sherlock Holmes, but there are other words with just as strong an association with the detective that would make for a far more exciting and interesting title for the show: Singular! Deerstalker! Trifles!

Elementary was a television series that, like BBC's *Sherlock,* brought Holmes and Watson into the present day. In fact, *Sherlock* co-creator Steven Moffat was very annoyed at *Elementary,* speaking out against its conception as being obviously lifted from his *Sherlock,* and you really can't blame him. But *Elementary* is its own thing - a much more humble, less showy crime show with long seasons of (approx.) 22 episodes across seven series. *Elementary* is really about addiction and how to overcome it - it's a character study of Holmes and how Watson and others help him stay sober. This is a Holmes who attends sobriety meetings.

I enjoy occasionally dipping into the series to rewatch certain episodes. Because I like it so much, I sometimes find myself binge watching until the early hours, when the hungry cats wake me up by poking me in the eye or jumping up and down on my man parts, presumably in revenge for being the targets of my paper missiles.

Jonny Lee Miller[101]is a very good-looking man with a huge adoring fanbase, but he often pulls a 'mugging' face that makes him look, to my eyes, uncannily like Beaker from *The Muppet Show*. I'd never tell him this to his face, should I be lucky enough to one day meet him, because he is by all accounts a nice man. And he could kick my teeth in without breaking a sweat. It is noticeable how, in contrast to BBC's *Sherlock*, where every effort is spent to make Benedict Cumberbatch sexy, Jonny Lee Miller is made to look unsexy and nerd-like (at least until he takes his shirt off), despite this Holmes being very sexually active.

This Holmes is a fascinating character. A recovering heroin addict who has relocated to New York City, he is a quirky, odd neurotic Englishman abroad. A very physical person (he regularly practices several martial arts), with a very closed-down, buttoned-up demeanour (he dresses like a stereotypical autistic 'idiot savant' - see Adrian Monk for a comparison), poor social skills and low emotional intelligence, he has a fascination with crime and a genius intellect. Jonny Lee Miller, perhaps the most athletic actor to ever play the part, might also be the smartest: he has an IQ of 124, and is a member of snobby brainy club Mensa (who couldn't even be bothered to reply to my email about how I'm so clever I decoded the hidden meaning in *I'm Too Sexy* by Right Said Fred, which

---

[101] I was pleased to learn that Jonny Lee Miller is the grandson of Bernard Lee, the first 'M' from the James Bond films.

I would be glad to share with them if they made me a member[102]).

Holmes is a consulting detective for the NYPD, working closely with Captain Gregson and Lieutenant Bell, assisted by his friend and 'sober companion' Dr Joan Watson. An expert linguist, escapologist, and cryptologist, with a photographic memory, and a brilliant understanding of forensics, and other subjects too numerous to list, this is a formidable version of Sherlock Holmes. In *Hounded*, Holmes is hired by Henry Baskerville to investigate the suspicious death of his brother, Charles Baskerville, whilst in a more character-based subplot typical of US television drama, Holmes also offers his help to a friend and colleague who is suffering from PTSD. This softer, open and empathetic side of Holmes is the result of many years' worth of character growth; by *Hounded*, Holmes is much more agreeable and sociable than he is in the first season.

Miller is excellent in the part - he has a superb voice, perfect for rattling off the rat-a-tat deductions, and a huge range, investing Sherlock Holmes with all manner of emotional responses; the *Elementary* Holmes is a compelling and fascinating character, and by far my favourite 21st Century version. Across seven seasons and 154 episodes, Jonny Lee Miller is the actor who has played Sherlock Holmes the most times to date. It's difficult to think of anyone who could do it any better.

Lucy Liu bears not the slightest bit of resemblance to Doyle's Dr John Watson because she is one of the most beautiful women in the world - in very much the way that Dr John Watson isn't. Native New Yorker, Ms Joan Watson is initially hired by Holmes's wealthy father to be Sherlock's live-in 'sober companion' - an expert in drug addiction who provides one-on-one assistance to newly recovering individuals.

---

[102] I've forgotten what it was now. Something about shirts. But there's definitely a coded message in the lyrics, and I urge all readers of this book to look for themselves, and if any of you solve the puzzle, please contact me, and I'll try again with the Mensa thing.

By *Hounded*, three seasons later, Watson is Holmes's partner as consulting detective, having nurtured Watson's inherent talents. The relationship is reciprocal because, as Holmes comes to acknowledge, Watson brings out the best in him - she teaches him the value of boundaries, personal space, privacy, empathy, and politeness; in effect, humanizing him and helping him through some very tough times. Holmes values Watson very dearly, considering her to be his best friend. She, in turn, is fascinated and beguiled by Holmes, and drawn completely into the world of criminal investigations, so much so that when Holmes leaves NYC for an extended period, Watson continues to consult for the NYPD and expands into taking on private clients.

A stylish dresser, the 5'3" Asian-American Ms Watson makes a striking contrast next to the tall, scruffy English Sherlock Holmes. It is to the credit of the considerable charm and talents of Liu that it is she who quietly dominates many of the scenes they share together. She portrays Watson as every bit as fascinating and complex as Holmes. This is a Holmes/Watson team of friends and equals who want to help people.

The most fun part of *Hounded* presents us with three ingenious versions of the deadly pooch. Cornwell, a glowing green chimera (a large bull mastiff cross bred with jellyfish DNA to give it bioluminescence) and an Enhanced Canine Asset, a 'War Dog' made to spec for the US military, which is stronger and faster than any other canine, and can be trained to kill on command - are revealed to be red herrings.

The *real* killer hound is Gus 5, a top-secret robot created to be used as a kind of superdog 'pack mule' for the US military. This thing is a hybrid robot made up of components from Devonshire Robotics and other inventions patented by the Baskervilles, equipped with seek-and-destroy programming which locks onto Henry. Its eventual downfall - trapped by Holmes in an empty swimming pool, looking forlorn and abandoned - is rather sad.

A middling episode from a terrific series, *Hounded* is not the very best of *Elementary*, nor the very worst. This is a series that's pretty solid across seven seasons, throwing up ingenious and decidedly odd cases that delightfully warp the police procedural format into something really quirky and compelling. This episode is only really a let down because it's the one about the most famous Sherlock Holmes book and the writing team don't really do anything particularly special with it, other than with the dog itself. The best bits are, as always, those scenes with Holmes and Watson - the pairing of Miller and Liu is one of the best Holmes/Watson partnerships across all media. They are superb actors and, together, they have an undeniable chemistry that makes them a pleasure to watch.

AW, SHUCKS!

Much has been written about the various legends of spectral dogs that inspired ACD to put pen to paper, resurrect his most famous creation, and have him chase down the Hound of the Baskervilles. Doyle had employed a whole menagerie of fearsome creatures in his works (both *The Speckled Band* and *The Brazilian Cat,* for instance, have villains using lethal creatures in complicated murder plots, and *The King of the Foxes*[108] and *The Green Flag* also centre around killer critters), so tales of hell hounds bounding out of the fog to terrorize generations of the same family was always going to set Arthur's big heart racing, his writing hand twitching. One of the likely inspirations for the Hound is Black Shuck, an East Anglian ghostly black dog which is said to roam the coastline and countryside of East Anglia, one of many ghostly black dogs recorded in

---

[108] *The King of the Foxes* is an excellent short story, published in *Windsor Magazine* in 1898, about a young alcoholic hunter who has been warned by his doctor that withdrawal from booze might result in him seeing phantoms; the hunter goes on a fox hunt and chases down a phantom fox which is revealed to be a great wolf: "At the same instant, a creature the size of a donkey jumped on to its feet, a huge grey head, with monstrous glistening fangs and tapering fox jaws, shot out from among the branches, and the hound was thrown several feet into the air, and fell howling among the cover. Then there was a clashing snap, like a rat-trap closing, and the howls sharpened into a scream and then were still."

folklore across the British Isles.

Another likely source for Arthur, once he had resolved to use Dartmoor as his setting, is the story of Squire Richard Cabell and the ghostly pack of hounds that haunt his tomb. Writers take ideas from anywhere and everywhere, and there's no doubt that a detective novel about a bloody big ghost dog killing generations of the same cursed family who live in the middle of a remote and forbidding wilderness (with a maximum-security prison nearby, for added thrills) is an absolute winner.

And since I would love to write a best-selling novel, earn a fortune and become an acclaimed, desired man of wealth and wisdom, I was thrilled to come across inspiration from, of all places, Instagram. You see, I follow an account called *weirdbristol*, which delivers to my feed all manner of information about unusual bits of my home city. On Halloween 2020, *weirdbristol* posted this:

A road in the village of Hallen, just north of Bristol, is said to be haunted by an enormous phantom dog with glowing red eyes. Known as a barghest, shuck or grim, in 1908 and 2004 witnesses claimed to see the dog morph into a donkey and walk on its hind legs before vanishing[104].

Well now, like Sir Arthur with the Black Shuck, that got my cold heart racing and my idle hand twitching. I knew I had to visit Hallen to get a sniff of the place and to hopefully see the ghost dog. I did a lazy bit of research as a cat climbed on my shoulders and went to sleep (why oh why do they do that?), and found a slightly more detailed report on the glorious website ParanormalDatabase.com, under the section Black Shucks, Hellhounds, and Other Black Dog Reports.

According to this new information, the exact location of the 'Morphing Shuck', as they've classified the thing, is a dead-end lane in Hallen, next to the M49 bridge. After wondering if a 'Morphing Shuck'

---

[104] There is a slew of amusing comments under the post, my favourite being by 'benostromo' who writes: "Great shrooms in Hallen"

had anything to do with Tony Hart[105], I looked up the location on Google Maps. Sherlock Holmes sent out to Stamfords (map specialists) in Charing Cross for a 'very large' Ordnance map of Dartmoor[106], but I've got a Google Maps app on my phone, installed by my sarcastic IT expert son, which means I can zoom right into the dead-end lane next to the M49 bridge and switch to street view. Alas, the Google Map car hadn't captured a Morphing Shuck when it drove through Hallen. I wonder if any paranormal activity has been caught by Google photographers when they mapped the Earth[107]?

Hallen is a two-hour thirty-minute walk from my home. I'm avoiding public transport, and all unnecessary journeys, following strict lockdown rules. I am permitted an hour's outdoor exercise a day, so clearly a five hour walk to and from Hallen is out of the question, particularly as I'd need at least an hour when I got there to munch on a salmon sandwich and examine the ground for footprints of a gigantic hound, meaning I'd be spending a minimum of *six* hours outdoors, during a pandemic. Clearly not going to happen.

That evening I sighed through dinner, dejectedly picking at my tagliatelle.

"What's up?" asked my wife.

"I can't go to Hallen," I whined.

"Where?"

"Hallen. By the Severn Bridge and Avonmouth, that whole industrial area. And I really only want to see a dead-end lane next to the

---

[105] Beloved kids' TV presenter and artist who was bothered by animated plasticine.
[106] Leslie Klinger goes into exhaustive detail on this in the annotated edition, quoting numerous sources who try to pin down the exact map Holmes was using. I adore this kind of thing!
[107] Do a search for 'Pigeon People of Japan' if you want to be unnerved by something captured by Google Maps. *shudders*

M49 bridge."

"Why do you want to go there?"

"It's for The Hound of the—"

"Yeah, of course it is."

"I'll have to wait till the end of lockdown."

"Paris. Barbados. Bermuda."

"What?"

"They're the places people are looking forward to going when lockdown is over. Nice places. Warm and happy. *You* want to go to look at a motorway bridge."

I couldn't explain it to my wife. I could barely explain it to myself. All I knew was that I wanted to write a best-selling novel and earn a fortune and become an acclaimed and desired man of wealth and wisdom, like ACD, and that I had to go to a bridge near a motorway to start my journey. That night, I dreamed I was there, in the dead-end lane, under the bridge. But the Shuck wasn't there. Instead, my cats were stood in a row, on their hind legs, beckoning me to approach. As I drew near it became clear that they wanted my salmon sandwich and that I wasn't going to be able to fend them off. I had a panic attack and I fell to the ground, clutching my heart, my face contorted and my body twisted, like Sir Charles Baskerville when he came face-to-face with the Hound. The cats ate my sandwich and ran away, leaving me for dead.

A DROOP OF THE GOOD STUFF

Droopy, Master Detective / Season 1 /Episode 6C / *Sherlock Droopy Gets Hounded* (Kids cartoon, 1993)

Seven minutes of brightly coloured, fast moving, laugh out loud mayhem, this is so good I watched it twice. The art is great, the gags are terrific, and the villain – McWolf – hilariously quick-change impersonates around a dozen characters in Baskerville Hall, folding a dash of Red Riding Hood and the Big Bad Wolf into the zany mix.

Droopy is yet *another* anthropomorphic funny animal on the scent of the horrible Hound. It strikes me that the lugubrious pooch (and his son, Dripple, who is basically a mini-Droopy) ought to team up with Scooby-Doo and Garfield and Chip n' Dale and Wishbone to form a sort of misfit super-posse, wisecracking their cowardly ways across lightning-lashed grotesquely misshapen moorland. I'd watch that. As long as Scrappy-Doo isn't in it, obviously. You could swap him out for Tom and Jerry, and add Bugs Bunny and Daffy Duck to the team. Hmmm...

From: @VinceStadon

To: @disneyplus

Hi there. I appreciate you're busy but could you please produce ASAP a cartoon based on The Hound of the Baskervilles, featuring Scooby-Doo, Wishbone, Droopy, Chip n' Dale, Tom & Jerry, Daffy Duck and Bugs Bunny as a misfit super-posse hunting the Hound?

Many thanks, Vince.

CHAPTER TWELVE

Sleep With a Dog, You Wake Up With Fleas

January 2021

THE BLOODY BIG BAT OF THE BASKERVILLES

LOCKDOWN OVER NEW YEARS was not a pleasant experience for anyone (and I'm so aware of how lucky I am compared to others), particularly since I had a panic attack and spent most of the holiday curled up in bed, reading HOUN - one final going away present from the year that hated humanity. Thanks, 2020!

I did manage to step outside at midnight on December 31ˢᵗ to see the fireworks and greet the new year. As my wife and I were stood at the gate, waving to our neighbours, a bloody big bat flew overhead. It was quite the biggest bat I've ever seen in the wild in the UK; the extraordinary sight took my breath away. Had I imagined it?

"Did you see *that?*" cried my neighbour excitedly. He'd seen it too!

"Yeah, wow, that was huge!" I replied.

"*Did you see that?*" repeated my neighbour with incredulity.

"Did *you* see that?" I replied. The "did you see that?!" thing was catching. But so was the excitement. It was a bloody big bat! At the stroke of midnight as the new year dawned!

We continued our "did you see that?!" exchange for a few more minutes. It was a batty bonding experience. Then my wife and I returned indoors, and I went to bed with a book as she stayed up, watching 80s and 90s pop videos on YouTube. She had the volume on the television too high and, from my bed, propped up reading about German Expressionist cinema, I could hear Kate Bush singing *Hounds of Love*, and my wife singing tunelessly along:

Help me, someone!

Help me, please!

HAT SONG

A cold January morning finds me sketching a bloody big dog on a bloody big sheet of cardboard, for reasons that I shall detail later in this chapter. Everybody is stuck indoors, aside from essential workers who are beyond amazing. The dawn of a new year feels not celebratory, but cautious; the world is on pause, I think, until the spring. And spring is a distant dream.

I drop two sweeteners in my decaff tea and head for my desk where the Deerstalker of Doom awaits. I've taken to singing a little song to it as I dip a trembling hand into its murky depths. I've borrowed the tune from *Goldfinger* by Shirley Bassey. My song goes:

Deer-stalker!

It's the hat, the hat that contains the Hounds!

And cost twelve pounds!

I briefly consider filming and uploading what is called, I'm told, a TikTok video of me singing to my Deerstalker of Doom, but the look of horror on my son's face as I tell him this convinces me that it would be unwise. I don't think TikTok is meant for fifty-one-year-old white men with a *Hound of the Baskervilles* obsession, and I think it prudent to wait until the launch of a social media platform that entirely fits my niche demographic.

The DoD is two-thirds empty now, by my rough guestimate. Most of the Hounds have run howling across the moor; only a few remain kennelled. What will be the next pick?

THE HOUND OF THE BENGALI-VILLES

Jighansa, starring Sishir Batabyal (B&W film, 1951)

My next pick takes me to India for *Jighansa,* the first Bengali screen adaptation of HOUN[108]. This effective and atmospheric film begins with a bang – a coach ride, a Hound baying, a scream. The editing is wonderful.

From here things get weird as we follow Conan Doyle up to a point, with Holmes-substitute detective Smarajit Sen (Shisir Batabyal) being called in to investigate the mysterious death of a wealthy and titled landowner and reports of a localised haunting, and Sen choosing instead to, err, send his friend and colleague Bimal to do the leg work. There's a terrific early scene of a dancer being lusted after by an obnoxious drunk who looks like Matt Berry from *Toast of London.* He goes to her room and makes unwanted advances towards her, she grabs a dagger and stabs him to death, then laughs hysterically and throws herself off a high balcony. It's perfectly in keeping with ACD and yet very Bengali.

Indeed, the contemporary-filmed bustling city streets of early 1950s (all cars and noise) and the contrasting wild beauty of the royal estate (mist rolling through swamps, etc.), filmed in crisp black and white, lends this film a real sense of place and time, every bit as vivid and intriguing as

---

[108] Very little is known about this film but at least two reputable sources credit it as being the first south Asian Holmes film.

late Victorian Dartmoor. Shisir Batabyal is a stocky, bowtie wearing, pipe-smoking sleuth who carries a warrant card and has a quiet authority, whilst Kamal Mitra as Bimal/Watson is taller, slimmer, with a pencil moustache and an easy charm. It's a shame these two actors and characters weren't in more Bengali 'Holmes' films.

The big change from Doyle (and as changes go it's a whopper) is the removal of the spectral Hound itself, substituted for a poor deaf and dumb porter who is employed as a killer[109] by dastardly villain Bikash Roy, who is secretly in line to the royal throne. The 'ghost' is a mysterious beautiful woman (Manju Dey), singing at night near the river, moving sensually through the mist-cloaked tall grass. She is beguiling and scary, her sinister laugh being genuinely unnerving.

The copy I sourced had no English subtitles and, because I don't speak a word of Bengali, I had to follow along as best I could. It helped that the film is visually appealing and atmospheric, and that I know the story of HOUN so well I can (and often do) find myself believing I'm living through it. And every now and again the odd English phrase is spoken – a "Please be seated", an "Excuse me, please", but sadly no "Elementary, my dear Bimal," or "Detective Sen, they were the footprints of a beautiful and mysterious singing woman who dances through the night, as well as a deaf porter who is being used by a villain for dreadful and murderous purposes!"

Jighansa was loosely remade in 1962 as the technicolor Indian Hindi-language psychological thriller film, *Bees Saal Baad*, which became an award-winning, super-smash (it was the top grossing box office hit of 1962) and lays claim to being by far the most successful screen version of *The Hound of the Baskervilles*, without really having anything much to do with it– a nice trick if you can pull it off.

---

[109] This might be a nod to Rondo Hatton's tragic 'Hoxton Creeper' from the Rathbone/Bruce-starring *The Pearl of Death* (1944), and the exploitative B-movie *The Brute Man* (1946)

I think HOUN Chapter Twelve, *Death on the Moor*, is my favourite chapter. It's certainly full of incident, not least the death of Selden as he is chased by the Hound (mistaking his scent for Sir Henry's) over the rocks in darkness until he slips, falls, and breaks his neck. Holmes and Watson initially believe the corpse they find to be that of their client and are full of remorse and regret. But on observing Selden's beard, they are delighted at the misidentification, positively leaping for joy as they realise Sir Henry is alive and that all is not lost. Immediately following this discovery, they meet Stapleton – Holmes coming face to face with the villain for the very first time. Holmes is filled with admiration for the psycho naturalist:

> "I told you in London, Watson, and I will tell you now again, that we have never had a foeman more worthy of our steel."

Professor Moriarty will soon cross paths with Sherlock Holmes to challenge that title with seemingly lethal effect, though confusingly for the reader, of course, he already has.

But before we get to all that, there's Cartwright to discuss. Because Holmes has brought the fourteen-year-old messenger boy with him to the moor (presumably living in rented accommodation in the village of Coombe Tracey); the lad has been supplying Holmes with food and clothing ("a loaf of bread and a clean collar – what does man want more?") and information.

Where to start with this... What do Cartwright's parents think about this? Aren't there child labour laws preventing the exploitation of minors? What exactly is Holmes doing to earn his fee (other than some background research) if Watson is doing all the interrogations of possible suspects and Cartwright is rushing around the moor delivering letters and supplies to Holmes as well as supplying further information on the case? In fact, if Holmes remained in Baker Street, and he had instead just sent Watson and Cartwright, would the investigation not have run just as smooth? And without Holmes, as the mysterious Man on the Tor, to drive Watson to distraction and unnecessarily muddying the waters, maybe things would have actually run better? Just how much is Holmes paying Cartwright, anyway? Is the lad keeping a record of the hours he's putting in? Why isn't Cartwright invited to join in the case officially, once Holmes steps centre stage? The boy's done an amazing job – don't just pack him off to London and forget all about him.

I know how these things go: if you cruelly ignore someone, they're going to turn against you. Cartwright will become resentful and bitter and he will grow into a formidable foeman bent on exacting revenge! Netflix, get to it.

I can't leave Chapter Twelve without commenting on Holmes's brilliant summation of the meaning behind the case and Stapleton's goal:

"It is murder, Watson – refined, cold-blooded, deliberate murder." How good is that? It sends chills down my spine.

DAY OF THE DETECTIVE

January 6th is Sherlock's birthday.[110] Happy birthday, buddy! Put your feet up, smoke an extra pipe, and let Mrs H and Dr W make a fuss of you all day. Perhaps Lestrade can pop round later with a juicy case that's baffling Scotland Yard. Perhaps brother Mycroft Holmes could send you a cake, hidden in which are top secret government papers that would bring

---

[110] This date was apparently chosen by Sherlockian Christopher Morley because it's the twelfth day of Christmas, and Holmes had made two references to Shakespeare's *Twelfth Night*. And because in *The Valley of Fear*, Holmes was grumpy on the morning of January 7th, meaning he is hungover, meaning he got out of his gourd the night before, meaning he was celebrating because it was his birthday. I can't argue with logic that watertight.

the British Empire to its knees if made public!

I have decided that I will spend this day doing things Sherlock Holmes would do - a mix of the physical, the intellectual, and the eccentric. I have jotted down a quick list:

1) Practice bartitsu
2) Adopt foolproof disguise
3) Solve a murder case
4) Kill the Hound of the Baskervilles

I had hoped to add 5) do some beekeeping[111] and 6) follow someone without them noticing me,[112] but Lockdown has scuppered these plans. I am confined to house and back garden and will have to make do.

THE STUDENT BECOMES THE MASTER

Bartitsu is mentioned by Holmes in *The Adventure of the Empty House* as the self-defence martial art he employed during his tussle with Professor Moriarty at the Reichenbach Falls in *The Adventure of the Final Problem*[113]. Unfortunately, I can't scrap with a balding mathematics professor over a Swiss waterfall, so I must make do with firing up a YouTube tutorial and making strange movements in front of my indifferent cats.

Bartitsu involves lots of punching with a straight arm, hitting with the flat of the hand, defending with a walking stick (I used a newly purchased Wilko's Magic Mop which promises to "clean tough marks without scratching"), and keeping a kind of bouncy balance. I kept thinking of the Fish Slapping Dance from *Monty Python's Flying Circus*, but after half an hour I was karate chopping and punching my way around

---

[111] My friend Tim keeps bees, and he had agreed to let me tag along to his hives with him. Hopefully this will happen another day.
[112] I'd planned to follow my younger brother for a day, as his eyesight is terrible.
[113] Though ACD spells it *baritsu.*

my room, listening to Carl Douglas's seminal disco classic *Everybody Was Kung-Fu Fighting*, feeling fast as lightning, confident that I'd mastered this eccentric martial art, and that I could handily defend myself from aggressive Napoleons of Crime who wish to do me in. I wished I had, as Inspector Clouseau has, a Kato-style man servant who could unexpectedly leap out of hiding to attack me, and to always keep me on my guard, but you can't have everything.

Over Christmas, I had ordered various elements I'd need to completely disguise myself, including: a false ginger wig, a hat, an eyepatch, an inflatable parrot to sit on my shoulder, a cutlass, and a hook. Only when I was dressed in the full disguise and admiring myself in the mirror did it dawn on me that I looked like a pirate, and that the disguise would be useless unless I was in the company of other pirates or at a fancy-dress party, or on the high-seas in a seventeenth century three-masted galleon, heading for Dead Man's Island. I sighed and stripped myself of the pirate disguise. It might come in useful one day.

Instead, I consulted my beloved *KnowHow Book of Spycraft*, pages 32-33 of which are all about 'Quick Disguises'. I learned how to change my look by combing my hair the wrong way, drawing new eyebrows onto my face, using a scarf to put my arm in a makeshift sling, and whitening my 'wrong way' hair with talcum powder. I decided not to use cocoa powder to make my face look browner because this is the twenty-first century and I'm not an insensitive bigot. There was also no need for me to tie a small cushion round my middle to make me look fatter as I already weep whenever I am brave enough to stand on the scales.

Disguise complete, I snuck outside, waited a few minutes, then knocked on the door. Would my wife recognise me when she opened the door? Yes. Yes, she did. She sighed, let me in, then resumed talking on the phone to her friend. I listened for a minute. She didn't mention me.

THE BOARD GAME'S AFOOT!

For my next activity of Being Sherlock, I decided to solve a case. I had already mastered the art of deductive reasoning as I'd amply demonstrated with my daughter's friends' pink selfie stick. With my powers of observation and imagination at their keenest, I knew I was ready to solve a baffling case.

I had been kindly gifted *221b Baker Street - The Sherlock Holmes Master Detective Game* for Christmas and was excited to finally play it. The box states that there are 75 cases, played by 2-6 players, aged 10+. I didn't think I'd be able to solve all 75 cases in one evening, but I was golden on the other two things: I was over ten years old (and had been for forty years, so I'd gotten the hang of it), and I had two to six other players in the form of my wife and my son whom I had to bribe with alcohol, cash and assurances this would be the one and only time they'd ever have to play a board game with me (they're still bitter, I think, about the game of *Battleships* I won against them five years ago; though it's true I employed sneaky and stealthy tactics to gain an advantage, I deny all accusations of cheating).

With glasses filled and the board set, we whiled away an hour on Case No. 1: The Adventure of the Unholy Man. Immediately, my face fell. I don't have what's called a poker face.

"What's the matter?" asked my wife, glugging down prosecco.

"Nothing... it's just... Well, where's the Hound?"

"What?"

"The Hound of the Baskervilles. I've read the case notes and there's absolutely no mention of a legendary ghost dog."

"How many stories have the Hound of the Baskervilles in it?" asked my son, knocking back Birra Moretti lager.

"Well one, obviously." I answered. Reader, do you now see the kind of people I have to deal with on a daily basis? People who think there's more than one Hound of the Baskervilles! Idiots. I snorted in my clear superiority, but my son thought I was choking on a BBQ flavour Dorito, instantly leaping into action, wrapping his arms around me, lifting me up and administering the Heimlich Manoeuvre until I managed to shake him off, assure him I was fine, and regain some dignity.

"There's only one Hound of the Baskervilles," I croaked. "There can be only one!" I added, like Christoph Lambert's preposterous Scottish immortal in *Highlander* (1986).

"Then why would there be a Hound of the Baskervilles in all the cases in this board game?" asked my son, finishing off the BBQ flavour Doritos. I'm positive they're not suitable for vegans, but that was on him.

He did have a good point, though. Had I really expected there to be a sequel case to HOUN in this board game? And perhaps sequel cases based on all the other stories? I think that was exactly what I had thought the game was all about, but that was foolish of me.

"You're right," I conceded, graciously. "I'm over it, it's beneath me, let's just crack on with the case. The game's afoot!"

My wife and son didn't get the reference. I had to explain it to them as they refreshed their glasses several times. Then we got on with the gameplay which involved rolling a die and moving a little Sherlock Holmes bust around a board dotted with various locations. The mini-Sherlocks were all different colours, and not based on the likenesses of actors, which was a shame. I fancied I might while away a few hours some time, busying myself with paint as I transformed the green piece into Arthur Wotner, the red into Jeremy Brett, and the black – the one I was using – into Wolf Ackva, who you may recall looks like Hugh Hefner.

As you move your Sherlock around the board you collect clues, which you jot down on your case file solution checklist until you hit upon the solution to the case. To be honest, though the Adventure of the

Unholy Man was a perfectly fine, clever little mystery (involving a preacher stabbed to death during a performance of *Hamlet*), my mind wandered often. The trouble is the Sherlock Holmes stories I've written tend to have more exciting elements to them: Exploding clowns! Evil telepathic cats! The Devil! Admittedly, these stories are comedies,[114] but I think I just enjoy really going to town with Holmes and Watson, so to speak, giving them thrilling adventures rather than detective stories. For I must also admit that I'm absolutely rubbish at solving whodunnits and even worse at dreaming up mystery plots. The developers of *221b Baker Street - The Sherlock Holmes Master Detective Game* are very clever fellows, and I tip my Deerstalker hat to them (or I would, if it weren't filled with slips of paper). But if Gibsons, the manufacturer, ever want to launch a new board game called *The Sherlock Holmes Wildly Silly Adventures Game*, I hope they give me call.

Of course, I solved the case first. It really doesn't matter that I got it completely wrong and (had the case gone to the Crown Prosecution Service) would have sent an innocent man to the gallows and allowed a killer to roam free... Because, in my head, the suspect was a criminal mastermind, running a network of German spies through a troupe of actors touring England with the Shakespeare Tragedies, which they were using as a front to assassinate British agents (each agent being killed in the manner befitting to each play). So, in a way, I was correct in every instance and was the true winner of the game that night, no matter what my wife says.

Admittedly my clever better half got the correct solution according to the prosaic limitations of the board game, but that's boring. I uncovered a plot that would have led to a world war, so actually everyone should be thanking me.

.

---

[114] Obviously, I'll let you be the judge of that.

For my final Sherlock Day thing, I got ready to kill the Hound. Earlier that morning I had drawn the beast onto thick cardboard, as I mentioned. I'd used the Paget illustration as a guide and drawn the animal to be five and a half feet long, and three foot tall – the thing was so massive it spanned across half my study. I was keen to be rid of the thing.

I eagerly unwrapped the Amazon package that had dropped onto my doormat a few weeks earlier. I had ordered a dart gun for £6.99 including P&P, and I was getting an itchy trigger finger. That dog was going down! To my dismay, however, I discovered I'd bought the wrong thing... I had in fact ordered something called the Bathtub Shoot 'Em Up: The ultimate in 'good clean fun'. Included in the box was a water pistol and a rack of flip down targets. No dart gun. Arse. Though obviously I was looking forward to using it later in the bath. But what to do now? The Hound was looking at me. I looked back at the Hound. I needed some kind of projectile. I looked at the pile of bills on my desk, and I had an idea! I would throw paper balls at the Hound of the Baskervilles until I knocked it over, thus 'slaying' the ghost dog and sending it back to hell!

I prepared by scrunching up around a dozen sheets of Final Demands and receipts from Amazon. I positioned myself six feet away from the Hound. I fired up my son's Spotify and wasted precious time trying to figure out how to get it to play Kate Bush's *Hounds of Love* before I gave up and had to settle for *Purely Educational* by Elder Island. God knows what that was about.

I threw cautiously at first, before I found a rhythm and got my arm loose and my aim straight. Soon I was hitting the Hound with every shot; the beast was beginning to wobble. But then two of my cats entered the room and sat watching me, then the Hound, like the strawberry-squaffing crowd at a Wimbledon tennis match. It was eerie. I threw another ball of paper and scored another hit, but then one of the cats started clawing at the Hound. Then the other one joined in. Both cats were now attacking the Hound! I holstered my throwing arm. I had no need to throw any more missiles. My cats were killing the Hound. Good cats! They had finally earned their keep, and I considered that the feline species had now been redeemed for that horrible night long ago in an English country village when I was locked in a toilet, naked, with an angry cat who immediately went on the offensive. Don't ask.

But then something most unexpected happened: I began to feel sorry for the cardboard dog! My cats can be vicious, and they weren't holding back. Claws and fangs were ripping into the cardboard, tearing it up like it was paper. Which it was, obviously, but thick paper. It was a massacre. I had to look away. And then I started to get angry at the cats – the brutes were attacking a poor defenceless cardboard dog. A dog I had spent ages drawing. I realised that I couldn't let it happen. God help me, I had to save the Hound!

I unholstered my arm, picked up a ball of paper, and threw it at one of the cats. Direct hit! The cat turned its attention to me as I hit it with a second paper missile. Then, a third missile hit the other cat. The Hound was free! I had saved it! My victory was short-lived, however, when I realised with mounting horror that the cats were now coming for *me*...

I fled the room and shut the door. I had a bath to calm down and relax after a hard day of being Sherlock Holmes. The Bathtub Shoot 'Em Up game was great fun, well worth the £6.99 inc. P&P.

The cats scratched at the bathroom door, but it only took me four hours of hiding before they gave up and wandered away. I emerged, clean and hungry, a Hound-killing/saving, case-solving, martial arts practicing, worthy successor to Mr Sherlock Holmes. I scoffed birthday cake and felt I had achieved all that any man could do that day.

THE SOUND OF THE BASKERVILLES

The Hound of the Baskervilles starring Nicholas Briggs (full-cast audio drama, Big Finish, 2011)

The Hound of the Baskervilles starring Carlton Hobbs (full-cast audio drama, BBC, 1961)

The Hound of the Baskervilles starring Kevin McCarthy (full-cast audio drama, CBS Radio Mystery Theatre, 1977)

The Hound of the Baskervilles starring Clive Merrison (full-cast audio drama, BBC, 1993)

Big Finish have been producing award-winning top tier audio drama for decades (their *Dr Who* range is exceptional) and their brand is a guarantee of quality. I loved this production of HOUN which is faithful without being slavish, and beautifully put together – the sound design by Martin Montague is so good I had to keep rewinding little bits to hear it again (Watson's narration as he arrives at Baskerville Hall, for one example - with all the background sounds of wind on the moor, a babbling stream, and lovely incidental music - made me squee with delight; the death of Selden, with the mournful baying of the Hound and the agonized cry of the convict, is also superbly done). Sir Henry has one too many 'by thunder!'s, perhaps, the postmaster is very 'mummerset', and the narration is over-descriptive at times, but these are mere quibbles. As Sherlock Holmes, Nicholas Briggs is sharp and brusque, though ready to laugh at his own folly – very much a 'thinking machine' obsessed with the case. But it is Richard Earl's splendid Dr Watson who steals the show – he is absolutely perfect in the role, the voice slightly gravelly, but always warm and intelligent. He is now one of my favourite Watsons and I look forward to hearing more of him. Lastly, the music by James Robertson is gorgeous and deserves to have its own release. All round, then, this production is hard to beat. Good job, Big Finish!

There are two available versions of BBC Radio HOUNs starring Carlton Hobbs as Sherlock Holmes and Norman Shelly as Dr Watson. Although the earliest version, from 1958, is creaky and crackly and stuffy and has the BBC Sound Effects Hound (yes!), it's perfectly fine entertainment, spread across six episodes that don't outstay their welcome.

But it's the *second* production – a brisk 90-minute version recorded three years later - that interests me more because the adaptor, Felix Felton, has done an injustice: having written in Mrs Hudson (she's not in the novel, sadly), a perfectly sensible thing to do, but the writer has given her only one line which is a silly thing to do and – gasp! – he has changed her name! Yes, Mrs Hudson has become, for one line only, Mrs Warren! Why? For God's sake, why?

Now, my hearing isn't in the best shape, even with top-of-the-range Bluetooth noise-cancelling Sony headphones (Christmas present from my wife) that my cats like to try to bite into, so it's entirely possible that I misheard the name and it is in fact Mrs *Watson* – John's wife - who knocks on the door to deferentially inform Holmes that "there's a man to see you, sir," and to be completely ignored by hubby Watson. Perhaps the Watsons are strapped for cash and Mrs W is working at 221b under Mrs Hudson's employ? Perhaps Mrs Watson winks saucily at her husband every time she is allowed into the shared flat with a tray of food or a telegram or to do some spring cleaning? Perhaps she is a live-in help and John sneaks out of his room at night to head to the servants' quarters? Perhaps, perhaps... The problem with the 'Mrs John Watson' theory is that the actress who delivers the line sounds like the Wicked Witch of the West from *The Wizard of Oz* (1939) and, unless Norman Shelly's Dr Watson has remarkably different tastes in romantic partners from all the other interpretations of the good doctor, I'm reasonably sure that this Mrs Watson is *not* John's type. The other theory I'm working on is that Mrs Hudson has married a Mr Warren, whomever he might be, and taken his name. And I'm hoping Mr Warren's first name is Warren.

Carlton Hobbs[115] – or 'Hobbo', as he was affectionately called – sounds like an actor doing a 'hero' voice – all strong and emotionless and detached. He sounds like he's been recorded separately from the rest of the cast, dropped in in post-production, and mixed way too high. It's like listening to a 1950's technicolour Biblical Epic God talking down to the likes of Charlton Heston from Heaven, only it's Sherlock Holmes talking to Dr Watson on Dartmoor. Though when I put it like that, it's pretty much the same thing.

Norman Shelley is a charmless, asthmatic, elderly Dr Watson who sounds like he needs a nap (and he has a very odd pronunciation of 'telegram', rhyming the second syllable with 'bum'), and 'young' Dr Mortimer sounds even older and more infirm than a great-great-grandfather on his deathbed. There's a jolly holly sticks Beryl Stapleton, a Scottish Eliza Barrymore, and a Mr Frankland who sounds like a Dalek. But the Hound is terrific, Selden's death cry is genuinely unnerving, and there's a sneaked-in 'elementary my dear Watson!' two minutes in which had me charmed from the start, so it's a mixed bag.

At 40 mins, the CBS Radio Mystery Theatre production, which begins with presenter EG Marshall reading a few lines from Francis Thompson's 1893 poem *Hound of Heaven*, moves so fast I thought I was listening to it at the wrong speed at first. There are even advert breaks for part-sponsors Buick Cars and Citizens Band Radio, stamping Americana all over this most English of stories with intriguing effect.

Kevin McCarthy (so brilliant in the 1956 *Invasion of the Body Snatchers*) makes no attempt at a British accent and the whiplash nature of the show means that *this* English listener didn't get the chance to grow accustomed to McCarthy's very American Holmes. As a result, a fine actor doing a decent job (aside from the odd fluffed line, and the weird

---

[115] Hobbs and Shelley played Holmes and Watson for BBC radio from 1952 – 1969, recording almost the entire Canon, and becoming the natural heirs to Rathbone and Bruce. Hobbs also joins that rare and intriguing group of actors to have played Holmes *and* Watson – Hobbs was Dr Watson to Arthur Wotner's genial Sherlock Holmes in a 1943 BBC radio production of *The Boscombe Valley Mystery*.

moment at the denouement where his Sherlock addresses the captive Beryl Stapleton as 'madame') is lost in the oddity of him sounding American while everyone else is trying for English accents with varying degrees of success. My favourite accent in this production belongs to the actress playing Mrs Barrymore – or 'Mrs Harris', as she's been renamed – who sounds like a cast member from *EastEnders*. Dot Cotton, perhaps (that's the only one I know, to be fair). With Mr Barrymore/Harris written out of the piece (aside from mentions in dialogue), it is left to Mrs Harris to cheerily greet Sir Henry on his arrival at Baskerville Hall not by welcoming him into his family home, but by warning him against crossing the moor in those dark hours when the powers of evil are exalted. I half expected the famous *EastEnders* 'dum-dum' cliff-hanger theme music to kick in. Bolstering the *EastEnders* feel is a 'luvaduck-guv-cor-blimey-ow's-yer-chimney-darlin' cockney cab driver who might well be channelling Dick Van Dyke[116].

    This is a decidedly odd adaptation; the briskness of the paired-down narrative leads to some strange and amusing bits such as Watson threatening to punch Sir Henry insensible if he doesn't immediately give up the hunt for Selden and return to the safety of the Hall(!), and Holmes saying goodbye to Watson without ever asking him to accompany Sir Henry to Dartmoor. Though I can forgive Holmes for sending Watson without consulting him, given that Dartmoor seems to have been relocated to Albert Square,[117] the world's most miserable piece of real estate. Not to mention the shameful rewriting of the iconic 'footprints of a gigantic hound!' as the anaemic and forgettable '*tracks* of a gigantic hound'... Jog on, son; jog on.

---

[116] Along similar lines, Alan Barnes' *Sherlock Holmes on Screen* quotes a review of actor Robert Duvall as Dr Watson in *The Seven-Per-Cent Solution* (1976) whose strangled English accent is described by *The New Statesman* as "I feah the fawg hez delayed arse."

[117] Fictitious location used in *EastEnders* where everybody is on drugs and having affairs and murdering people and burning down pubs, so far as I can make out from the little bits I've seen.

I'd never in a million years have thought that the best opening to a version of HOUN would be the comfy, warm tones of stuffy sitcom star Donald Sinden telling the bloody story of the Curse of the Baskervilles, but marathoning *The Hound of the Baskervilles* in all media has certainly thrown up a few surprises. Beyond the jolt of realising Donald Sinden is the perfect Sir Charles, nothing else about the 1993 *Hound of the Baskervilles* acclaimed two-part BBC audio play, starring Clive Merrison and Michael Williams,[118] is much of a surprise, *per se*. It is instead just as roundly excellent as I'd hoped and expected. Dramatist Bert Coules is in love with Holmes and Watson, and it shines through every second of this lovely production, not least in the extra bits of character business he's given to the duo, shining little spotlights on their friendship. The gentle teasing between them is a joy:

WATSON: Obvious now you point it out.

HOLMES: What happened to, "Holmes, that's amazing!"?

WATSON: You're mistaking me for the man in *Strand* Magazine.

There's a charming scene of Watson singing happily as he returns from a day at his gentlemen's club, followed by Mrs Hudson imploring him to get Holmes to stop filling the room with noxious tobacco smoke. Mrs H being played by the incomparable Judi Dench – wife of Michael Williams – is the icing on a scrumptious cake.

There are many excellent Holmes and Watson pairings, and every fan has their favourites, but it's not too controversial to say that Merrison and Williams might be the most authentic. They are nothing less than perfect in every one of the splendid Bert Coules adapted Holmes stories they appeared in, and this series is certainly a contender – with the first Jeremy Brett series – for the best Sherlock Holmes series of them all. I bought the first series on CD many years ago, and I've listened to them dozens of times, enjoying revisiting this team as I do Brett/Burke, Rathbone/Bruce and Miller/Liu. Indeed, around the same time I bought

---

[118] Merrison and Williams are the only actors to have starred as Holmes and Watson in all 60 of ACD's stories. Bert Coules oversaw every one of them.

the Rathbone/Bruce radio plays from the 40s,[119] sponsored by Grove's Bromo Quinine[120] and Petri Wine. I would often switch between the two different series – creaky old-time radio with Rathbone and Bruce, and dynamic, sophisticated audio drama with Merrison and Williams. I suspect that somewhere in that mix is the perfect version of Sherlock Holmes outside of Doyle.

Bert Coules had earlier adapted HOUN for BBC radio in 1988 with Roger Rees as Holmes and Crawford Logan as Watson. Although I'm sure it's terrific, I've not been able to source a copy. Nor have I had any luck in finding radio adaptations of HOUN starring Nicol Williamson (an excellent screen Holmes in *The Seven-Per-Cent Solution*) and Edward Petherbridge. Collecting is not an easy (or cheap) hobby; sometimes it's best to just give up the search and abandon all hope. Life's easier that way.

DAMN YOU, CORONAVIRUS!
The Hound of the Baskervilles starring Eille Norwood (Silent film, 1921)
The Hound of the Baskervilles starring Robert Rendel (B&W film, 1931)

I sip some decaff tea and flick through the latest issue of the splendid *Sherlock Holmes Magazine*[121] as I ponder what to do about Eille Norwood. I've just fished out his Hound from the Deerstalker of Doom, but I've no way of watching it. A print exists, but it's at the British Film Institute. My plan had always been to book a viewing in London and write about my escapades there. But that can't happen until the coming summer (hopefully), so I'm rather stymied as my editor wants this book in the spring, and I'm a little frightened of her. It's not the same as with other

---

[119] *The New Adventures of Sherlock Holmes* ran for a decade on US radio. Happily, lots of them survive and are in surprisingly good condition, though sadly the Rathbone/Bruce audio adaptation of HOUN is lost.
[120] It's some kind of flu medicine, apparently, popular with the US army.
[121] I'm still waiting for someone to launch *Hound of the Baskervilles Monthly*.

Hounds that I can't see because I can't source a copy (or because I can't source a copy where none exists); the Eille Norwood *Hound of the Baskervilles* exists and I *can* see it – but not today, not for this book. I'm dejected.

Norwood was the Jeremy Brett of his day.[122] In just two years, he starred in forty-seven short Sherlock Holmes films, then played the detective on stage in London. I've read that his starring role in *The Hound of the Baskervilles* is, like Jeremy Brett's over sixty-years later, the best thing in a rather disappointing affair.

I munch on toast and stop two cats from killing each other (these two are in a lifelong blood feud) as I'm struck by another miserable realisation – not only do I have to skip the Norwood Hound, I won't be able to watch the first British talkie version of the Hound, made a decade later and starring Robert Rendel, because again I'd need to see it at the BFI. Arse. That's two versions I don't get to see.

Ah well. There's always a revised second edition, right? You'd pay for that, wouldn't you, dear reader?[123]

·

---

[122] In fact, his real name was Anthony Edward Brett, so he was quite *literally* the Brett of his day!

[123] I'm guessing no.

CHAPTER THIRTEEN
Black Dog
January 2021

A BAD CASE OF GAS

THIS MORNING I STUMBLED across a peculiar newspaper clipping from the *La Crosse Tribune*, Wisconsin, 1909:

> **DOYLE'S BOOK IS CAUSE OF INSANITY**
> BOSTON, Mass., April 8 – After reading Sir Arthur Conan Doyle's *The Hound of the Baskervilles* which tells of a ghostly dog that tears the throat of Sir Hugo Baskerville and leaves him dead on the moor, Marcus J Long, 65, chopped to pieces all the keys and strings of the piano, smashed a $1,000 violin and then committed suicide by inhaling illuminating gas.

I really know what to make of that. There's clearly a lot to unpack. I mean, first, what the hell is illuminating gas[124]? Why did Mr Long chop up a piano and smash to bits a very pricey violin? Did he have other musical instruments that he left intact? Was there something about the piano and the violin in particular that made him destroy them so violently before taking his own life? Why is HOUN being dragged into this? Did

---

[124] It's just gas for lighting, according to Google. Scientific American has this to say: "The illuminating gas made in large gas works, and used almost universally for lighting the buildings and streets of large cities throughout the civilized world, is composed of products of the distillation of bituminous coal." There you go: illuminating stuff about illuminating gas. I'll bet you're so glad you bought this book.

he read the novel in its entirety, and then immediately set about his piano/violin massacre and subsequent suicide by illuminating gas? It's all a bit of a puzzle.

What bothers me most, though, is that Marcus Long only seems to have read HOUN *once* before it drove him insane. I've read it dozens of times. What's it doing to *me*?

UP PERISCOPE!
Der Hund von Baskerville starring Carlyle Blackwell Snr (Silent film, 1929)

Today's pick from the DoD is a bit of a cheat, in that I'd picked it a month ago, but put it aside (with an 'IOU' in German, and a doodle of the Hound) until I received a copy of the glorious and expensive Blu-ray, courtesy of Father Christmas (or, more likely, my wife). My problem was that, owing to me being at least ten years behind technologically than the rest of the world, I don't own a Blu-ray player. My son came to the rescue by lending me his Xbox, setting it up for me, and supplying more sarcasm than a lesser man could have withstood. But I took it all in good humour, for I was happy to retrieve the 'IOU' today because I had been looking forward to seeing this film, knowing its reputation as something special.

I'm happy to report that it has not been overpraised. It really is something special – a moody, strikingly photographed, thrilling Expressionist horror. An extreme close-up of scary Stapleton (Fritz Rasp) looking monstrously unhinged is as unnerving as the melodramatic reveals of Lon Chaney's Phantom of the Opera or Conrad Veidt's Cesare from *The Cabinet of Dr Caligari* (1920). And with Barrymore played by an actor who eerily resembles Bela Lugosi, the horror film comparisons are strengthened.

Certainly, the wonderful, expansive, and atmospheric sets for the moor and Baskerville Hall are the equal of the glorious and justly celebrated ones for Universal's cobweb-strewn Castle Dracula and Victor

Frankenstein's lightning-lashed laboratory. Elsewhere, eyes move behind statues. Men with burning torches scour the desolate moor during a tremendous thunderstorm. Shadows creep up the stairs. A cat plays with a ball as a terrified Dr Watson sits up in bed, gun in hand, listening to movement in the house...

I think this is a clear candidate for the best-directed version of HOUN. Austrian-born director Richard Owswald had scripted the 1914 version of HOUN, and had gone onto direct dozens of well-regarded German films (including adaptations of *The Picture of Dorian Grey* and *Around the World in Eighty Days*). He was one of many Jews who was forced to flee Nazi Germany, and find a home in Hollywood. I've yet to see any of his other films, but on the strength of *Der Hund von Baskerville* alone I'd have no hesitation in regarding him amongst the other great directors of the time, such as Fritz Lang (*Metropolis*, 1927) and Friedrich Wilhelm Murnau (*Nosferatu,* 1922).

Long considered lost to time, a print of *Der Hund* was found in Poland in 2009. Experts from around the world and from diverse communities[125] have worked together to lovingly restore this film (there's one section where only still photographs remain), and a stirring new score by the conductor, composer, pianist and violinist, Guenter Buchwald[126].

Star Carlyle Blackwell is an American-Brit and certainly looks like a leading-man version of Sherlock Holmes, with his big hair and square jaw. He looks great in a deerstalker and long leather coat flapping in the wind. The shot of Watson seeing Holmes silhouetted on the Tor is terrific.

---

[125] Filmmuseum Muenchen and San Francisco Silent Film Festival; the restoration was overseen by film preservationist Rob Byrne.

[126] A pioneer of the renaissance in silent film music, Buchwald has accompanied silent films for thirty-eight years with a repertoire of more than three thousand titles. And he has conducted orchestras worldwide from Iceland to Romania, Tokyo to Zurich.

This Watson is an odd sort – a chain-smoking, gun-toting nervous fool who looks like Harry Enfield[127]. At one point he throws open a pair of double doors so dramatically he reminded me of Patrick McGoohan in the opening titles to mind-blowing 60s spy series, *The Prisoner*. Inventively, Holmes's hiding place on the moor is not in a prehistoric stone hut, but deep in an underground cave. To gain entrance, Watson climbs through the gap in some giant twisted tree roots. The sequence has about it the magical air of *Alice in Wonderland*. Down in the cave, he finds signs of habitation – a lantern, a tin of crab meat, and a top-of-the-range periscope that looks out onto the moor.

This had me wondering how Holmes was supplied. I imagined the following exchange between the detective and his fourteen-year-old ally, the dependable Cartwright:

"Mr Holmes, about this list of things you need me to get for you..."

"Problem, Cartwright?"

"Well, sir, it's just that there aren't many shops on the moor. The lantern I can get, no problem."

"Excellent."

"The tinned crab meat... That might be tricky, sir. There aren't any crabs on the moor as far as I know."

"I'm sure an enterprising village shopkeeper could import tinned goods from a wholesaler, perhaps from nearby Plymouth which, being a port, I'm certain will be replete with all manner of tasty aquatic crustaceans."

"You may be right about that, Mr Holmes. But what about a top-of-the-range periscope, sir? A village storekeeper couldn't send out for one of those, I reckon, no matter how enterprising the fella might be."

"You are aware, I hope, young Cartwright, that there is a naval base in Plymouth? A very well supplied naval base?"

"Err..."

---

[127] British comic actor best known for his sketch shows. He does a lot of work for charity, but doesn't like to talk about it.

"Problem, Cartwright?"

"Err, it's just... Well, it seems like you're asking me to break into a naval base and steal a periscope for you, Mr Holmes."

"Yes, and?"

"Nothing, sir. I'll get right on it, Mr Holmes."

"Thank you, Cartwright. Now, about those magazines I requested..."

NETWORK RAIL APOLOGISES FOR THE LATE ARRIVAL OF THE 4:10 FROM PADDINGTON

Cartwright gets two short lines in HOUN Chapter Thirteen, *Fixing the Nets*: waiting eagerly at Coombe Tracey train station, the real hero of this classic novel greets Holmes by asking if he has "any orders, sir?" On being sent home to London on the next train with instructions to telegram Sir Henry some nonsense about a possible lost pocketbook, the lad replies, "Yes, sir." And then he fetches a telegram, hands it to Holmes, and vanishes from *The Hound of the Baskervilles*. But not from our hearts. Never from our hearts.

The telegram is from Inspector Lestrade who says he'll be arriving with a warrant card at five forty – though if west country trains were running anything like they do these days (pre-Covid-19), I'd not bother to turn up on the platform to greet the policeman until at least six fifteen.

Meanwhile, Sir Henry has been delighted to see Holmes again, then baffled and hurt by the detective's immediate departure for London, utterly perplexed by Holmes's instruction to do the one thing he has been warned he must never do: walk alone across the moor at night, after he's had dinner at the Stapletons, and when the powers of darkness are exalted. Poor Sir Henry. Never has a Canadian been so comprehensively mindfucked by so many weird English people.

FAMILY'S ALWAYS AWKWARD

Sherlock Holmes has barely stepped foot inside Baskerville Hall before he observes that the seventeenth century portrait of Sir Hugo Baskerville bears a striking resemblance to Jack Stapleton. This got me curious to know if any of my own devilishly handsome distant relatives bear a striking resemblance to me.

After Googling '17th century Stadon' with no luck other than some disturbing fan fiction, I signed up for a trial with an ancestry database thing with similarly disappointing results. If ever I'm famous and invited to appear on *Who Do You Think You Are?*[128] then I'm going to be a crushing disappointment to the producers – no royal blood, hangmen, heroes, or people of distinction in my lineage; the Stadons are nondescript nobodies. I know my dad and my uncle had criminal pasts, but that's all I know. (I'm fairly sure that my uncle was in a mob that ran the seaside resort of Weston-super-Mare – which conjures up all manner of silly images of ice cream extortion rackets and beefy mobsters on the beach telling terrified kids that they love the little sand castles they've built but "it would be a shame if anything happened to them, oops, clumsy me.") Whispers and rumours, nothing solid, nothing factual.

I considered paying the full fee to My Heritage, which would give me access to criminal records and the like, but it would cost me £73 and I can't afford it. I've spent too much on pricey books from small publishers. My dad's criminal history must remain for the time being a mystery, like the rest of his life before I was a young adult, for although I lived with him throughout my childhood and teens, I was fearful of him which created a distance between us. I don't even know when and where he met my mother.

At any rate, my half-arsed research had produced nothing useful so I decided to make up a long-distant relative, based on wicked Sir Hugo, and create a portrait of the fellow based on my likeness. Behold: the

---

[128] BBC series where celebrities like Stephen Fry go through a 'journey' into their family histories so that they can shed a tear or two when it inevitably gets to a cynically contrived soppy bit.

devilish Sir Hugo Stadon (1601 – 1640), wicked and profane squire of Stadonville Hall!

SIR HUGO STADON
1601 - 1640

THE HOUND OF THE BOLSHEVIKS
Vasily Livanov as Sherlock Holmes in *The Adventures of Sherlock Holmes and Dr Watson: The Hound of the Baskervilles* (TV movie, 1981[129])

---

[129] Alan Barnes in *Sherlock Holmes on Screen* recommends Series 2 as 'the high watermark' for this wonderful series of Holmes adaptations. I'm keen to watch them all to see if I share his opinion. Barnes and I don't always agree – in *Kiss Kiss Bang Bang,*

My room is so cold this morning that The Deerstalker of Doom has icicles hanging from the brim. I put on extra clothing, then more extra clothing, and drink hot tea as I examine the slip of paper that will decide today's fate.

Ah, we're off to Russia, to watch the acclaimed Vasily Livanov version of HOUN. I think it's only fitting because today is colder than the snow in Moscow. And when I look outside, I see there is, in fact, snow in Bristol today.

The kitten is sat at the window, watching the snow fall. Occasionally she will raise a paw and try to catch snowflakes. I am charmed by the sight. It's her first ever snow! But then one of the grumpy older cats jumps up and smacks the kitten with its paw, knocking the poor little one to the ground. Nature is cruel. I let the little one out of the back door into the garden and it runs around in the snow, leaving the footprints of a tiny cat, before deciding snow is too cold and weird for her, and running back inside, into the warm.

As my wife goes out for a walk to buy vodka and to build a snowman, I settle down and watch Vasily Livanov do his stuff. The kitten joins me after a while.

And what a delight this version is! Beautifully shot in rich colours, extensive location filming (with the snowy Russian wilderness making an excellent Dartmoor) and a terrific Holmes and Watson, this had me captivated from beginning to end. There's a charming sequence leading up to the end of Part One, with a drunk Sir Henry and Dr Watson tipsily discussing Beryl Stapleton (with whom Henry has fallen for, love-at-first-sight style) and the relevance of Beryl's remarks about blossoming orchids, before the two men discover the Barrymores signalling to escaped convict Selden – much to Sir Henry's utter bafflement – then recklessly decide it would be a hoot to go out on the moor in their drunken state, at night, to

---

his unauthorised book on James Bond films (co-authored with Marcus Hearn), he gives a critical mauling to Timothy Dalton as Bond in *Licence to Kill*, a film I think is bloody marvellous. So there, Alan!

208

hunt down the escapee... Only to find themselves sobering up very quickly indeed when they hear the baying of the Hound.

I laughed out loud when Part Two sees the two men nursing horrendous hangovers in Baskerville Hall the next morning, with Henry asking Barrymore to please speak more quietly, then looking queasy and aghast at the bowl of gloop his butler has served for breakfast.

Henry is played for laughs throughout, and it works brilliantly: we first see him wrapped in furs, looking like a Canadian bear, excitedly and restlessly prowling his hotel like an eager puppy. I also loved the gorgeous score (played by the Leningrad State Philharmonic Orchestra), the genuinely scary hound (with mask!), the sleepy cat in the Dartmoor Post Office, and Vitaly Solomin as a bright, endearing, capable Dr Watson.

My favourite thing of all, however, is a scene where Holmes tasks Cartwright with:

(a) Memorising the names and locations of twenty-three London Hotels, in five seconds

(b) Memorising an article in yesterday's edition of *The Times*, in three seconds

(c) Visiting each hotel in turn, bribing a porter to show him the previous day's waste, searching through the waste to locate the relevant edition of *The Times*, then discarding it if the article does not have holes in it from where someone had cut out certain words to use as in a threatening letter to Sir Henry Baskerville

(d) To complete these tasks and report to Holmes at 221b Baker Street by early evening

I've read this passage from HOUN dozens of times, but it was only when I watched it dramatized in this Russian version that it struck me how ludicrously demanding Holmes is. I mean, talk about asking for the moon! Memorize twenty-three London hotels in five seconds? Could *you* do that? I certainly couldn't and I'm amazed Holmes would expect a fourteen-year-old boy to do it, then visit each one in turn, rummage through disgusting waste (this is a hundred years before the introduction of recycling bins), identify a specific article from a specific edition of a specific newspaper... Blimey. Most fourteen-year-old boys can barely remember the names of their siblings because their brains are filled up with utterly useless trivia about computer games or Marvel movies (or in my case, Sherlock Holmes).

To be fair, in the novel, Holmes doesn't tell Cartwright he only has five seconds to memorise the list, nor does Vasily Livanov's Holmes in this excellent Russian HOUN. But Vasily only shows Cartwright the list for (at most) five seconds. I know enough about the production of films to know that the scene would have been shot multiple times (hundreds of times, if Stanley Kubrick had directed it[130]) and that dozens of smart people would have watched the scene back many times in the editing suite; if it wasn't ever their intention to do the five seconds thing then they would not have let it remain in the finished print. Therefore, we can safely deduce that it was intentional and that Sherlock Holmes really expected Cartwright to easily memorise twenty-three London hotels in under five seconds. But of course, this was all merely my opinion. Maybe I was making a fuss over nothing. Perhaps it really is easy to memorize twenty-three London hotels in under five seconds? I had to test my hypothesis.

"Are you busy?"

"Yes, go away. Unless you're pouring me more gin." My wife was watching a repeat of *Agatha Christie's Poirot* on ITV4. She prefers Christie to ACD. I can't for the life of me understand why.

"I thought you went out for vodka?"

"I did."

I waited. No explanation was forthcoming, so I let it drop. "Can you please see if you can memorize the names of twenty London hotels I've written down in my special notebook? In five seconds."

"What? No. Why?"

---

[130] Kubrick was busy with *The Shining*, but I can't be alone in thinking that a Kubrick Sherlock Holmes film would have been enticing.

"It's for the Hound of the B—"

"Of course it is, I don't know why I bother to ask."

"It'll only take five seconds. Literally." I showed my wife my mobile phone which has an app on it with a useful timer countdown thing that also tells the time in New York, Petaluma California, and Moscow.

After much persuasion – involving me promising to do certain chores and cutting my wife in on a percentage of any money I might make from sales of this book – my wife finally agreed. She took a big gulp of pink gin, then on my go she stared at the list. I stopped the timer at five seconds.

"The Strand, the Hilton, the Hard Rock... and, err, the Park Plaza."

"That's only four. Cartwright had to remember twenty-three."

"Yeah well, it's late, I'm tired, I've had gin, and anyway fourteen-year-olds have sharper brains."

"I didn't, when I was fourteen."

"Colour me surprised. Now leave me alone with Poirot."

I left her alone. Though not before telling her who the killer was[131].

There is a statue of Livanov and Solomin as Holmes and Watson outside the British Embassy in Moscow. I would love to go there and see it. My wife has been to Moscow (indeed, she got her degree in Russian History and Politics) back in the late 80s as the Soviet Union collapsed. She loves the city. A return visit appeals to her.

Me, my wife, and the kitten, in Red Square, in the snow. The kitten can catch the snowflakes as they gently fall. It's a nice dream to have.

---

[131] I was wrong. I got my Poirots mixed up.

CHAPTER FOURTEEN
Beware of the Dog!
February 2021

WE COULD BE HEROES JUST FOR ONE DAY

I AM HEADING FOR the finish line. There are a scant few Hounds remaining in the Deerstalker of Doom, and only two chapters from Mr Doyle to engross me. But Chapter Fourteen, as one might expect from a chapter titled *The Hound of the Baskervilles*, is an absolute corker! This is the title track on the album, the *L.A. Woman/Born in the USA/ Band on the Run* meaty epic that towers over everything else on the record. This is David Bowie's *Heroes*.

And what heroes we have, what heroic things they do: using a hapless baronet as bait for an attack dog! Shooting a poor animal to death! I mean, that's a very uncharitable way of looking at it, but I really don't like the Hound dying. I always hope they'll calm the animal, take it to a vet, rehabilitate it and then give it to a dog-lover who will cherish it for the rest of its happy life. The pitiful dog doesn't even get a name – that's why I've been calling it Hound with a capital 'H'.

I wonder if Sir Arthur was ever bitten by a dog and is using HOUN (and his other Sherlock Holmes stories) to exact revenge on the canine species. My younger brother, Troy, was bitten by our family dog – a black poodle named Prince – and he still bears the scar on his cheek like a

German duellist. But Troy, unlike Sir Arthur, grew up to be a dog lover[132] and, in fact, owned a high street pet store. That's a much healthier attitude.

The Hound is shot and killed by Holmes and Watson firing at the animal as it bounds out of the wall of fog. One bullet wounds it, then Holmes fires five more shots and puts it out of its misery. Being men of courage and ability, Holmes and Watson do not hesitate. They spring into action and run towards the danger and face the monstrous Hound. Lestrade, however, acts differently: on hearing the beastly roar, Scotland Yard's finest gives a yell of terror and throws himself face down on the ground. So, that was well worth him making the trip from London, then! I can well imagine his Chief Super at Scotland Yard calling him into his office to have a quiet word with him:

CHIEF SUPER: I see you've put in an expense form for 'train journey to Devonshire', Inspector. Surely you're not expecting the Met to pay for your holidays?

LESTRADE: No, sir, that journey was for official police business.

CHIEF SUPER: Really? I haven't seen any case files pertaining to crimes in Devonshire. That's outside our jurisdiction, Inspector.

LESTRADE: There isn't a case file, sir, as the whole business is wrapped up now.

CHIEF SUPER: And what is your involvement in this "wrapped up business" in the west country?

LESTRADE: I was asked to go to Devon to make an arrest, sir.

CHIEF SUPER: Oh, so you've made an arrest?

---

[132] In the service of a poor gag, I do Sir Arthur a grave injustice here, because by all accounts the great man was a dog lover.

LESTRADE: No, sir.

CHIEF SUPER: Do you have a suspect?

LESTRADE: I did, sir, a big ghost dog. But it's dead now, sir.

CHIEF SUPER: You killed a vicious dog?

LESTRADE: No, sir. I was curled up in a ball, sucking my thumb, when the dog was killed, but I heard it, sir.

CHIEF SUPER: You went to Devon to make an arrest which you failed to do. The suspect was, and I quote, 'a big ghost dog' which you failed to destroy because you were scared. And you expect the Metropolitan Police Force to reimburse you?

LESTRADE: Yes, sir.

CHIEF SUPER: Get out of my office, Lestrade.

LESTRADE: Right away, sir.

ANXIETY IN THE UK

I still get very anxious, quite a lot of the time. I worry a lot, about my health, my family, my friends, my cats, and the awful fact that millions have succumbed to a deadly virus.

I often get pains and twinges in my chest – aches, or heartburn, or indigestion – and my body panics, thinking it's something serious, and I must keep control. I'm getting much better at holding back full-blown panic attacks, but it can be tiring. I sometimes lose my balance, so I walk around feeling a bit dizzy; this can go on for a few days, and it can get a little disorientating. It feels a little like being drunk, but without singing Beatles songs very loudly until I'm told to shut up by my wife who is trying to sleep. It's probably a chemical thing in my ear; I should ask my doctor, but I don't want to bother my GP with something so trivial. Besides, I've seen so many health professionals, had so many consultations and tests, that I just want to go a few months without seeing a doctor, except ones with space-time machines and terrible hair.

Looking at screens bothers me, gives me headaches, so I take regular breaks when I'm writing, and sometimes I go weeks without switching on my PC. Any bright light is a problem - they can trigger migraines with auras, which are a bit scary. I keep catching glimpses of light in the corner of my eye and worry that I'm about to experience a migraine. Candlelight used to bother me, but now I've got used to it and find it quite comforting. I put a log in the fire in my study, light a candle, and settle down with one of my cats to read *The Hound of the Baskervilles*.

Talking Italian
L'Ultimo dei Baskerville starring Nando Gazzolo (TV serial, 1968)

It was past 1am and I couldn't sleep, so I awkwardly manoeuvred myself out of bed without disturbing the snoozing cat sprawled out like a mutant fluffy starfish and headed into the study, inexorably to the Deerstalker of Doom. This hat generates weird and dangerous hypnotic powers, like the blue energy cube-things in the Marvel movies or the Ark of the Covenant. I am completely under its spell. Like a mindless zombie, I reach out a hand and pull a Hound from the hat. Then I kneel before it and mutter an incantation:

"Deerstalker of Doom, I am forever and always in tautology your obedient acolyte. Your awesome cloth power is supreme, your majesty unparalleled in the realm of men's silly hat wear. I am yours to do your bidding, oh Deerstalker of Doom, but only after I've had a cup of tea and a slice of toast, or perhaps the leftover chicken and mushroom pie which I could heat up without much fuss."

My pick is *L'Ultimo dei Baskerville*, the only Italian version of HOUN (and I immediately wished I had some pasta or pizza to reheat, but I didn't). It's a three-part, three-hour, black and white epic from the late 60s.[133] I watched all three parts in one sitting, making notes, until I collapsed, bleary-eyed at 4:30am, sinking into a deep sleep where I dreamed about next door's dog howling in the night, but I couldn't see it or identify the breed except that it sounded Italian somehow, so perhaps it was a ciao-wah[134]. The copy I watched had no English subtitles and I don't speak Italian. The hours just flew by.

Episode 1 begins promisingly: a bravado tracking shot through Baskerville Hall to the midnight chimes of a grandfather clock, and Sir Charles walking the Yew Alley to his doom, is mixed with Selden already on the loose. It becomes apparent that some significant shifting of plot furniture has happened. The most obvious example is Holmes accompanying Watson to Baskerville Hall and only later, near the end of part 2, does the detective leave the narrative to pretend to be in London. It is Watson who reads aloud the Curse of the Baskervilles – not at Baker Street (which we never get to see), but sometime after he's already a guest at Baskerville Hall. The same scene has the 'keep away from the moor' letter delivered to Sir Henry by Barrymore.

Surprisingly, all this works well – particularly a scene of Holmes and Watson walking to Baskerville Hall, shot on a sunny day in verdant countryside. The detective examines the scene of Sir Charles's death as a small crowd look on in awe and Watson carries the luggage. I was amused by Holmes lighting his pipe and casually tossing away the match, contaminating the crime scene. In Part 3, when Holmes reappears in the nick of time to save Watson from the embarrassment of accusing Dr Mortimer of being the villain (Watson having been following the doctor on the moor as the latter man whistles for his missing dog – or for the

---

[133] The HOUN adaptation is the final three episodes of a short season called *Sherlock Holmes*, following *The Valley of Fear*, again adapted over three hour-long episodes.
[134] Sorry, that's a dreadful joke.

Hound, as Watson suspects), the detective is sporting altogether more casual clothing: a white roll neck sweater and natty jacket. Looking cool, Sherlock!

Much screen time is invested in the burgeoning romance between smooth Sir Henry and a rather odd Beryl Stapleton who enjoys playing weird music on some kind of steam pipe organ as if she's in Iron Butterfly.[135] Elsewhere, there's an impish, chess-playing Stapleton who keeps a stuffed toucan in his weird house of plants. Barrymore the butler looks like the funny one from the Monkees[136] and is dressed throughout as a Regency-era page boy. There's a new servant at Baskerville Hall, called Perkins, who lingers in the background but doesn't actually do anything.[137] Stapleton gets his own assistant – a brute who also lingers menacingly in the background, but doesn't actually do anything.[138] There's a preponderance of crash zooms into the portrait of Sir Hugo. The end of Part 2 hilariously has the actors standing stock still as the credits roll.[139] I half-expected a fly to land on Barrymore's nose.

The Hound is a confusing mix of shots that, at various points, makes the beast look like a harmless little Yorkshire Terrier with white rings around its eyes, then a ferocious attack dog that's been dubbed by the MGM lion.

Overall, I rather enjoyed this Italian TV Hound and, though I found it dragged in parts, I keep in mind that it wasn't supposed to be

---

[135] San Diego rock band, best known for the 1968 hit *In-A-Gadda-Da-Vida*, with its epic organ solo, which was used to unnerving effect in the climactic shootout of *Manhunter* (1986), Michael Mann's brilliant, stylish adaptation of the first Hannibal Lecter novel, *Red Dragon* by Thomas Harris.

[136] Mike Nesmith, apparently – the one in the woolly hat.

[137] This might be Perkins, the young groom at Baskerville Hall, who has somehow aged sixty years overnight. Perhaps he had been listening to the tedious, never-ending Clive Nolan and Oliver Wakeman prog rock album.

[138] This might be Anthony, the man Holmes describes in Chapter Fifteen, who assists Stapleton in looking after the Hound when the Stapletons are in London. Or it might be my friend Tony, on magic mushrooms. Who knows?

[139] Lampooned mercilessly by the 1982 short-lived US TV comedy *Police Squad!* from the makers of *Airplane!* (1980).

watched all in one go, over fifty years later, by an insomniac who doesn't speak a word of Italian.

KILL COUNT

HOUN Chapter Fourteen has Stapleton, his batty murder scheme in tatters, scarpering across the Grimpen Mire to make his getaway, only to perish -- supposedly. Watson surmises that "down in the foul slime of the huge morass which had sucked him in, this cold and cruel-hearted man is forever buried." What a pity - I'd have liked to have seen Mad Jack back for a few more clashes with Holmes, perhaps each time accompanied by an exotic animal, covered in phosphorous. A rhino here, a Mongolian gerbil there... Stapleton's malevolent menagerie could have been a winning spin-off franchise. Netflix, are you listening?

If we are to take Watson's (and Holmes's) word for it, and Stapleton is indeed a gonner, then his death is the last mortality of the novel. The full tally, in chronological order, runs:

Yeoman's daughter (dies of exhaustion, stress, and fright)

Sir Hugo Baskerville (throat ripped out by the Hound of the Baskervilles)

Various Baskerville men throughout the ages (meet suspicious violent deaths) *

Rodger Baskerville (cause unknown)

Fraser, tutor at the Yorkshire school run by Stapleton (cause unknown) *

Three children at the Yorkshire school run by Stapleton (died during an epidemic) *

Sir Charles Baskerville (heart failure brought on by chronic anxiety and exertion from running away from the Hound of the Baskervilles)

Two Moor ponies (swallowed by the Grimpen Mire)

Dr Mortimer's spaniel (eaten by the Hound of the Baskervilles)

The Hound of the Baskervilles (shot to death by Sherlock Holmes and Dr Watson)

Jack Stapleton (alias Vandeleur, Rodger Baskerville Jnr) (swallowed by the Grimpen Mire)*

* These deaths are reported, rather than shown. Indeed, Fraser the tutor is only mentioned by Holmes in the final chapter, and the deaths of the three schoolchildren are related to us very briefly by Stapleton when he initially meets Watson. The deaths meted out to various Baskerville heirs are so vague as to be meaningless.

SUSTAINED BY BURNING INDIGNATION

Readers of HOUN on first publication would have read a chapter a month in the *Strand* magazine, starting in August 1901, concluding nine months later in May of 1902. Luckily, impatient readers could buy the first hardback edition of the book in March 1902 when it was published by George Newnes Ltd. 25,000 copies were printed in England, with a further 15,000 copies for India and the British Colonies later in April, and 70,000 for America. It cost six shillings, which in today's currency, if I've done my maths right (always doubtful) is 30p.[140] First Editions pop up for sale at starting prices of £3,000 – significantly out of my budget. But you never know, if I sell twenty thousand copies of this book, I might be able to surprise my wife one day with a HOUN First Edition. I'm sure she'll be thrilled.

---

[140] According to ChurchillCentral.com, "a pound was worth twenty shillings and each shilling was worth a dozen pennies. Today, a shilling from Churchill's England has the purchasing equivalent of 5 pence in the decimal currency system. Of course, this isn't reflective of the worth of rare coins." Obviously, I would have preferred a website dedicated to Victorian currency, but each one I tried was a nightmare to navigate, so I gave up. Effort is just not my thing.

Reading a chapter at a time over nine months was commonplace for the Victorians, but is decidedly uncommon in the twenty-first century, the age of Netflix boxsets. I started reading HOUN in September and now, in February, I have only one chapter left to enjoy. When I last read the novel, I did so across the full nine months, in the company of many other Sherlock Holmes fans across the globe. The instigator of this reading was the noted Sherlockian, Max Magee. In August 2019, Max set up an email mailing list and each month he would send out a scan of the original edition of the *Strand* featuring a chapter of *The Hound of the Baskervilles*. Recipients would then discuss various topics of interest arising from each instalment. My life is just a thrill-a-minute, isn't it?

I asked Max if we knew much about Doyle's writing habits when penning HOUN, and Max kindly sent me in the direction of the December 1924 edition of the *Strand* in which Sir Arthur has an article titled *How I Write My Books*. Here, ACD explains his working method:

> "As to my hours of work, when I am keen on a book, I am prepared to work all day, with an hour or two of walk or siesta in the afternoon. As I grow older, I lose some power of sustained effort, but I remember that I once did ten thousand words of *The Refugees*[141] in twenty-four hours. It was the part where the Grand Monarch was between his two mistresses and contains as sustained an effort as I have ever made. Twice I have written forty-thousand-word pamphlets in a week, but in each case, I was sustained by a burning indignation, which is the best of all driving power."

On top of that, Arty was a prolific letter writer – he'd correspond with several friends and colleagues every day and his letters were loooong. Clearly, the man was an unstoppable writing machine!

---

[141] *The Refugees: A Tale of Two Continents* is an historical novel set in seventeenth century France. It was published in 1893.

It occurred to me that my output might well see a substantial increase if I, like Sir Arthur, was to write always with burning indignation. My wife says I'm a grumpy old man, always railing at the world, but I think of myself as a quiet, placid type who doesn't like to cause a fuss. I don't have the energy for burning indignation, especially since I'm feeling a bit bloated from scoffing all that chicken and mushroom pie in the middle of the night: I have burning indigestion.

There is, however, one thing guaranteed to raise my hackles, and that is unfairness. Which brings me back to Sir Arthur, and to Bertram Fletcher Robinson.

HERE'S TO YOU, MR ROBINSON!

This book has so far given scant mention to poor Bertram Fletcher Robinson which is only fitting as he was practically erased from *The Hound of the Baskervilles* for decades. He is the ghost that haunts every single version of HOUN, and every word written about it. Recent years have seen renewed interest in him and the part he played in the creation of HOUN. It's nice to see him getting the credit he deserved because there is no doubt that, without Robinson, *The Hound of the Baskervilles* would never have been written.

The story goes that Robinson and Doyle met aboard *Briton*, a steamer ship returning to England from South Africa in July 1900. Robinson was the editor for *The Daily News*, as well as a close friend of P G Wodehouse,[142] who was, like every other notable person of the age, an acquaintance of Conan Doyle, *the* A-List Celeb of Victorian writers.

The two men met again in March 1901, in Cromer, Norfolk where they stayed at the Royal Links Hotel and played a few rounds of golf until the bloody English weather forced them indoors. Sitting by the fire, drinking brandies, the men got to discussing ghost stories and folklore. Inevitably, the talk turned to Black Shuck, then to Robinson's own

---

[142] Wodehouse and Fletcher Robinson collaborated on several short comedy plays.

knowledge of ghost dogs on Dartmoor, where he lived. Doyle was inspired and suggested that the two of them should write a novel together. Doyle began drafting straight away in his hotel room, then, in April, he joined Robinson in Dartmoor. Together they explored the Moor and were driven around by Robinson's coachman, named Harry Baskerville. Then the plan went awry, and Doyle completed the book on his own. Quite why Robinson did not join Doyle in the writing process is unknown. The original intent was for a full collaboration – we know this for a fact because Doyle wrote to his editor at the *Strand* about the idea and stated:

"I must do it with my friend Fletcher Robinson, and his name must appear with mine. I can answer for the yarn being all my own, my own style without dilution, since your readers like that. But he gave me the central idea and local colour and I feel his name must appear."

But Doyle would later state that every word of the novel was put down on paper by himself alone. Fletcher Robinson was credited only as a footnote in the *Strand*, then later as a thanks in the book.

It may well have been Sherlock Holmes who pushed Fletcher Robinson out of a full collaboration. Quite early in the writing process, Doyle realised he needed a detective to explain away the ghost dog as something explicable and, since he'd already created arguably the most famous detective of all, he simply resurrected Holmes for the book and set the adventure years before the detective's supposedly fatal tumble from the Reichenbach Falls. Fletcher Robinson, who had nothing whatsoever to do with Sherlock Holmes, was therefore surplus to requirements. Ultimately, no man matches up to Holmes.

Another reason for Holmes's inclusion in the book was to cash in on the success of the smash-hit stage play *Sherlock Holmes*,[143] written by and starring the American actor William Gillette. Doyle had written a

---

[143] Gillette was in his mid-30s when he wrote and starred in *Sherlock Holmes* and 79 when he gave up the part in 1929, after 1,300 performances. A silent film was made of the play in 1916 and lost for just under a century; quite wonderfully, prints were discovered in France in 2014.

Sherlock Holmes play himself, but Gillette had completely rewritten it[144] and, after a 'triumphant opening' in New York and an 'instant success' at the Garrick Theatre on Broadway, he had taken it on tour across America, to packed houses and critical acclaim. The play was scheduled to be produced at the Lyceum Theatre[145] in London (after a run in Liverpool) in the autumn of 1901, and Doyle no doubt understood that this would lead to renewed interest in Sherlock Holmes. None of this had anything to do with Fletcher Robinson who seemed to have been quietly pushed aside. ACD had a new Holmes story and no need for BFR. Them's the breaks.

In 1903, when he was back full-time writing Sherlock Holmes stories for absolute mountains of cash, Doyle used another winning Fletcher Robinson idea – involving a mysteriously appearing bloody thumbprint at a murder scene - for part of *The Adventure of the Norwood Builder*, one of the stronger stories from *The Return of Sherlock Holmes*.

Robinson died tragically young, at 36, from typhoid and peritonitis. A strange occult theory soon surfaced that poor Robinson had died because of a Mummy's Curse[146] – specifically a mummy-board which was donated to the British Museum in July 1889. Dating to Thebes in the late 21st/early 22nd Dynasty, the mummy-board is a wooden inner coffin lid, painted with the mummified body of a woman, possibly from the temple of Amen-ra, King of the Gods. Robinson had extensively researched the mummy-board for an article he wrote for (but which was mysteriously never published in) *The Daily Express* in 1904. Like Sir Charles Baskerville, Robinson became convinced that a curse was hanging over

---

[144] During the rewrite process, Gillette telegraphed Doyle: "May I marry Holmes?" Doyle responded: "You may marry him, or murder or do what you like with him."

[145] Managed by *Dracula* author Bram Stoker, yet another of ACD's acquaintances. He palled around with some famous chums, Sir Arthur did. I'm jealous. Why aren't any of my friends noted writers of gothic romances? Bah!

[146] This curse was also, at one time, thought to have been responsible for the sinking of *The Titanic*, which is nonsense of course... Unless a mummy was hiding in the iceberg. Ice Mummies from the Deep!

him and that it would lead to his untimely death. Three years later, he was dead, the poor sod.

Sir Arthur wrote that Robinson's death "was caused by Egyptian 'elementals' guarding a female mummy, because Mr Robinson had begun an investigation of the stories of the mummy's malevolence. The immediate cause of death was typhoid fever, but that is the way in which the elementals guarding the mummy might act." All very peculiar and fascinating. These days, you simply don't get enough Egyptian Mummy Curses bumping off *Daily Express* journalists, more's the pity.

As I sit here munching on toast and (Robinson's) strawberry jam, hoping I don't get more burning indigestion, I'm looking at a photo of Bertram. He looks to be a serious man with a serious moustache, a man who'd walk the moor without fear. I salute him, for without him there would be no *Hound of the Baskervilles*, and I would not be writing this book. Though I probably *would* be munching on toast with strawberry jam and worrying about indigestion.

CHAPTER FIFTEEN

Let Sleeping Dogs Lie

February 2021

HERE COMES THE SUN

THE OTHER MORNING, I wandered lonely, thinking of HOUN, and saw bright yellow daffodils in bloom. I felt like William Wordsworth having a bliss trip in the Lake District.

Birds are singing loudly in the mornings now, as dawn brings warmth. The days are warmer, brighter, longer. Winter is retreating and spring is coming, and a zing of optimism is in the air. Lockdown will be over before spring turns to summer, and my vaccination appointment is drawing near.

I am sleeping more soundly, with no nightmares. I even chat to my neighbour over the fence and ask him about his dog,[147] I have the sense of change in the air, of dark clouds parting, of sunlight. It's been a long cold lonely winter.

---

[147] He denies ever having a dog or, indeed, being my neighbour. Hmm. I may have mistaken a complete stranger for my neighbour. I think that's what I did – I mistook a complete stranger for my next-door neighbour.

The final chapter of HOUN is essentially one long monologue from Holmes as he explains what the book was actually all about. He has already moved on to two important cases (one in France) and explains that Baskerville is but a hazy memory for him now, before going into forensic detail on every single aspect of the case. What a guy!

We learn that Stapleton bought the Hound from Ross and Mangles, the dealers in Fulham Road. I was disappointed to learn this shop is fictitious as I would have loved to have shopped there, particularly if they were holding a sale. Holmes surmises that Stapleton took the Hound home on a train on the North Devon line, then walked it miles across the moor so that no one would see them. I hope master and dog bonded during the journey. I hope the Hound had some small happiness in its life. Remember, there are no bad dogs, only bad owners.

Stapleton, of course, isn't really called Stapleton. He's the son of Rodger Baskerville. His real name is probably Redginald Baskerville, or Rudpert Baskerville or Ridchard Baskerville. What is it with these Baskerville boys and their unnecessary 'D's? Reader, have you ever known a Rodger with a 'D'?[148] Of all the wretched villainy on display in HOUN, the extra D in Rodger is to me the most egregious.

Beryl's real name was Beryl Garcia, apparently, which strikes me as odd. Were there many nineteenth/early twentieth century South American women named Beryl? I'd be fascinated to know.[149] Holmes says that Beryl has been helping him with the details of the case, so it would seem the young woman is recovering from her ordeal, for which I'm glad.

We learn nothing more of Laura Lyons, though, who had been so cruelly used by Stapleton. Perhaps Dr Watson could return to Coombe

---

[148] There's at least one other character named Rodger in the Sherlock Holmes Cannon: Rodger Presbury, in the *Adventure of the Three Garidebs*. This Rodger, like his namesake, is a rotten sort.

[149] There's no footnote regarding Beryl's name in the Leslie Klinger annotated HOUN, nor in my trusty Oxford Press edition. I invite Sherlockians to email me their thoughts, should they have any.

Tracey with a bunch of flowers and a much less aggressive attitude. Perhaps he could work his considerable Dr Watson charm, and perhaps Laura Lyons could become the second Mrs Dr Watson? Or is it the third? Wedding bells at Baskerville Hall, a spring wedding, and a happy ending all round. The newlyweds could even buy a big dog and name him Roger Moor[150].

---

[150] Sorry.

It's Health & Safety Gone Mad

The Hound of the Baskervilles[151] starring Nikolay Volkov (Russian TV serial, 1971)

For my penultimate pick from the DoD, I have a 50/50 chance of either the Russian TV thing from 1971 or the Richard Roxburgh BBC thing from the early aughties. Drumroll please....

Break out the vodka, we're back to Russia! This, then, is my final black and white version, my final serialised version, and my final foreign language version. I'm a little sad. I'll miss these strange Hounds from long ago and far away. They're like old fairy tales, told in a visual grammar that has lost none of its charm.

Beginning and ending with Dr Watson narrating to the camera, featuring an amusingly cheap sequence where Holmes and Watson look out of the window at Baker Street to observe Sir Henry being followed along a London Street and describe the action to the viewer like they're presenting *Jackanory*[152] (also, the Northumberland Hotel is basically just a room with lots of curtains), this two-part Russian television play is otherwise well staged and remarkably faithful to the novel. Dr Mortimer even gets to spend a few minutes groping Holmes's skull.

There are some lovely Sherlockian touches – Watson writing the telegram Holmes is dictating to him on his shirt cuff, Holmes stabbing a letter to the wall (though it takes the actor[153] two goes!) and effective, creepy

---

[151] *Sobaka Baskerviley* is the English translation; *Собака Баскервилей* is the Russian title.

[152] British kids TV show which featured celebrities narrating children's books.

[153] Actor Nikolay Volkov who is very good in the role, also played Holmes in Russian TV versions of *A Study in Scarlet* and *A Scandal in Bohemia*. He resembles a rather chubby Frank Langella. I couldn't find out much about Volkov except that, as Sherlock Holmes, he carries a Nagrant M 1895 pistol; this scintillating fact is courtesy of the Internet Movie Firearms Database. Did you know there is an Internet Movie Firearms Database? Well, now you do. I spent hours searching through all the actors who have played Sherlock Holmes to find out what weapons they used on screen and, because I am me, I forgot to write anything down, so it was a complete waste of time. I even had

night photography. But, aside from Stapleton looking alarmingly like David Lynch, only two things leapt out at me:

1) The first part is so slow it appears to be happening in real time. It takes Holmes and Watson over ten minutes to examine and discuss Dr Mortimer's walking stick. The reading of the Curse of the Baskervilles goes on for at least another twenty minutes. Imagine a version of HOUN in real time – the story takes place over weeks (months, if we start at the death of Sir Charles, centuries, if we start with the Hound doing in wicked Sir Hugo). I would actually love to see a weeks' long adaptation of the book with a live feed from Baskerville Hall. Sort of a *Big Brother Baskerville*: "Day nineteen in the Big Brother Baskerville Hall, and Dr Watson is talking to Laura in the garden..."

2) This version of HOUN made me more anxious than any other version because what's depicted on screen is a friggin' health and safety nightmare. The floors of Baskerville Hall are decked with large square tiles that are so loose, I'm amazed Barrymore doesn't trip on them as he's creeping around at night with a lit candle. And everywhere in the hall are antlers, lying on the ground or hanging from the walls. Razor sharp antlers, just waiting for Watson to fall onto them and have his face gashed open or for Sir Henry to drunkenly impale himself on them after a night at the local Coombe Tracey boozer. Stapleton needn't bother with the Hound – he simply has to get Sir Henry plastered and let the lethal décor of Baskerville Hall do all the murdering for him.

This reckless disregard for safety extends to Dr Watson's actions, sadly, for he has taken to sleeping with a loaded pistol in his hand[154] and

---

to go back to the site to write this entry, and even then, I forgot to write down the make of gun and had to go back *again*.

[154] The Internet Movie Firearms Database let me down here, for they don't have an entry for Dr Watson's (Lev Krugly) pistol. I'm going to guess it's an unspecified Service Revolver as that's the gun from the original stories. Who knows? Maybe someone can update the IMFDB and email me when it's done. But by then, I'll almost certainly have forgotten all about this subject and I'll just assume the email has been sent to me by mistake. Up to you.

chain-smoking cigars! I wondered if, at some point, we'd cut to Baker Street to see Sherlock Holmes shooting up cocaine while he's investigating the most celebrated case of his career, but no production team, even one as lackadaisical with H&S rulings as this reckless Russian TV crew, would be idiotic enough to ever do that, surely?

CHOOSE THE HOUND OF THE BASKERVILLES

The Hound of the Baskervilles starring Richard Roxburgh (BBC TV movie, 2002)

It is a Saturday night in late February and I am excited. This is unusual because I'm rarely excited, particularly not during the month of February. I am excited because tonight is the night that my journey comes to an end – the final pick from the Deerstalker of Doom! Hooray! I feel there should be cake and bunting and a marching band playing *Who Let The Dogs Out?* But there isn't, there's just me, my very patient wife and Chinese takeaway. Attentive readers will have already guessed which lonely Hound lurks in the depths of my hat (not least because it's spelled out above this paragraph) and I have to say that I'm rather pleased with which one it is because it means that fate has decreed that my HOUN binge is bookended by two BBC versions! That's a satisfying bit of symmetry. Who says there isn't a God?

The Hound of the Baskervilles, starring Richard Roxburgh, has taken rather a battering from Sherlockians over the near-enough two decades since it was first broadcast, but I think a lot of the criticism is unfair. I can remember enjoying it back on Boxing Day, 2002, and being surprised at the vitriolic reaction it received on online message boards such as Scarlet Street. Am I out of step with received Sherlockian opinion? Am I a bit of a rebel? A man who walks on his own? Like a drifter born to walk alone. A man who's made up his mind, who ain't wastin' no more time. A man who'll walk along this lonely street of dreams.

I was delighted to have the very pleasant company of my wife for this momentous viewing. She has, thus far, steadfastly avoided joining me in watching black and white silent German films and Chip n' Dale Rescue Rangers, but she very graciously agreed to watch Richard Roxburgh with me, on the understanding that this is the last ever version of HOUN that I'll watch. She is pleased that this madness will very soon be over and amused by the idea of anybody on Earth being remotely interested in buying a copy of this book. I'm hoping to prove her wrong by this book becoming a surprise best seller. Then buying her a holiday. To the Reichenbach Falls.

We were living together with two young children (five and three) back in 2002. My mum had died about six years earlier, so my dad was staying with us for a few days over Christmas. He liked to drink in the afternoons, come home to snooze, then watch TV with us in the evenings. I wish now that I knew him better and that I loved him more. My mum was a sweetheart and easy to love, while my dad was a difficult man and I have always felt a disconnect from him. Watching Richard Roxburgh race across the moor I feel an ache, a longing for my parents, long since gone from my life. I look across to my wife and she squeezes my hand, and I am glad of the comfort. But then she squeezes harder and nods at her wine glass and I understand that she wants me to pour her another glass.

This version of HOUN begins brilliantly, perhaps better than any other version, with a strikingly directed and edited sequence that depicts the inquest into the death of Sir Charles, intercut with flashbacks to him walking to his doom, and a second flashback to Selden escaping from prison and being chased across the moor. Muddy, brutal, exciting and clever, this is the perfect way to grab the viewer's attention. The rain-lashed moor has never looked more bleak, desolate and forbidding. You wouldn't want to be there.

"We've been there," says my wife.

231

"Well, no, actually we haven't, as this was filmed in Yorkshire," I inform her.

Nothing else in the film matches the thrilling opening – aside from a very brief jump-scare as the Hound appears suddenly at the window during a séance – but the production is roundly good, with extensive location filming and interesting cinematography. There are numerous changes to Doyle's work, the best of which being a secret passageway in Baskerville Hall, and the worst of which – a needless change to Stapleton's motive.

There's an excellent Dr Mortimer (John Nettles in straggly long hair and beard), Beryl Stapleton (Neve McIntosh) and Stapleton (Richard E Grant at his most scenery-chewing). There's a Christmas party (with a scary Father Christmas and costumed Hound), as well as a scene of Watson performing an autopsy – all good stuff.

But my impression of this version is of hostility. Everybody seems to be on edge and aggressive. Sir Henry grabs Barrymore, Holmes grabs a cabbie, Watson grabs Beryl, Selden grabs Sir Henry, Holmes grabs Watson ("Take your hands off me!" hisses Watson). Watson punches Stapleton, Stapleton decks Lestrade and shoots Watson... It's a feast of teeth-gritted, lapel grabbing testosterone.

The relationship between Holmes and Watson is very odd indeed – these men don't seem to like each other at all, with Watson openly telling Holmes that he doesn't trust him.

"I don't like this Watson," says my wife. And I share her opinion. I like the actor, Ian Hart, very much and I'm aware he's striving to bring something new to an old character, but I think it's a fatal mistake to rob Holmes and Watson of their deep respect and friendship. Watson, in particular, is symbolic of compassion and courage and the best of men; without those qualities, the cold moor has no sanctuary, and *The Hound of the Baskervilles* has no heart. I do love how rock hard he is, though – having been shot in the shoulder, he still manages to get up, find a path along the moor to Holmes, and rescue his imperilled detective chum from the Grimpen Mire with nothing more than his well-tailored jacket and his goddam macho determination, goddamit.

The most controversial aspect of this film is the drug use. Ten minutes into the film, having just been commissioned to investigate what will become the defining case of his career, Richard Roxburgh's Sherlock Holmes gets out his drugs kit, wraps a tube around his arm, fills his syringe with a seven-per-cent solution of cocaine, and shoots up. He does it again near the denouement, upstairs at Baskerville Hall, on Christmas Eve. I half expected him to do it a third time as he's struggling for his life in the Grimpen Mire. And again over the end credits, accompanied by Iggy Pop's *Lust for Life*. Choose Life. Choose a job. Choose a consulting detective agency. Choose a family curse. Choose the footprints of a gigantic hound, choose hansom cabs, telegrams, and tinned crab meat. Choose Baker Street, Baskerville Hall, and The Reichenbach Falls. Choose to cross the moor when the powers of evil are exalted. Choose anonymous threatening letters. Choose Bertram Fletcher Robinson. Choose Lestrade and Scotland Yard. Choose a Deerstalker Hat and an Inverness Cape. Choose life...

But why would I want to do a thing like that? I chose not to choose life. I chose somethin' else. And the reasons? There are no reasons. Who needs reasons when you've got Holmes?

It 'Aint Over Till The Big Dog Howls

My 2020/2021 HOUN odyssey is over. I have read all the books, played the games, heard all the audio versions, and watched (near enough) all the film versions, TV versions, cartoon pastiches and YouTube oddities. On my TV screen, twenty Sherlock Holmes's have unloaded 120 bullets into twenty hellhounds. Close to two dozen hounds have ripped out the throats of Sir Hugos. A Charing Cross Hospital ward worth of forgetful Dr Mortimer's have left walking sticks behind at Baker Street, and a (Fifth Northumberland Fusiliers) platoon of Dr Watsons have choked on smoke-filled rooms of noxious pipe tobacco. Jack Stapleton has failed in his dastardly plan, no matter what medium he's tried it out in, making him literature's most inept villain. I raise a glass to him.

This marathon has brought poor Beryl Stapleton to life for me more so than any other character. All the women in *The Hound of the Baskervilles* have a rough go of things, but none more than Beryl who has been abused for decades. It's upsetting to think of the cruelty inflicted on her by the loathsome Stapleton and I wish nothing but happiness for her now that she is free of him. I've read many sequels to HOUN, but I think if I were ever to write one myself, it would place Beryl at the centre of the narrative, making her the protagonist of a sweet and charming little mystery.

I've also been struck yet again by the excellence of Sir Arthur's prose. I don't believe the man ever put pen to a clumsy sentence. HOUN sees him at his best. The book is by far the best written, most evocative and gripping of the Holmes Canon and, for me, stands as a high watermark in Conan Doyle's career and, indeed, in English literature. Quite frankly, the popular novel doesn't get any better than this.

The end of my journey also brings relief from the dreams and nightmares I've been having. In my dream state, I often felt like Sir Charles Baskerville, having lived with fear for many weeks, running for his life on the moor as the Curse of the Baskervilles reaches out through demonic agencies to take his life. Though in my case, it was the Wind of the Stadons blowing through the palm trees of my mind, while the demonic agents are a bunch of mad and grumpy cats rather than phantom hell hounds. I am glad that my sleep is troubled no more.

The end brings with it farewells. Soon I will stop receiving emails from Amazon.co.uk, recommending me books on Dartmoor and the life of William Shatner. My doormat will no longer be thudded with morning deliveries of German silent film Blu-ray discs. My YouTube feed will cease being all about ASMR detectives who will put you to tingly sleep. My life will be Baskerville free. I'm sure I'm going to miss it. I look forward to reading it again next year, sat in my garden, scoffing tinned crab meat with the cats, and admiring my growing palm tree. Though, I keep wondering if I should perhaps convince my wife we should move to Dartmoor, get a dog, live out our dotage crossing the moor on Tuesdays, when the forces of evil (i.e; the rock band The Darkness) are exalted.

It is time, then, to hang up my Deerstalker of Doom, put my Oxford Press edition of HOUN back on the shelf and bid adieu to Sherlock Holmes and *The Hound of the Baskervilles*.

DAMN LIES AND STATISTICS

Some statistics, then. Everyone loves a good statistic – or at least 80% of the adult population do, according to something I read once. My stats are as follows:

I have watched twenty screen adaptations, which is approximately 40 hours of Hound on Moor action. I've listened to six full cast audio adaptations and six spoken word readings of the novel. I've watched five documentaries, five cartoons and three kids' shows. I've heard two prog rock albums and attended a production of a stage play, all of which adds a further twenty hours, bringing my total to 60 hours. I've played a computer game (total six hours play) and completed a 1000-piece jigsaw puzzle. I have read twenty-two books about *The Hound of the Baskervilles* – that's over a million words. I estimate I've spent roughly £650, mostly on cat treats, alcohol bribes, and out-of-print books. My Hound Days lasted twenty-eight weeks or 196 days.

In my HOUN marathon, Sherlock Holmes has been played by twenty actors, mostly English, but also including three Germans, two Canadians, two Russians, two Americans, one Italian, and one dog. The oldest actor to play Holmes in a HOUN adaptation was genial old Arthur Wotner, at sixty-two; the youngest was Bruno Güttner, at a sprightly, jazzy twenty-eight. The average age works out to be forty-three – eight years older than the character in the book.[155] Two Dr Whos have played Sherlock Holmes,[156] and one *Star Trek* Captain has played Stapleton. One actor (Denholm Elliot) played two Dr Mortimers. Shamefully, only one POC has played Costa Rican Beryl Stapleton.

The average length of Dr Watson's moustache is four inches, though several Watsons were clean shaven (including Dudley Moore, Martin Freeman and Lucy Liu – coincidentally the three shortest Watsons).

No Sir Henrys were played by Canadians, by thunder!

The Hound has been played by an assortment of breeds including Mastiff and Alsatian, though by far the most popular breed cast as the Hound is the Great Dane. Blitzen, the Great Dane dog actor in the Rathbone '39 film, went under the alias 'chief' – mainly because German named dogs weren't getting much work during the war. Four HOUN adaptations were partly filmed on Dartmoor and one production – the Stewart Granger US TV film - used old sets from the Bela Lugosi *Dracula* for the Baskerville Hall interior.

There you go, some nice, useless stats. I did think to count lightning strikes and thunderclaps in every version, but I forgot about it somewhere along the line, by thunder!

---

[155] HOUN is set in 1889 (we know this because of the inscription on Dr Mortimer's stick), and Holmes was born in 1854 - we know this because Holmes is sixty in 1914, according to *His Last Bow*.

[156] Three, if you count Nicholas Briggs from Big Finish, who played Dr Who in an audio drama series and lent his likeness to a sorta Dr Who in a comic strip in *Dr Who Magazine*.

WORD COUNT

As I write this, I occasionally look up at my wall to see the poster of my play, *Sherlock Holmes and the Adventure of the Devil's Whisper*, which pits Holmes, Watson and the *Dracula* author Bram Stoker against a villainess from the Hermetic Order of the Golden Dawn who scathingly critiques Dr Watson's prose, a cab driver with exacting standards of pedantry, and a much-in-demand housemaid with remarkable cleaning powers. I'd written it mainly because I'd hugely enjoyed a book called *Sherlock Holmes vs Dracula* by Loren D. Estlemen, but I had come away a little irked that Holmes had bought wholesale into the idea of vampires – something he would never do, no matter how high he got on coke. Hence, I had the detective rip Stoker's fantasy to shreds in my silly play. I'd always felt a little guilty about doing it, though, as if I were bringing the snark undeservedly to Stoker.

My gaze falls upon my bookshelf of *Dracula* books. It's been a while since I read the novel. I hear that there is a new big screen *Dracula* film in production, due to hit cinemas exactly a century after the release of *Nosferatu* (1922), the remarkable first *Dracula* film. As always when a new version is released into the wilds, I wonder if I might watch all the other films in preparation. And then I remember the bat that had flown overhead on New Year's Eve. Surely that was a sign? Surely I should start looking at flights to Transylvania...

Thunder booms and lightning flashes the sky. In the eerie silence that follows, the temperature drops. My room gets very cold and I shiver.

From far away in the distance comes a long, low moan, indescribably sad. It fills the whole air and yet, it is impossible to say whence it came. From a dull murmur, it swells into a melancholy, throbbing moan once again.

"The bitterns are back, then," says my wife, pouring two glasses of wine.

SHERLOCK HOLMES ACTORS & THEIR DOG DOPPELGANGERS

GREYHOUND

BASIL RATHBONE

BEAGLE

PETER CUSHING

FIELD SPANIEL

BENEDICT CUMBERBATCH

PHAROH HOUND

JEREMY BRETT

WELSH TERRIER

JONNY LEE MILLER

BULL MASTIFF

TOM BAKER

JACK RUSSELL TERRIER

WISHBONE

An Exhaustive List of The Hound of the Baskervilles Across Media

(Or At Least All the Ones I Binged for This Book)

* Indicates I've included it in this book

* * Indicates a copy exists but I couldn't source one in time

* * * Indicates no copy is known to exist at time of publication

The Hound of the Baskervilles (novel by Sir Arthur Conan Doyle, 1902) *

Der Hund von Baskerville - Alwin Neuss (silent film serial, 1914-1920) *

Das dunkle Schloß - Eugen Burg (silent film, 1920) * * *

The Hound of the Baskervilles - Eille Norwood (silent film, 1921) * *

Der Hund von Baskerville - Carlyle Blackwell Snr (silent film, 1929) *

The Hound of the Baskervilles - Robert Rendel (B&W film, 1931) * *

Der Hund von Baskerville - Bruno Güttner (B&W film, 1937) *

Silver Blaze (Murder at the Baskervilles) - Arthur Wotner (B&W film, 1937) *

The Jack Benny Program / Episode ? / *The Hound of the Baskervilles* - Jack Benny (comedy radio skit, 1939) *

The Hound of the Baskervilles - Basil Rathbone (B&W film, 1939) *

Jighansa - Sishir Batabyal (B&W film, 1951) *

Der Hund von Baskerville - Wolf Ackva (TV movie, 1955) * * *

The Hound of the Baskervilles – Carlton Hobbs (BBC full-cast audio drama, 1957) *

The Hound of the Baskervilles - Peter Cushing (technicolour film, 1959) *

Bees Saal Baad - Sajjan (Technicolour film musical, 1961) * *

Sir Arthur Conan Doyle's Sherlock Holmes - Peter Cushing / Season 2, Episodes 4&5 / *The Hound of the Baskervilles* (BBC TV serial, 1968) *

L'Ultimo dei Baskerville - Nando Gazzolo (TV serial, 1968)

The Hound of the Baskervilles - Nikolay Volkov (TV movie, 1971) *

The Hound of the Baskervilles - Stewart Granger (TV movie, 1972) *

The Hound of the Baskervilles – Kevin McCarthy (CBS full cast audio drama, 1977) *

The Hound of the Baskervilles - Peter Cook (comedy film, 1978) *

The Adventures of Sherlock Holmes and Dr Watson - Vasily

Livanov / Season 1, Episodes 6 & 7 / *The Hound of the Baskervilles* (TV movie, 1981) *

The Hound of the Baskervilles - Tom Baker (six-part TV drama, 1982) *

The New Scooby and Scrappy-Doo Show / Season 1, Episode 3 / *The Hound of the Scoobyvilles* (TV kids cartoon pastiche, 1983) *

The Hound of the Baskervilles - Ian Richardson (TV movie, 1983) *

Sherlock Holmes and the Baskerville Curse - Peter O'Toole (TV Movie, animated, 1983) *

The Hound of the Baskervilles - Jeremy Brett (TV movie, 1984) *

The Hound of the Baskervilles – Nicol Williamson (full cast audio drama, 1984) * *

On the Scent of the Baskerville Hound (TV documentary, 1989) *

Chip 'n Dale Rescue Rangers / Season 1, Episode 8 / *Pound of the Baskervilles* (TV kids cartoon, 1989) *

Garfield and Friends / Season 3, Episode 9a / *The Hound of the Arbuckles* (TV kids cartoon pastiche, 1990) *

The Hound of the Baskervilles – Clive Merrison (full cast audio drama, 1993) *

The Hound of the Baskervilles – Edward Petherbridge (full cast audio drama, 1993) * *

Droopy, Master Detective / Season 1, Episode 6C / *Sherlock Droopy Gets Hounded* (Kids cartoon, 1993) *

241

Wishbone / Season 1, Episode 8 / *The Slobbery Hound* (TV kids show, 1995) *

Nightmare: Birth of Horror / Series 1, Episode 4 / *The Hound of the Baskervilles* (TV documentary, 1996) *

The Hound of the Baskervilles According to Spike Milligan (comedy novel, 1997) *

The Moor (mystery novel by Laurie R King, 1998) *

Bobaka Saskerviley: The Bound of the Haskervilles (TV parody film, 1998) **

Sherlock Holmes in the 22nd Century - Jason Gray Stanford / Episode 4 / *The Hounds of the Baskervilles* (TV animated series, 1999) *

The Hound of the Baskervilles - Matt Frewer (TV movie, 2000) *

George Shrinks / Season 2, Episode 13 / *The Hound of the Bath-Ervilles* (TV kids cartoon, 2001) *

West Country Tales: Dartmoor, Devil Dogs and Conan Doyle (TV documentary, 2001) *

The Hound of the Baskervilles - Richard Roxburgh (BBC TV movie, 2002) *

Great Books - *The Hound of the Baskervilles* (TV documentary, 2002) **

The Hound of the Baskervilles (Prog Rock concept album by Clive Nolan and Oliver Wakeman, 2002) *

The New Annotated Sherlock Holmes / Volume 3 - The Novels: *The Hound of the Baskervilles* (annotated version of the novel by Leslie S Klinger) *

The Hound of the Baskervilles - Javier Marzan (comedy stage production, 2007) *

Sherlock Holmes was Wrong: Re-opening the Case of the Hound of the Baskervilles (non-fiction book by Pierre Bayard, 2008) *

Sherlock Holmes and the Hound of the Baskervilles (PC adventure game, 2010) *

Selden (Short film pastiche, 2010) *

Professor Moriarty: The Hound of the D'urbervilles (pastiche novel by Kim Newman, 2011) *

The Baskerville Legacy (Pastiche novel by John O'Connell, 2011)

The Watson Files / Season 2, Episode 1 / *The Hound of the Baskervilles* (amateur full-cast audio pastiche) *

Mark of the Baskerville Hound (pastiche novel by Wilfred Hueffel, 2011) *

The Hound of the Baskervilles – Nicholas Briggs (full-cast audio drama, 2011)

Sherlock - Benedict Cumberbatch / Season 2, Episode 2 / *The Hounds of Baskerville* (TV series, 2012) *

Hounds of the Baskervilles: From Devil Dogs to Sherlock Holmes (collected essays and stories, edited by Timothy Green Beckley and William Kern, 2012) *

Deadtime Stories / Episode 5 / *The Beast of Baskerville* (US Kids TV drama, 2013) *

The Hound of the Baskervilles - Seamus Dever (full-cast audio drama, 2014) *

Castle Secrets & Legends / Season 1, Episode 3 / *The Hound of the Baskervilles* (TV documentary, 2014)

The Hound of the Baskervilles (Prog Rock concept album by

Looking-Glass Lantern, 2014) *

Baskerville - A Sherlock Holmes Mystery (Stageplay by Ken Ludwig, 2015) *

Elementary - Johnny Lee Miller /Season 4, Episode 16 / *Hounded* (TV episode, 2016) *

The Hounding of Peers Baskerville (pastiche novel by Orlando Pearson, 2017)

Warlock Holmes – The Hell-Hound of the Baskervilles (pastiche novel by G S Denning, 2017)

Sherlock Holmes and the Beast of the Stapletons (pastiche novel by James Lovegrove)

Sherlock Holmes and the Hound of the Baskervilles (Lego YouTube adaptation, 2020)

APPENDIX TWO

Glow-in-the-Dark Stuffed Bunnies

Sherlock: Hounds of Baskerville Tweetalong

The participants are: Robin Bailes (@DarkCorners3); Kyle Borcz (@KyleBorcz); Morton Duffy (@Morton100); James Leech (jamesdleech); Julio Angel Ortiz (@jaowriter); Fazia Rizvi (@faziarizvi); Kev F Sutherland (@KevFComicArtist); Kim Woo (@gelfling1220)

@VinceStadon #FootprintsOfAGiganticHound Here we go - the game's afoot! (I've already scoffed my cake. No will power!)

@DarkCorners3 #FootprintsOfAGiganticHound Where do I get my cake?

@jaowriter I'm catching the episode on NETFLIX. I love the TV-14 Warning that pops up: "Substances, language, smoking." If Holmes isn't doing an 8-Ball by the end of this episode, I will consider this entire episode a failure.

@faziarizvi Fair warning - I'm about to live tweet an episode of BBC's *Sherlock* for #FootprintsOfAGiganticHound. I had pimento cheese sandwiches and watermelon instead of cake, Vince. Forgive me.

@KyleBorcz Bourbon: check, #Sherlock Series 2 blu-Ray: check. Let's do this.

@faziarizvi I grew up reading the original stories. But I'm an American, and it's been *mumble-mumble* years... I didn't remember them very well. When I first saw this modernized version of the character, I was delighted to see things I did remember.

@gelfling1220 The cake is probably long since gone, but I'm sure there's still plenty of tea left, right? #Hotbeverage

@VinceStadon Great opening - very effective. And that looks like the real Dartmoor. And a real Basset Hound.

@gelfling1220 Moody opening. I don't know - the Hound actually looked pretty cute? (Puppy!)

@jamesdleech HOUN usually starts with a walking stick; certainly an attention grabber to switch it for the harpoon from *The Adventure of Black Peter*

@KyleBorcz Great entrance by Benedict Cumberbatch

@jaowriter Can you imagine if a PoC tried to take public transportation all covered in blood? Do you they they'd even make it 10 feet? But Holmes can do it... Four tweets in and I'm already bringing in current events. Vince, it's not too late to stop me.

@VinceStadon Cumberbatch is a very shouty Holmes. It's a very big performance.

@jaowriter Sherlock doesn't have time for your bullshit. Or idle chit-chat.

@jamesdleech nods to Holmes' drug habit: we're led to believe that "I need some" refers to that, it turns out to be cigarettes. Then a clunky ref to wanting something "7% stronger": a nod to Meyer's *The Seven-Per-Cent Solution*, which made it a full-blown addiction.

@faziarizvi Loved Holmes's reaction to the iconic cap. I also liked the subtle shift of the aspects of Holmes's addition to trying to give up cigarettes (even though the hard stuff is still present in the series).

@jamesdleech Holmes is certainly more abrasive than in other portrayals, and it's all about context. He calls Watson's mind "placid, barely used". There are similar lines in other versions, but here it's a response to Watson asking him to show Mrs Hudson empathy

@VinceStadon Una Stubbs is a brilliant Mrs Hudson. And never once does she ask Holmes to 'give us a clue'.

@gelfling1220 Mrs Hudson is seriously the best.

@VinceStadon This 'Holmes is bored and needs a case' scene is reminiscent of *The Private Life of Sherlock Holmes*, complete with seemingly small and silly case request turning out later to be connected. The *Cluedo* joke is great, though.

@gelfling1220 I very much would like a webisode showing the *Cluedo* incident. I also wonder who else they roped into playing.

@KyleBorcz Martin Freeman gets paid the big bucks to be one of the best reactors on television.

@Morton100 Having watched the series for fun and research you reach the point of knowing some of the lines. My favourite is the doorbell rings, fingers point and in unison Holmes, Watson and an unknowable number of us all say "Client!"

@VinceStadon It's disconcerting not to have Dr Mortimer and the walking stick and the manuscript and so on.

@KyleBorcz Well, they skip over Mortimer bringing the case and go right to Henry.

@jamesdleech Russell Tovey, the werewolf from *Being Human*, as the character haunted by the hound of Baskerville. nice touch.

@VinceStadon Russell Tovey's ears are by far the most terrifying thing in any adaptation of *The Hound of the Baskervilles*.

@gelfling1220 Russell Tovey was a fascinating choice for this - I can't help but wonder if he was chosen as a winky nod to George Sands, his werewolf in *Being Human*

@KevFComicArtist Find myself v bad at tweeting while watching a TV show. But Russell Tovey's accent deserves some comment.

@VinceStadon Fun bit with Holmes showing off deductions - Cumberbatch is at his best in scenes like these, where Holmes is just bursting for applause.

@jaowriter Having never read the source material but watched (and enjoyed) the Robert Downey Jr. films. I'm guessing the trope of Holmes noticing all the tiniest details is prevalent in the books? I like how Mark Gatiss' script modernizes this & applies humor.

@VinceStadon Replying to **@jaowriter:** Yes, that's very much Holmes's superpower - "the observation of trifles" from which he can form a hypothesis. A bit like noticing your wife has had her hair done, and reasoning that it's your anniversary and you'd better nip out quick to buy some flowers (not that this has ever happened to me!).

@gelfling1220 I love the breakfast deduction.

@jamesdleech The analysis of Henry's morning on the train, and Watson's exasperation at it, is much more like it.

@jaowriter "If I wanted poetry I'd read John's emails to his girlfriend. Much funnier..." SHERLOCK IS A SAVAGE.

@VinceStadon Martin Freeman sighs. Let's count them.

@jaowriter Annnnnnnnnd #FootprintsOfAGiganticHound has been called!

@gelfling1220 "Say that again" "Mr Holmes, they were the #FootprintsOfAGiganticHound" He said the thing!

@KyleBorcz There's the line! My favorite line from when I played Mortimer (and 16 others) in Ken Ludwig's *Baskerville* in 2018! Perfect for the hashtag: #FootprintsOfAGiganticHound

@jamesdleech They introduce the notion of Holmes pretending not to go to Dartmoor, only to then discard it. Not sure of the logic there, other than subversion of the original story for the sake of it?

@VinceStadon Replying to **@jamesdleech**: All it needs is The Clash's *Should I Stay or Should I Go?*

@gelfling1220 Sherlock's back and forth about whether or not he's going to Dartmoor was needlessly confusing.

@DarkCorners3 Dispensing of Holmes for half the book was a stroke of brilliance by Conan Doyle. And it's a shame this version didn't have the sense to stick to it.

@VinceStadon Holmes is driving the land rover because Martin Freeman can't drive. That's my one and only piece of #*Sherlock* trivia.

@KevFComicArtist The music while they're in the car sounds like *Chitty Chitty Bang Bang*.

@gelfling1220 I know why they filmed it this way, but it always strikes me as odd for Sherlock to know how to drive.

@jamesdleech Holmes dresses in a suit for this trip to the country; the original story popularised the image of him in the deerstalker and Inverness Cape, although it was never mentioned in the books. We've seen him turn his nose up at 'the hat' earlier in the episode.

@VinceStadon Hero shot of Benedict Cumberbatch's Holmes, long black coat flapping in the wind, atop the craggy tor. Like he's in *Torchwood*, if they had craggy tors in Cardiff. Do they have craggy tors in Cardiff?

@Cardiff No.

@gelfling1220 Ah, gotta love the modern BBC drama tradition of standing pensively atop a high platform, long coat flapping dramatically in the wind.

@Morton100 Replying to **@VinceStadon:** Confession time - I own a replica of the coat that flaps and billows like a flappy, billowing thing.

@VinceStadon Replying to **@Morton100:** It's a wonderful coat, and I'm sure you look fab in it! I think we should start a trend of selfies taken on craggy tors, in long coats, billowing in the wind.

@Morton100 Replying to **@VinceStadon:** We're a tad short on craggy tors in East Anglia, unfortunately. But we have wind.

@faziarizvi When I first saw this scene on the rock, I thought it was weirdly dramatic - until I discovered it recreated a famous painting/sketch (that I can't find now) of Sherlock Holmes.

@Morton100 A nod to the painting *Wanderer above the Sea of Fog* by Caspar David Friedrich. Double points for referencing the canon also.

@jamesdleech I mean, why WOULDN'T you draw on this painting for this story?

@VinceStadon The photography is gorgeous!

@faziarizvi Okay, living in Texas, seeing what looked like farmland referred to as "in the heart of this ancient wilderness" just makes me snort every time.

@VinceStadon Replying to **@faziarizvi:** We live on a tiny island. Any spot of land without a WH Smiths with a cafe' inside it constitutes an ancient wilderness to us.

@VinceStadon The west country bumpkin accents are... a thing. You get the feeling sometimes that nobody in TV or films has ever been south of London.

@KevFComicArtist 'Mummersetshire' accent from tour guide.

@faziarizvi Aw man, seeing this little town, pub, etc. is making me really feel the "stay at home, can't travel, pandemic ya know" thing hard.

@VinceStadon Replying to **@faziarizvi:** Yeah, me too. Though of all the places on Earth, Dartmoor would be high on the list of places you'd be highly unlikely to catch the virus - on the other hand, your chances of being eaten alive by a giant, spectral hound are vastly improved. Swings and roundabouts.

@VinceStadon Our first "we're not gay" gag in the pub. There are more "we're not gay" gags in #*Sherlock* than any other thing ever.

@Morton100 I remember this episode is where we learn that John Watson likes crisps (from the Cross Keys pub).

@VinceStadon Replying to **@Morton100:** What crisps does Watson like the most? Cheesey Wotsits? Bacon Frazzles?

@Morton100 The crisps would have to be vegetarian if Martin Freeman had to eat them, and the Cross Keys sold them, it's a vegetarian establishment, so I'd guess Plain or Salt and Vinegar.

@VinceStadon The Grimpen Mire becomes the Grimpen Minefield, Baskerville Hall becomes a research lab. Smart scripting.

@KevFComicArtist Getting such a Pertwee *Dr Who* vibe from the Baskerville installation and those UNIT uniforms.

@jamesdleech Watson using his military bearing to preserve their cover. No matter the adaptation I will always pop for Watson being useful.

@faziarizvi John goes from being worried about faking their way into a government installation to enjoying making use of his military I.D.

@jaowriter I was sceptical when the whole "infiltrate the base using stolen credentials" plot thread started, but I actually like the mental countdown Sherlock is running and the overlays onto the world around them of the computer security checks. Nice tension.

@jamesdleech More lens flares in this lab than a JJ Abrams opticians' appointment.

@gelfling1220 Animal count: 4 so far Hound, Pig/boar (referenced), Bluebell the Bunny, Lab Monkey.

@VinceStadon And another "we're not gay" gag, minutes after the first one. A record even for #*Sherlock*!

@gelfling1220 "Rats the size of dogs..."

@Vince Stadon Replying to **@gelfling1220:** Reference to The Giant Rat of Sumatra - one of the cases mentioned fleetingly in the books. See also the classic & problematic *Dr Who* story *The Talons of Weng Chiang*, which uses a gigantic ball of fluffy cuteness to bring it to life in all its terrifying glory.

@faziarizvi Nice use of the location for the shot through the industrial pipes. I love so much of this series' cinematography. It's photographic and like a series of paintings and portraits.

@VinceStadon "Did we just break into a top-secret military base to investigate a rabbit?" Best line in this.

@faziarizvi I really wanted a glow in the dark stuffed bunny after this episode.

@VinceStadon Replying to **@gelfling1220, @faziarizvi:** I'm most interested in this poor rabbit's story, and feel it deserves to be given its own mini-*Sherlock* episode: *The Bunny Coronet.*

@VinceStadon I don't think I can get used to Holmes and Watson calling each other Sherlock and John. It feels wrong and icky, like walking in on your parents having sex.

@KyleBorcz I want to go to this location so badly and wander around at night.

@VinceStadon Another "we're not gay" gag, as Holmes and Russell Tovey's ears explore the moor.

@KyleBorcz Well played by Benedict Cumberbatch, the sight of the hound has proper shaken him.

@KevFComicArtist Very odd depth of field trickery in that pub scene. Not sure it didn't distract slightly.

@VinceStadon Replying to **@KevFComic:** Framing a shot with the mighty Cumberbatch schnoz taking up half the screen feels like a weird choice.

@jaowriter The scene where Sherlock confesses to Watson what he saw and that he is afraid is fascinating. Interesting camera work on the close-up of Sherlock's profile in the foreground and Watson in the background creating a sense of claustrophobia.

@jamesdleech This seems to be a makeshift attempt to replicate a split dioptre, using two shots and a feathered split screen. Doesn't entirely work.

@jamesdleech Watson calls Holmes "Spock", which is appropriate.

@faziarizvi "Oh, alright. Spock." lol (I love moments like that, when something that's a huge part of our cultural heritage is done again and again and then in one incarnation incorporates a reference to something ELSE that's a huge part of our cultural heritage.)

@VinceStadon Martin Freeman sigh no.3, after he storms out of the pub. To be fair, everybody sighs after they storm out of a pub, not just Martin Freeman.

@jaowriter The truth behind the Morse code is pretty damn funny.

@jamesdleech Putting a dogging gag in *The Hound of the Baskervilles* almost makes up for ditching that subplot.

@VinceStadon Martin Freeman sigh no.4 after psychiatrist Dr Mortimer storms off from their date.

@Morton100 Replying to **@VinceStadon:** One could get absolutely blottoed quite quickly playing John sighs Bingo.

@gelfling1220 I forgot about the whole 'Watson-constantly-wants-a-date' thing.

@faziarizvi Well, to be honest, I'm with the offended psychiatrist there, John. You WERE trying to get info out of her under false-ish pretences.

@faziarizvi Lestrade!! GREG Lestrade. Lol. There is so much going on in this scene, from the appearance of the inspector, to the books inspection, to the sugar.

@gelfling1220 "Is that why you're calling yourself 'Greg'?!" "...that's his name" Poor Lestrade!

@VinceStadon Replying to **@gelfling1220:** I think he's only given the initial 'G' in the stories so I always thought his name was Gerald, to rhyme with Lestrade.

@gelfling1220 Replying to @VinceStadon: Heh! I mostly enjoyed this as a take on the "I thought his name was Agent" type gag.

@KyleBorcz Reused shots of Holmes on the rock, or redone?

@jamesdleech Huh. They've gone back to that shot. Why bother with the "getting lost" contrivance at the start if you're going to do it again in a context that makes more sense (although I suspect this is just recycling a shot they liked).

@jaowriter With the shot of Sherlock standing on the rocky outcrop and the stirring music, I half-expected him to burst into song. Has there been a musical episode of *Sherlock*? We need this now.

@VinceStadon "Winding your way down on Baker Street..."

@gelfling1220 Animal number 5: lab mice!

@KyleBorcz Great sequence with John and the Hound in the lab. Intense, scary. Well shot. Freeman acting his socks off, only to have Holmes come in and under cut it.

@gelfling1220 The disorienting hyperstimulation of the lights and sounds is really effective.

@jaowriter The flashing light motif is reminiscent of an episode of *Fringe*. I'm betting it's the root cause of the hallucinations.

@faziarizvi The suspense and fright here was good. First there's the concern Watson's walking into a biological agent, then the unsettling lights and then the gothic horror feel of the rest of it.

@gelfling1220 Was this the first instance of the Mind Palace in the show? I'm sort of glad they didn't keep this awkward manifestation of it... it has not aged well.

@KevFComicArtist His mind palace is a very silly place.

@Morton100 If Holmes has a Mind Palace, Watson has a Mind Bungalow but John does the most that solves the case.

@KevFComicArtist Hound acronym? Well that's rubbish.

@VinceStadon Project HOUND makes people paranoid and scared, like a Nigel Farage Brexit broadcast. But here comes the Hound! It's... er... hmm.

@Morton100 What a manky-looking hound.

@DarkCorners3 Oh the BBC shouldn't do CGI.

@gelfling1220 That CGI, yikes!

@VinceStadon Russell Tovey is completely wrong for this - he seems like he's always been a nervous wreck on the edge of collapse, only kept upright by his ears.

@VinceStadon Of course all episodes of *Sherlock* must have explosions in them. And I can't say I disapprove. Though my wife fancies Clive 'Little John from *Robin of Sherwood'* Mantle and was not pleased to see him be blown sky high.

@VinceStadon Martin Freeman sigh no. 5 when he realizes Holmes drugged him.

@jamesdleech I don't think even Rathbone's Holmes, who regularly engages in trickery and mockery, would pull that drugging trick on his Watson. Too cruel, regardless of the intent.

@DarkCorners3 This angers me. I assume they're using *The Devil's Foot* or what Stamford in *Study in Scarlet* says as justification, but I do not buy Holmes doing this and certainly not enjoying it.

@VinceStadon And a Moriarty coda, just to annoy me. Actually, I wouldn't mind a cocktail called a Moriarty Coda. Two-parts vodka to one-part Guinness, with ice from the Reichenbach Falls.

@jaowriter The problem with starting *Sherlock* with this episode: I have no idea who the guy in the asylum ward is. But I guess I'll just to KEEP WATCHING Eh, later.

@Morton100 Replying to **@jaowriter, @VinceStadon:** Too late to warn you, you are doomed! The best place to start is with series 1 episode 1. Caveat it goes from believable to ever-increasing absurdity with some massive hand-waving over plot points.

@KevFComicArtist Finished it. Good fun. Conclusion: I can't tweet and watch *Sherlock* at the same time. Sorry.

@DarkCorners3 And I'm finished. As I remember; just a collection of references hammered together with no story logic or sense.

@Morton100 Bio-weapon chemistry rather 'meh' but actor chemistry is one of the most enjoyable aspects so that earns a big 'yeah' from me.

@jamesdleech Overall, not an episode I'm fond of. Too cruel, for one. It contains *that* mind palace scene that Twitter rolls out to mock every now and then, but they never include the lines preceding it that set up his pompousness. Some bright spots, but not a fan.

@jaowriter So, the episode was okay. For a first-timer like me, Cumberbatch and Freeman buoy this episode that winds up feeling like re-heated *X Files/Fringe*. The twists are okay, but I can't help but wonder if the government experiment angle hurts the story.

@faziarizvi HOUN was never one of my favourites of the original stories, but its atmosphere made an impression. This modernized version doesn't feel as intensely gloomy, but the story speaks to our fears of patented genetic manipulation and military research.

@VinceStadon Thanks to everyone participating - I hope you all wear long black coats that flap in the wind, as you stand like a hero on a craggy tor, listening to the howls of a gigantic hound and/or the sighs of Martin Freeman.

APPENDIX THREE

The Hound of the Baskervilles (abridged)

by Vince Stadon

A very silly & very short play

Int. 221b Baker Street. Sherlock Holmes is examining a walking stick. Dr Watson is asleep. There is a knock on the door.

HOLMES Come in!

Dr Mortimer enters. Holmes throws him the stick.

HOLMES You are Dr Mortimer and I know everything about you from your stick, including the fact that you're learning Spanish, but have only mastered one word. Don't bother arguing, simply tell me what is in the mid-18th century document, and the latest edition of the *Devon County Chronicle,* that has brought you here from Dartmoor.

DR MORTIMER Who's that?

HOLMES Dr Watson. Let him sleep, he'll be coming with you to Dartmoor later.

DR MORTIMER *(reads from document)* The Curse of the Baskervilles!

Enter Sir Henry Baskerville and an actress who will play all the female roles, dressed as a maid. She is holding a balloon.

SIR HENRY Arse!

DR MORTIMER Wicked Sir Hugo Baskerville was an evil and wicked man.

Sir Henry puts on an evil beard to become Sir Hugo, pulls a pin from a pocket and bursts the balloon.

DR MORTIMER He fancied a servant girl, but she was having none of it.

The Servant Girl knees Sir Hugo in the groin. She runs off.

SIR HUGO This very night I render my body and soul to the Powers of Evil so that I might but overtake the wench! Saddle my mare and unkennel the pack!

Sir Hugo pretends to be on horseback, chasing the maid across the moor. They fight, Sir Hugo pulls a knife, kills the Servant Girl.

DR MORTIMER Wicked Sir Hugo killed the girl, but then there came a terrible howl...

Enter the Hound of the Baskervilles – an actor in a dog onesie – howling.

DR MORTIMER And it was curtains for Wicked Sir Hugo.

The Hound and Sir Hugo fight. Sir Hugo drops dead, the Hound exits.

HOLMES Is there much more of this? I'm a busy man.

DR MORTIMER Last week, Sir Charles Baskerville fell foul of the Curse.

Enter Sir Henry, in Evil Beard, carrying a balloon, and the Servant Girl.

DR MORTIMER Sir Charles was nothing like Sir Hugo.

Sir Henry pulls off his Evil Beard and hurls it away, then he gives the balloon to the Servant Girl who curtsies and then exits.

DR MORTIMER It was me who found Sir Charles's body on the moor.

Sir Henry drops dead.

DR MORTIMER His face was horrible. And around the body were footprints...

HOLMES Were they: a) a man's; b) a woman's; or c) those of a gigantic hound?

DR MORTIMER Mr Holmes, they were the footprints of a gigantic hound?

HOLMES So C, then?

DR MORTIMER Si. You were right about me learning Spanish.

HOLMES I'll take the case, but only if I can send Dr Watson with you to Dartmoor. His snores are giving me a headache.

WATSON *(snores himself awake)* What'd I miss?

Interior, Baskerville Hall. SFX: Thunder, lightning. Enter Sir Henry (now with Canadian accent and wearing a racoon hat), hobbling in just one boot. Dr Watson follows him.

SIR HENRY By thunder, my new home Baskerville Hall is gloomy. I know I'm the new heir who has inherited everything, but I should have stayed in Canada. I shoulda paid heed to this anonymous letter.

WATSON *(reads the letter)* "I yearn to be held in your manly arms again, for by thunder, you make me weak with desire."

SIR HENRY No, the other side.

WATSON *(reads the letter)* "As you value your life or your reason keep away from the moor."

SIR HENRY Oh, it's 'reason', yeah that makes more sense. I read it as 'raisin'. You know, dried grapes. Do you get them in England?

Enter Mrs Barrymore, tiptoeing, carrying a candle.

WATSON *(whispering to Sir Henry)* Where's Mrs Barrymore going at this time of night?

SIR HENRY *(whispering to Dr Watson)* She seems to be signalling to someone out on the moor!

Dr Watson approaches Mrs Barrymore, taps her on the shoulder. She turns round and shushes him, puts the candle on the floor, produces two semaphore flags and begins an elaborate message.

WATSON Look, there's someone out there on the moor, returning the signal!

SIR HENRY By thunder, you're right!

WATSON It must be the convict, Selden, the Notting Hill Murderer who has recently escaped from nearby Dartmoor Prison! I wonder what they're saying to each other.

SIR HENRY You know, in Canada I learned morse code with the Mounties. They were such a fine bunch of guys. Rugged. Strong.

WATSON And...?

SIR HENRY And by thunder, it sure broke my little heart to have to leave them to come here to—

WATSON No, I mean, what's the signal?

SIR HENRY Oh. Let me see... "Y... M... C...A... They have everything for you men to enjoy! You can hang out with all the boys... It's fun to stay at the YMCA..."

Exit Mrs Barrymore, dancing.

Exterior, The Moor, the next morning. Thick fog. Enter Stapleton with a butterfly net, scampering around like a ballet dancer. Dr Watson enters from the opposite direction.

STAPLETON Hello there, you must be Dr Watson, here with Sir Henry Baskerville, on request of Consulting Detective Sherlock Holmes who has heard all about the Curse of the Baskervilles and the mysterious recent death of Sir Charles Baskerville from Dr Mortimer. How do you do?

WATSON Hello, you seem remarkably well informed. I'm getting red flags that you're the villain of the piece.

STAPLETON *Laughs*

WATSON *Laughs*

SFX: The Hound of the Baskervilles!

WATSON What was that?

STAPLETON What was what?

WATSON That noise, just then.

STAPLETON Probably a bird. A penguin or something. Maybe an albatross. Who knows?

SFX: *A man's agonising death screams!*

WATSON What was that?

STAPLETON What was what?

Enter Holmes.

HOLMES That, my dear Watson, was a man's agonizing death screams!

WATSON Holmes! I thought you were in London!

HOLMES No, I've been here all the time, enjoying Mrs Barrymore and her brother Selden, the Notting Hill Murderer who's recently escaped from nearby Dartmoor Prison signalling disco anthems to each other at night. I particularly enjoyed *Staying Alive.* But come, there's not a moment to lose, Sir Henry is in danger!

Stapleton exits as Holmes and Watson rush around the moor! They halt when Holmes spies something high on the tor...

HOLMES Look, Watson!

Enter Selden, the Notting Hill Murderer, backing away from the Hound. The Hound pounces and Selden screams and then drops dead as the Hound lets out its' bloodcurdling cry and bounds away into the fog.

SFX: The Hound of the Baskervilles!

WATSON Sir Henry! I shall never forgive myself for having left him to his fate!

HOLMES I am more to blame than you, Watson. In order to have my case well rounded and complete, I have thrown away the life of my client. It is the greatest blow which has befallen my career. And now I'll never get paid.

WATSON Perhaps he is still alive? You might get him to sign a cheque?

Holmes and Watson hurry to the body. Watson turns it over to see the face.

WATSON It's not Sir Henry!

HOLMES Thank God! It must be Selden, the Notting Hill Murderer who has recently escaped from nearby Dartmoor Prison.

Enter Sir Henry and Beryl Stapleton in a romantic clinch. Beryl wears a Beauty Queen sash that has the legend MISS COSTA RICA, 1899

SIR HENRY Say, by thunder, what's all the commotion?

HOLMES Sir Henry!

WATSON *(appreciatively)* And hello, Miss!

SIR HENRY Allow me to introduce to you fellows to my fiancée, Beryl Stapleton.

WATSON Wow, you Canadians work fast! Is it the snow?

SIR HENRY What?

BERYL Miss Costa Rica, 1899. Should have been 1900 as well, but they gave it to the mayor's daughter, and she was barely a 7.

SIR HENRY Mr Holmes, I thought you were in London!

HOLMES That is what I wanted you to think. Had my presence been known, it would have alerted our formidable opponent....

Enter Stapleton

STAPLETON Mr Holmes! How delightful to see you...

HOLMES I'll bet it is. *(mimes the 'I'm watching you!' hand signal)*

BERYL Jack, dear brother, I am engaged to Sir Henry!

STAPLETON Oh, excellent! You must come to dinner tonight, Sir Henry, at Merripit House. You'll need to walk alone through the moor across the fog, in darkness. How's that sound?

SIR HENRY Will there be raisins in the dessert?

STAPLETON Do you *want* there to be raisins in the dessert?

SIR HENRY I mean it's not a deal breaker, but yeah, sure.

STAPLETON Till tonight, then. Come, Beryl!

Exit Stapleton and Beryl.

WATSON Holmes, do you really think it's safe for Sir Henry to be alone on the moor at night?

HOLMES Good point, Watson. Sir Henry, would you mind writing me a cheque?

Exit all.

Ext. The Moor. Night. Fog.

Sir Henry, still wearing only one boot, is strutting his stuff as he walks across the moor to keep his date with his fiancée Beryl. He is singing Staying Alive *by the Bee Gees. Suddenly he hears:*

SFX The Hound of the Baskervilles!

He freezes in his tracks, looks around fearfully.

Enter The Hound, stalking Sir Henry through the fog. Sir Henry sees it, backs away slowly.

SIR HENRY Good doggie... good doggie... Stay there... Who's a good boy then, eh? Who's a good boy? Who's a god little doggie then, eh? You is! Yes, you is! You's a good boy! Who's a good boy, then, eh? You is! Yes, you is!

In slow motion, the Hound leaps at Sir Henry who falls to the ground, the Hound on top of him. They fight for their lives. Holmes and Watson enter, revolvers in hand.

HOLMES Here boy!

The Hound startles at the sound, climbs off Sir Henry, and faces Holmes and Watson, growling.

WATSON A hound it was, an enormous coal-black hound, but not such a hound as mortal eyes have ever seen. Fire burst from its open mouth, its eyes glowed with a smouldering glare and its hackles and dewlap were outlined in flickering flame. Never in the delirious dream of a disordered brain could anything more savage, more appalling, more hellish, be conceived than the dark form and savage face which broke upon us out of the wall of fog.

HOLMES Finished?

WATSON Yes.

HOLMES Good. Now fire, Watson!

Holmes and Watson fire six shots each at the Hound which whimpers in pain and falls to the ground, dead. Holmes rushes to the Hound. Watson rushes to Sir Henry.

WATSON He's alive.

HOLMES It's dead. Poor thing.

WATSON Good shooting, Holmes!

HOLMES Sadly not, I missed with every shot.

WATSON Then how—

HOLMES *(Picks up a boot)* It must have choked on this - Sir Henry's missing boot.

WATSON I wondered why he was always limping. I just thought it was a Canadian thing.

Enter Beryl, who runs to Sir Henry as he stirs.

BERYL Henry!

SIR HENRY Beryl! Say, am I too late for dessert?

BERYL Oh, Henry! I didn't want to betray you, but I had no choice!

HOLMES It was you who sent the anonymous letter.

BERYL Yes!

HOLMES You've been working with your brother, Stapleton. Though, he's not really your brother, is he?

Enter Stapleton.

STAPLETON You're a very clever man, Holmes.

HOLMES I know.

WATSON Yes, it's true, he's very clever.

SIR HENRY Yes, there's no doubt about it, most clever indeed.

BERYL Just super-smart and intelligent and clever, the whole brainy package.

WATSON A walking brain box, a thinking machine.

SIR HENRY Absolutely nobody smarter, by thunder.

BERYL Smart is the new sexy, and he's got it all to spare.

SIR HENRY I wouldn't go that far...

BERYL A smouldering hunk of pure intelligence, a deep thinking, deeply passionate, sexy, desirable, ravishing—

SIR HENRY (interrupting) Alright, yes, he's clever, we get it!

STAPLETON Clever you may be, but you've met your match in me, Holmes! *(to Beryl)* Come here, dear wife.

BERYL No! I'll have no more to do with you! I'm with Henry now. Or Sherlock. Preferably the latter.

SIR HENRY Beryl!

HOLMES And Stapleton isn't even your real name is it, Stapleton? Or should I say, Rodger Baskerville, son of long-thought dead younger brother to Charles, and next in line to the Baskerville fortune?

STAPLETON Damn you, Sherlock Holmes! Time I scarpered! Only I know a safe way through this perilous stetch of moorland, pocketed with bog holes, known as the Grimpen Mire where one false step yonder means death to man or beast! Goodbye!

Exit Stapleton.

HOLMES He'll not get far.

WATSON How can you possibly know that?

HOLMES Because of what I've really been doing on the moor all this time... (*He produces a trowel or other digging instrument*) Digging new bog holes!

SFX: Stapleton cries out: Help! Help!

SIR HENRY Did you hear that?

WATSON Hear what?

Everybody laughs. Enter Inspector Lestrade, rushing in with a revolver.

LESTRADE Holmes, Watson, Sir Henry, ravishing beauty queen, I have come to help you solve this case!

WATSON You're too late, Inspector Lestrade. Holmes has everything wrapped up.

BERYL Yes, he's just yummy.

LESTRADE Oh.

HOLMES *(throws an arm round Lestrade, they walk off together with Sir*

Henry and Beryl) Let me tell you all about it, Lestrade... Come along, Watson!

WATSON *(sits sleepily on the ground)* It's been a tiring case, Holmes, I'm just going to get a little rest... *(Falls asleep)*

HOLMES *(enters, sees his friend asleep)* Good old Watson. *(removes his Inverness Cape and drapes it over his friend, exits.)*

SFX: The Hound of the Baskervilles!

WATSON *(wakes with a start)* What was that...?

END

BIBLIOGRAPHY

221 BBC - Writing for the World's Only Complete Dramatised Canon and Beyond by Bert Coules (Gasogene Books, 1998)

Arthur Conan Doyle, Sherlock Holmes and Devon by Brian W Pugh, Paul R Spiring & Sadru Bhanji (MX Publishing, 2010)

A Sherlock Holmes Handbook by Christopher Redmond (Simon & Pierre, 1993)

An Actor and a Rare One: Peter Cushing as Sherlock Holmes by Tony Earnshaw (Scarecrow Press, 2001)

A Study Guide for Sir Arthur Conan Doyle's The Hound of the Baskervilles Edited by Ira Mark Milne (Gale, 2010)

Bending the Willow: Jeremy Brett as Sherlock Holmes by David Stuart Davies (Calabash Press, 2001)

Bertram Fletcher Robinson: A Footnote to The Hound of the Baskervilles by Brian W Pugh and Paul R Spiring (MX Publishing, 2008)

Conan Doyle: The Man Who Invented Sherlock Holmes by Andrew Lycett (Weidenfield & Nicholson, 2007)

Cut to Baker Street by Nicko Vaughn (MX Publishing, 2019)

The Encyclopaedia Sherlockonia by Jack Tracy (New English Library, 1977)

England's Secret Weapon: The Wartime Films of Sherlock Holmes by Amanda J Field (Middlesex University Press, 2009)

The Films of Sherlock Holmes: 60 Years: 1931-1991 by Scott V Palmer (Self-published, 2017)

From Holmes to Sherlock: The Story of the Men and Women Who Created an Icon by Mattias Boström (Mysterious Press, 2007)

The Game Is Afoot: The Story of The Sherlock Holmes Films Series, Starring Basil Rathbone & Nigel Bruce by Adam Roche (Self-published, 2017)

German Expressionist Cinema: The World of Light and Shadow by Ian Roberts (Wallflower Press, 2008)

Granada's Greatest Detective: A Guide to the Classic Sherlock Holmes Television Series by Keith Frankel (Fantom Films Limited, 2016)

The Hammer Story: The Authorised History of Hammer Films by Marcus Hearn and Alan Barnes (Titan Books, 2007)

The Hound of the Baskervilles: Hunting the Dartmoor Legend edited by Philip Weller (Devon Books, 2001)

How Very Interesting! Peter Cook's Universe and All That Surrounds It Edited by Peter Gordon, Dan Kieran and Paul Hamilton (SnowBooks, 2006)

The Life of Sir Arthur Conan Doyle by John Dickson Carr (John Murray, 1949)

Memories and Adventures: An Autobiography by Sir Arthur Conan Doyle (Cambridge University Press, 1924)

The Public Life of Sherlock Holmes by Michael Pointer (David & Charles, 1975)

Sherlock Holmes & the Fabulous Faces: The Universal Pictures Repertory Company by Michael A Hoey (BearManor Media, 2014)

Sherlock Holmes: Behind the Canonical Screen Edited & Introduced by Lyndsay Faye and Ashley Polasek (BSI Press, 2015)

Sherlock Holmes on Screen by Alan Barnes (Reynolds & Hearn Ltd, 2002)

Sherlock Holmes on Screens (various volumes) by Howard Ostrom & Thierry Saint-Joanis

Sherlock Holmes on the Stage: A Chronological Encyclopaedia of Plays Featuring the Great Detective by Amnon Kabatchnik (Scarecrow Press, 2008)

Sir Arthur Conan Doyle at the Cinema: A Critical Study of the Film Adaptations by Scott Allen Nollen (McFarland and Co., 2014)

Starring Sherlock Holmes by David Stuart Davies (Titan Books, 2001)

The Television Sherlock Holmes by Peter Haining (Carol Publishing Group, 1994)

Who on Earth is Tom Baker? by Tom Baker (HarperCollins, 1997)